Translation and Translation Studies
in the Japanese Context

Advances in Translation

Series Editor:
Jeremy Munday
Centre for Translation Studies, University of Leeds, UK

Advances in Translation publishes cutting-edge research in the fields of translation studies. This field has grown in importance in the modern, globalized world, with international translation between languages a daily occurrence. Research into the practices, processes and theory of translation is essential and this series aims to showcase the best in international academic and professional output.

Other Titles in the Series:

Corpus-Based Translation Studies
    Edited by Alet Kruger, Kim Wallach, and Jeremy Munday

Global Trends in Translator and Interpreter Training
    Edited by Séverine Hubscher-Davidson and Michał Borodo

Music, Text and Translation
    Edited by Helen Julia Minors

The Pragmatic Translator
    Massimiliano Morini

Quality in Professional Translation
    Jo Drugan

Retranslation
    Sharon Deane-Cox

Translating the Poetry of the Holocaust
    Jean Boase-Beier

Translation, Adaptation and Transformation
    Edited by Laurence Raw

Translation as Cognitive Activity
    Fabio Alves and Amparo Hurtado Albir

Translation, Humour and Literature: Translation and Humour Volume 1
    Edited by Delia Chiaro

Translation, Humour and the Media: Translation and Humour Volume 2
    Edited by Delia Chiaro

Translation and Translation Studies in the Japanese Context

Edited by
Nana Sato-Rossberg
and
Judy Wakabayashi

Advances in Translation

B L O O M S B U R Y
LONDON • NEW DELHI • NEW YORK • SYDNEY

Bloomsbury Academic

An imprint of Bloomsbury Publishing Plc

50 Bedford Square	1385 Broadway
London	New York
WC1B 3DP	NY 10018
UK	USA

www.bloomsbury.com

Bloomsbury is a registered trade mark of Bloomsbury Publishing Plc

First published in 2012 by the Continuum International Publishing Group Ltd
Paperback edition first published 2013

British Library Cataloguing-in-Publication Data
A catalogue record for this book is available from the British Library.

ISBN:	HB:	978-1-4411-3982-5
	PB:	978-1-4725-2650-2
	ePDF:	978-1-4411-1885-1
	ePUB:	978-1-4411-1459-4

Library of Congress Cataloging-in-Publication Data
Translation and translation studies in the Japanese context/
edited by Nana Sato-Rossberg and Judy Wakabayashi.
p. cm. – (Continuum advances in translation studies)
Includes bibliographical references and index.
ISBN 978-1-4411-3982-5 – ISBN 978-1-4411-1885-1 (PDF) –
ISBN 978-1-4411-1459-4 (Ebook) 1. Translating and interpreting–Japan.
I. Sato-Rossberg, Nana. II. Wakabayashi, Judy.
P306.8.J3T723 2012
418'.020952–dc23
2012011977

Typeset by Newgen Imaging Systems Pvt Ltd, Chennai, India

Contents

Series Editor's Preface

The aim of this new series is to provide an outlet for advanced research in the broad interdisciplinary field of translation studies. Consisting of monographs and edited themed collections of the latest work, it should be of particular interest to academics and postgraduate students researching in translation studies and related fields, and also to advanced students studying translation and interpreting modules.

Translation studies has enjoyed huge international growth over recent decades in tandem with the expansion in both the practice of translation globally and in related academic programs. The understanding of the concept of translation itself has broadened to include not only interlingual but also various forms of intralingual translation. Specialized branches or sub-disciplines have developed for the study of interpreting, audiovisual translation, and sign language, among others. Translation studies has also come to embrace a wide range of types of intercultural encounter and transfer, interfacing with disciplines as varied as applied linguistics, comparative literature, computational linguistics, creative writing, cultural studies, gender studies, philosophy, postcolonial studies, sociology, and so on. Each provides a different and valid perspective on translation, and each has its place in this series.

This is an exciting time for translation studies, and the new Advances in Translation series promises to be an important new plank in the development of the discipline. As General Editor, I look forward to overseeing the publication of important new work that will provide insights into all aspects of the field.

Jeremy Munday
General Editor
University of Leeds, UK

Notes on Contributors

Beverley Curran is a professor teaching linguistic, cultural, and media translation in the Department of Global Culture and Communication at Aichi Shukutoku University in Nagoya. Her publications include *Theatre Translation Theory and Performance in Contemporary Japan: Native Voices, Foreign Bodies* (St. Jerome Publishing, 2008). She is the current editor of the *Journal of Irish Studies*.

Irmela Hijiya-Kirschnereit is professor of Japanese Studies (Literature and Cultural History) as well as the director of the Friedrich Schlegel Graduate School for Literary Studies at Freie Universität, Berlin. From 1996 to 2004, she was director of the German Institute for Japanese Studies (DIJ) in Tokyo. She is editor of the series Japanische Bibliothek (Japanese Library) with Insel Publishers (34 vols between 1990 and 2000) and of Iaponia Insula with Iudicium Publishers (25 vols to date) and coeditor of *Großes japanisch-deutsches Wörterbuch* [Comprehensive Japanese-German Dictionary] Vol. 1, 2009. Her research interests include modern and contemporary Japanese literature, identity discourses, cultural translation, and culinary studies.

Ken Inoue is a professor of Comparative Literature at the Graduate School of Arts and Science, the University of Tokyo, Japan. He has recently published *Bungō no Hon'yakuryoku* [Great Writers' Ability to Translate: Translations by Writers in Modern Japan] (Takeda Randomhouse Japan, 2011) and edited *Hon'yakubungaku no shikai* [Perspectives on Literary Translation: Translation and Cultural Transformations in Modern Japan] (Shibunkaku Co. Ltd., 2012).

Akira Mizuno is a professor of the Department of English at Aoyama Gakuin University, Japan. He is also the secretary-general and vice-president of the Japan Association for Interpreting and Translation Studies (JAITS). His research interests are in Interpreting and Translation Studies.

Makiko Mizuno is a professor in the College of Humanities at Kinjo Gakuin University, Japan, where she teaches interpreting and translation theories and skills. She is the vice president of the Japan Association for Language and Law. Her research interests include linguistic analysis of court interpreting and community interpreting in general.

Minako O'Hagan is a senior lecturer at Dublin City University, Ireland, affiliated with the Centre for Translation and Textual Studies. She has been involved in cutting-edge interdisciplinary translation technology research, with a main interest in emerging practices of translation. She has been an investigator on a number of funded research projects, ranging from a feasibility study on machine translation for computer-aided subtitling to a study of localized video games based on player biometrics. She has recently edited a special issue (10/2011) of the journal *Linguistica Antverpiensia* on the emerging phenomenon of translation crowdsourcing.

Emiko Okayama is a research fellow in the Asia Institute at the University of Melbourne. She has published in the areas of translation history, historical linguistics, modern Japanese literature, and Japanese visual culture.

Nana Sato-Rossberg is a lecturer at the School of Language and Communication Studies, University of East Anglia, United Kingdom (Yakult Lecturer). Her research interests include intergeneric translation (manga—film), non–mother tongue writing, translation of oral narratives, cultural translation, and the relationship between translation and power. Among her recent publications are *Translating Culture: Creative Translations of Aynu Chanted-Myths by Mashiho Chiri* (Sapporodō Press, 2011) and the edited volume *Translation Studies* (Misuzu Press, 2011).

Kayoko Takeda is professor of translation and interpreting studies in the Graduate School of Intercultural Communication at Rikkyo University, Japan. Her research interests include sociocultural aspects of translating and interpreting, translator and interpreter education, translation and interpreting history, and translation technology. She is the author of *Interpreting the Tokyo War Crimes Trial* (University of Ottawa Press, 2010).

Akiko Uchiyama is a lecturer in the School of Languages and Comparative Cultural Studies at the University of Queensland, Australia. Her research interests are in social, cultural, and literary aspects of Translation Studies.

Judy Wakabayashi is professor of Japanese translation at Kent State University. She is coeditor of *Asian Translation Traditions* (St. Jerome Publishing, 2005) and *Decentering Translation Studies: India and Beyond* (Benjamins, 2009). She has a particular interest in Japanese translation history.

Introduction

Judy Wakabayashi and Nana Sato-Rossberg

Japan has often been portrayed as a "translation superpower" and Japanese history as a history of translation. The vital role of written and oral translation in Japan has led to a considerable body of research and thinking on this topic. Yet despite Japan's standing in the world, little information has been available in English about Japanese practices of translation over time, much less Japanese discourses on translation. This scholarly oversight signifies a missed opportunity to broaden our understanding of translation as an international and culturally constructed phenomenon. In recent years, encouraging steps have been taken toward rectifying this situation, with the publication of some noteworthy (although often narrowly focused) English-language narratives about translation in Japan.[1] The present volume adopts a different approach by bringing together a range of perspectives on the part of scholars of Japanese translation who are generally familiar with the contemporary Euro-American discipline of Translation Studies (TS) and who combine these understandings with Japan-inflected insights. The editors' hope is that the historical and contemporary contexts and perspectives introduced here will help inform and extend translation scholarship.

This book has five main focuses—(1) TS as a culturally situated academic discipline in Japan, (2) aspects of Japanese translation history, with a particular focus on the role of translation in society and in the creation of new genres and written styles, (3) the rendition of minority and diasporic voices in Japanese translation, (4) the translation of Japanese literature and video games outside of (and back to) Japan, and (5) the emerging field of community interpreting in Japan. The 11 chapters offer insights into practices, norms, and thinking that are rooted in contexts and trajectories different from those of translation in Europe and North America. They portray some of the dynamics and complexity of phenomena relating to written and oral translation involving the Japanese language—mostly into Japanese, but also from Japanese—as well as Japanese discourses on this topic.

Most of the chapters originated as papers presented at the first international conference on TS in Japan (organized by Nana Sato-Rossberg at Ritsumeikan University in January 2010). Many were originally in Japanese but have been rewritten in English, and all have been revised in line with the conventions and expectations of English academic writing and with the addition of background information about Japanese history, society, and literature necessary for a more international audience. The diverse backgrounds of the contributors—they include an Australian, a Canadian, and a German, while five of the Japanese contributors live and work outside of Japan—reflect the internationalization of Translation Studies and Japanese Studies and add richness to the content and perspectives, rather than being restricted to a solely emic or etic outlook.

Instead of common themes emerging from these essays, what is offered here is a range of topics and perspectives, indicative of the multifaceted nature of translation practices in Japan as well as thinking and research on translation and TS in the Japanese context. The connecting thread is the Japanese language itself and the situations in which it has functioned as the source or target language or as the object of theorizing in connection with the act of translation. Given this diversity, it is impossible to present here a comprehensive or even a balanced overview of the breadth and depth of Japanese translational practices, thinking, and research. Nevertheless, the chapters in this volume single out certain prominent features that might prompt critical reflection and encourage further research into this understudied site of translation so as to foster a more truly multinational dialogue. It is hoped that the present volume can make a small contribution to further cross-fertilization of ideas in this field, with Japan acting not just as a recipient of imported thought but as a source of ideas of potential interest and relevance to TS researchers working in other contexts.

* * *

For readers who are not familiar with the Japanese language or Japanese history, it will be helpful to sketch out some of the key background that underpins the contributions to this volume. Understanding the evolution of translation in Japan requires, first, grasping the relationship between the Japanese language and that of Japan's most influential neighbor, China. Since ancient Japan lacked a writing system of its own, it adopted the expedient of borrowing characters from China—long regarded by the Japanese as a superior civilization—even though the Chinese and Japanese languages belong to unrelated language families.

Since individual Chinese characters (known in Japan as kanji) can represent both sound *and* meaning, they could be used to represent the same meaning in Japanese, regardless of the verbal form used there to convey that meaning. Hence, Chinese characters were read in Japan not only in an approximation of the original Chinese pronunciation (known as the *on*-reading [Chinese or Sino-Japanese reading]—e.g. the Chinese word *shän* 山, meaning mountain, read in Japan as *san*), but also assigned the altogether unrelated pronunciation of the Japanese word having the same meaning (known as the *kun*-reading [Japanese reading]; in this example, 山 also read as *yama*).

By the early Heian period (794–1185), the Japanese had developed a method known as *kanbun kundoku* (literally, "Japanese reading of Chinese texts") that involved physically (or even just mentally) adding reading-order marks to texts written in Classical Chinese, reading Chinese nouns in their *kun*-reading, using predetermined equivalents for verbs and adverbs, and adding Japanese grammatical indicators. This allowed those Japanese trained in this method to access the meaning of Chinese texts directly, without needing translations. It was not until the late seventeenth century that translations in the "conventional" sense of the term appeared in Japan, triggered by the importation of Chinese novels written not in Classical Chinese but in vernacular language, which was not amenable to the longstanding practice of *kanbun kundoku*. Over time, these various influences from China had an enormous impact on the writing of original texts in Japan and also on translations. This resulted in a plethora of styles of written Japanese that ranged from ones that hewed to Classical Chinese in varying degrees to ones that eschewed Chinese influences and instead adhered to the norms of indigenous style, which similarly ranged from Classical Japanese to the pseudoclassical style of literary Japanese and, eventually, a style that "unified" the spoken and written styles.

By about the ninth century, the Japanese had in fact invented their own writing system—actually, two systems, collectively known as kana. The physically rounded hiragana phonetic syllabary and the more angular katakana phonetic syllabary (nowadays mainly used for writing borrowed foreign words) were both formed by simplifying Chinese characters. Although their invention made it possible to represent the Japanese language without resorting to Chinese characters, factors such as the established prestige of the imported script, its more concise representation of concepts, and the presence of numerous homophones meant that the indigenous scripts played an ancillary rather than central role. With the eventual introduction of the Roman alphabet, Japanese writers and translators now have four writing systems on hand, and their interplay can be used creatively to achieve different effects, such as emphasis, playfulness, or transgression.

After many centuries in which Japan's contacts with other cultures were confined to its Asian neighbors (predominantly China and South Korea), the sixteenth century witnessed the arrival of Europeans and their languages and cultures. The Portuguese, Spanish, Dutch, and English were motivated by proselytization or trade prospects, rather than military conquest, but fear of their superior knowledge and technology and their possible intentions soon led the Japanese government (the shogunate or *bakufu*) to expel all Europeans except the Dutch, who were not interested in spreading Christianity and were regarded as a useful source of information. They were, however, confined to a tiny island in the harbor of Nagasaki in western Japan, and the country entered a period of enforced national isolation for over 200 years, although contacts with Asia continued. Nagasaki was far from the cultural centres of Edo (present-day Tokyo) and Kyoto, yet the knowledge introduced from Europe and translated by the professional translators stationed in Nagasaki (as well as their knowledge of the Dutch language itself) was immensely influential in these cultural centers during the Edo period (1603–1868).

In the mid-nineteenth century, Japan's isolation was brought to an end with the arrival of American ships. Concurrent political changes led to power shifting out of the hands of the shogunate, with a nominal restoration of the emperor in what was known as the Meiji Restoration of 1868. This momentous change in Japanese society led to a decisive and rapid shift from Dutch and other European languages to English as the primary source language for translations, a situation that continues to the present. In their encounter with European languages in the Edo and early Meiji periods, the Japanese drew on the existing mainstream model for accessing the meaning of foreign texts—that is, the practice of *kanbun kundoku*—and contrived to adapt it for use with source texts written in European languages. Although these efforts were not very successful or long-lived, soon being overtaken by approaches less constrained by the physical form of the source texts, the legacy of this source-oriented approach survived to varying degrees in the more conventional translational approaches that superseded the *kundoku* method. The influence of European styles on Japanese writing (and translations) added to the existing mix of written styles, and a major challenge for writers and translators in the Meiji period (1868–1912) was to develop a written language more suited to the needs of a rapidly modernizing society. In the ensuing decades, translation in Japan has moved closer to what is usually understood by the term "translation" in English, while still showing evidence of its historical roots. Translation continues to act as a major innovative force in Japanese society today.

* * *

The opening essay by **Kayoko Takeda** examines institutional and social aspects that have helped shape the academic discipline of TS in Japan in recent years. In line with calls for a sociology of TS, she focuses on the academic identity and backgrounds of Japanese researchers, while recognizing the existence of a translation discourse and training infrastructure independent of academic institutions. After surveying Japanese academic writing on translation before TS began to have an impact, Takeda suggests that the concept of translation norms is the imported concept that has had the most impact. She relates the characteristics of TS in Japan to three main institutional and social factors: (1) a growing emphasis on practical aspects of language teaching at universities, (2) contacts with non-Japanese researchers, and (3) a "translation-friendly" cultural and publishing environment (although this does not explain the time lag in the emergence of TS in Japan). All three factors can be expected to lead to greater research on translation. The role played by non-Japanese scholars highlights the blurring of international academic boundaries and the importance of international exposure, as does the growing number of Japanese who have studied TS overseas. Another distinguishing feature of TS in Japan is the prominence of publications by graduate students, which bodes well for the future but suggests weaknesses in the current infrastructure. Takeda concludes with some suggestions "for furthering the discipline in Japan and at large."

The essay by **Judy Wakabayashi** offers a complementary discussion of the state of TS in Japan today, but situates this emerging discipline within a broader regional context. She juxtaposes the Japanese situation not only with TS in the West, but also with developments in TS in Japan's neighbor China, which has been grappling for some time now with the relationship between local and imported ideas and methodologies relating to translation. After surveying the arguments of "progressive" translation scholars in China, who are keen to learn from TS in the West, and "conservative" translation scholars, who valorize traditional Chinese ideas on translation, Wakabayashi suggests that this ongoing debate might prove instructive for translation scholars in Japan, who in the past decade have been eagerly embracing Western theories without fully examining their appropriateness in Japanese circumstances or considering what existing ideas might be sidelined in the process. Although these first two chapters adopt somewhat different viewpoints, together they highlight the desirability of a more thoughtful integration of "Western" and Japanese approaches to the study of translation.

The contribution by **Emiko Okayama** traces the footsteps of Kanzan Okajima, an influential translator of vernacular Chinese in the early eighteenth century who moved between several different cities and occupations in his lifetime. Drawing on Anthony Pym's principles of focusing on translators and their professional intercultures, Okayama takes the innovative step of combining these principles with the interference model developed by Ayssar Arida in the field of urban studies to understand the personal and social interactions in this particular translator's networks and his various roles as an intercultural agent. She demonstrates how Okajima's diverse activities contributed to the popularization of Chinese vernacular novels and the formation of a new literary genre in premodern Japan. Her essay also highlights the distinctive practice of *kanbun kundoku* (also known as *wakoku*) and how this blurs the familiar dichotomy between source and target languages. Okayama calls for further consideration of this practice from a perspective informed both by Japanese realities and TS.

Akiko Uchiyama examines how one of the leading Meiji-period intellectuals, Yukichi Fukuzawa, embraced and assimilated foreign elements in order, paradoxically, to resist Western dominance through his translation works (including translation in the broad sense of rewriting). Uchiyama's primary concern is the social and cultural, rather than linguistic, aspects of Fukuzawa's "manipulative" translation work as a means of introducing Western civilization in a manner adapted to Japanese circumstances and as a means of strengthening the nation against possible colonization. Her approach illustrates how a postcolonial framework can provide insights even in situations without formal colonization. In an interesting instance of the cross-fertilization of ideas that is possible through the globalization of TS, Uchiyama also draws on the framework of Brazilian "cannibalistic" translation because of the "digestive" elements present in Fukuzawa's approach to translation, whereby he emphasized what he regarded as important for Japan's "nutritional needs." Uchiyama's awareness of directionality and certain differences between the Brazilian approach and Fukuzawa's approach again highlights the importance of site-based understandings when applying theoretical frameworks.

The chapter by **Akira Mizuno** traces changes in translation norms in the early and mid-Meiji period, focusing specifically on stylistic norms in translations of fiction and nonfiction works, with this latter category being of particular interest as Japan emerged from its national isolation and attempted to learn about the West. Mizuno's close analysis demonstrates that the mainstream norm in terms of the type of language used in translations underwent substantial changes in this period as a result of (1) the gradual disappearance of lexical elements, grammatical constructions, and situations derived from literal translations of Chinese classics, and (2) the incorporation of new lexical and grammatical elements and situations derived from translations of European-language works. He suggests that one of the factors prompting these changes was an initial translation norm that emphasized the source languages. Whereas most studies of style in translations focus on shifts between the source and target languages and on the style of individual writers or translators, Mizuno focuses on changes within the stylistic norms of the target language itself. His findings confirm, yet also modify, Gideon Toury's claim as to the concurrent existence of a mainstream norm, previous norms, and emerging norms, as Mizuno concludes that changes in norms can occur as a gradual process prompted by "internal forces or necessities," with little overt competition.

The paper by **Ken Inoue** explores the interaction between translation and creative writing from the 1920s through to the postwar period, focusing particularly on two translators who helped signal a break with traditional literary style through the influence of foreign literary styles. Ritsu Oda's literal reproduction of the short sentences and perfective verbs in Ernest Hemingway's *A Farewell to Arms* in 1930 arguably constituted a kind of mistranslation, but it was underpinned by Oda's interest in and empathy with Hemingway's realism and lack of sentimentality, and it subsequently gave rise to a new "hard-boiled" literary style that influenced many postwar Japanese novelists. Similarly, Tatsuo Hori's translations of some paragraphs by Marcel Proust in the 1930s taught him how to render prose depicting a stream of consciousness into long sentences, and a Proust-like style subsequently played an important role for modern Japanese novelists in shaking up the established mode of writing fiction. These two case studies illustrate the important formative effect of translations—even very literal translations—on Japanese literary genres and writing.

Set against the background of the Japanese government's annexation of the island of Hokkaido in the late nineteenth century and the subsequent "assimilation" of the indigenous Ainu people, the chapter by **Nana Sato-Rossberg** makes a careful analysis of how two researchers' different approaches to the Japanese translation of Ainu place-names reflect differing understandings of the Ainu worldview and how to convey this to Japanese readers. Place-names are not often a matter of interest for scholars of TS, and it is only fairly recently that the translation of minority and indigenous languages has attracted some attention. Sato-Rossberg highlights both of these relatively neglected aspects, emphasizing how place-names often reflect and convey indigenous knowledge and culture. After sketching in the historical background and comparing the translations in an Ainu place-name dictionary compiled in 1891 by a Japanese researcher with the translations in a dictionary compiled in 1956 by an ethnologist of Ainu origin who translated from his "mother tongue" (Ainu) into his "first language" (Japanese), Sato-Rossberg relates these translations to the concept of "thick translation," with its emphasis on valuing the meanings and belief systems of minority cultures.

Beverley Curran extends the volume's horizons further by examining the tension between interlingual and intralingual translation in texts emanating from diasporic contexts. Taking up two English novels written by Canadian Nikkei (second-generation Japanese immigrants), both of which make strategic use of Japanese expressions within the English text, Curran analyzes how these expressions, with their particular relationship to the Japanese and English languages as well as to the history of Japanese migrants in Canadian society, were handled differently by the two translators when the novels were rendered into Japanese. She focuses in particular on the orthographic dimension (which has been largely overlooked in TS in the West) and the potential of the four different writing systems and phonetic glosses used in Japanese (and their mixture and the ability to create custom-made combinations of characters) to convey a meaning that transcends the graphic forms. This offers additional options for translators into Japanese, even though the translators studied here failed to exploit these possibilities to the full. Curran's chapter highlights how superficially similar techniques can stem from different motivations on the part of the translators and how diasporic writing merits study as a resource for understanding translation in general.

The chapter by **Irmela Hijiya-Kirschnereit** addresses issues of Japanese literature as a literature of the world, shifting the focus from translations into Japanese to translations from Japanese. She discusses a relatively new phenomenon called pretranslation, whereby some Japanese authors make their texts more readily accessible to international audiences by avoiding cultural specifics and/ or elaborating on cultural specifics that are self-evident to readers of Japanese but not international audiences. These writers also sometimes formulate their sentences in a way that will facilitate transposition into a European language (usually English), while a further strategy for making Japanese literature "fit" for world literature entails heavy editing on the part of translators and publishers. In reflecting on these pretranslation strategies, Hijiya-Kirschnereit suggests problems involved in these procedures and questions the notion of "world literature." She concludes by sketching some consequences for authors, translators, publishers, critics, and readers.

In a chapter emblematic of the changing language industry and the impact of new technical capabilities on source texts, translation strategies, and expectations of translations, **Minako O'Hagan** turns to video game localization, which does not fit readily into existing genre categories and entails changes in the nature of language transfer because the source texts are in digital (coded) form. She focuses on a novel practice known as reverse localization. This is used when Japanese games that had been introduced into the North American market with voiced English dialogue are subsequently given subtitles in the Japanese market that differ somewhat from the original Japanese, so as to allow Japanese gamers to enjoy the flavour of the English version. O'Hagan notes that the source code of games represents a strong physical link between source and target texts, so that localized games are not "wholly separate entities" severed from the source text. She emphasizes how the entertainment element shapes the micro- and macrostrategies (including considerable liberties) adopted at the linguistic, technical, and cultural levels. Given Japan's leading position as a creator of video games, reverse localization is suggestive, she argues, of one way in which a Japanese perspective can contribute to the field of TS. Coincidentally, O'Hagan draws on the Brazilian metaphor of cannibalist translation, as does the chapter by Akiko Uchiyama.

The contribution by **Makiko Mizuno** is significant not just as the only chapter on interpreting, but also because it focuses on community interpreting, a long-neglected area in Japan, which does not have a strong history of migrant intake. Mizuno examines community interpreting practices (particularly in the legal and healthcare fields), as well as Japanese research on this topic. The recent increase in migrant workers has led to growing interest in this topic, in line with a new understanding of community interpreting as a way of guaranteeing the human rights of non-Japanese-speaking residents. This attention has been most notable in connection with legal interpreting, prompted largely by the use of interpreters in the recently introduced system of lay judge trials, where the interpreter's mode of expression takes on greater importance than in conventional trials. Legal interpreting is the only government-regulated area, with other community interpreting services being largely provided by volunteers. Unlike in many countries, sign language interpreting is not regarded as part of community interpreting but as a matter of government welfare services, and there is a certification system for sign language interpreting but none for community interpreting. In addition to issues of compensation and quality control, Mizuno highlights how institutional and market factors and the lack of interpreters competent in the most-needed languages have hindered a comprehensive and systematic approach to community interpreting in Japan.

* * *

For the convenience of English readers, Japanese names are written here with the family name last (rather than following the Japanese practice of placing it first). It is common in Japan to refer to certain well-known literary figures by their personal name (often a pen name) rather than their surname, and that practice is followed when appropriate. In general, the Japanese in these chapters is transliterated into the Roman alphabet to assist those who cannot read the three Japanese scripts, but the original Japanese scripts are retained when necessary to convey a particular point made by the author. Macrons are used in transliterated words to indicate long vowels, but they are not used in common place-names such as Tokyo and Kyoto, in personal names where that person's preference is not to use macrons or where macrons were not used in a cited English publication including that person's name, and in words that have found their way into English dictionaries.

Note

1   Douglas Howland's *Translating the West: Language and Political Reason in Nineteenth-Century Japan* (2002), Hiroko Cockerill's *Style and Narrative in Translations: The Contribution of Futabatei Shimei* (2006), Indra Levy's *Sirens of the Western Shore: The Westernesque Femme Fatale, Translation, and Vernacular Style in Modern Japanese Literature* (2006) and her edited volume *Translation in Modern Japan* (2011), and Beverley Curran's *Theatre Translation Theory and Performance in Contemporary Japan: Native Voices, Foreign Bodies* (2008).

1

The Emergence of Translation Studies as a Discipline in Japan

Kayoko Takeda

Introduction

The main purpose of this paper is to examine the state of Translation Studies (TS) as a discipline in Japan. Some texts are available as a general introduction to the overall landscape of scholarly work on Japanese translation (e.g. Kondo and Wakabayashi 1998; Mizuno 2007a; Teplova 2009), but the recent surge in the number of publications and academic activities related to TS in Japan warrants a closer look at their features and the surrounding contextual factors. Although some picture of the Japanese discourse on translation will emerge in the course of this paper, the main focus is on the institutional and social aspects of the discipline: how TS as an academic field has started taking shape in Japan, what factors have contributed to this development, and the academic backgrounds of those participating in the efforts to establish TS as a distinct discipline in Japan.

The attention to the academic identity and backgrounds of researchers is prompted by the recent calls for a sociology of TS. Along with the trend to pay more attention to the social dimensions of translating and translators (e.g. Pym et al. 2006; Wolf and Fukari 2007), there have been contextualized discussions of how the discipline itself has developed, providing geopolitical and sociocultural analyses of the institutionalization of TS (e.g. Simeoni 2007a, 2007b, 2008; Toury 2008; Pym 2011). This paper aims to make a modest contribution to this line of self-reflection by revealing how TS is starting to establish itself in Japanese academia. It should be emphasized that this does not present a complete picture of discussions and writings on Japanese translation, as some have taken place independent of institutional settings, as indicated later. Against the backdrop of the debate over the "de-Westernization" or "internationalization" of the discipline (e.g. Hung and Wakabayashi 2005; Hermans 2006; Tymoczko 2009; Wakabayashi and Kothari 2009), consideration is also given to how researchers in Japan, in their study of phenomena associated with Japanese translation, are addressing concepts, theories, and approaches developed by Western translation scholars.

Although Interpreting Studies is often considered to be a subdiscipline of TS (e.g. Shlesinger 2004; Pöchhacker 2004), this paper does not address the state of research on interpreting in Japan. As discussed below, collective efforts to advance interpreting research took off much earlier in Japan than those for translation research, and the recent developments discussed in this paper do not involve interpreting research. It should also be noted that the standard Japanese rendition of the word "translation" (*hon'yaku*) refers only to written translation and does not include interpreting (*tsūyaku*). "Translation Studies" has been generally translated as *hon'yaku-gaku* or *hon'yaku kenkyū*, which indicates that in Japan the discipline addresses only written translation. "Interpreting Studies" is generally translated as *tsūyaku-gaku* or *tsūyaku kenkyū*, implying that it is a parallel discipline to TS, not a component of TS. Therefore "translation" and "Translation Studies" are treated here in a narrower sense than what these English terms can encompass.

The paper first provides a brief overview of academically oriented writing on translation in Japan before the turn of the millennium. It then lays out a series of key events and publications in the past several years that signify a heightened level of interest in translation as an object of academic inquiry and the emerging institutionalization of the discipline in Japan. The primary focus is on the academic association, conferences, and journals that are related to TS as a discipline, as well as works produced within this particular community. The findings about the main concerns and methods are analyzed from both local and global perspectives, paying attention to social and cultural factors in Japan and the global reach of TS. In closing, suggestions are made for furthering the discipline in Japan and at large.

Early works

As reflected in the plurality of what the word English "translation" and the "equivalent" word in other languages can stand for (e.g. Tymoczko 2007: 54–106; Hermans 2007: 137–56; Halverson 2010), academic inquiry into translation can derive from a variety of perspectives and research objectives. In the Japanese context, scholarly writings on translation range from linguistic analysis of translation shifts (e.g. Naruse 1978), didactic texts (e.g. Kawamoto and Inoue

1997; Saitō 2007a), and examinations of machine translation[1] to reflections on the role translation has played in the cultural, social, and political history of Japan (e.g. Maruyama and Katō 1998; Levy 2011) and critical theorizing of the act of translating (e.g. Sakai 1997; Morinaka 2006). For the purposes of this paper, however, the following review of early works focuses on those that pioneered an extensive discussion of translation as the core object of research (rather than as a pretext for a larger topic in philosophy or comparative literature, for instance) and/or sought to formulate the study of translation as a discipline in its own right in Japan.

The most prolific scholar of Japanese translation to date is probably Akira Yanabu, who since the 1970s has devoted his academic career to the study of *hon'yaku-go* ("translation words"—i.e. words newly coined to translate foreign concepts). Yanabu's elaborate examinations of how *hon'yaku-go* came into existence and how they have affected the development of the language and culture of modern Japan recently became more accessible to a wider audience through English publications (Yanabu 2009, 2011). Largely unaware of theories and research methods developed within TS in the West,[2] some of Yanabu's works seem to lack evidence-based argumentation and critical theorizing. Nevertheless, his extensive reflections on the history of translation methods in Japan remain an indispensable asset to researchers of Japanese translation, and his insights into the attraction of unfamiliarity found in *hon'yaku-go* (the "cassette effect" or "jewelry box effect"; see Yanabu 2009) might prompt other scholars to seek empirical evidence and theoretical grounding for his observations.

Despite his pioneering and extensive work on translation, Yanabu has never explicitly called for the establishment of a new discipline dedicated to translation issues, and nor has he actively interacted with scholars in the international community of TS. The first text to propose the study of translation as an academic field in Japan was probably Naruse (1978). Unlike the many self-reflective essays written by renowned translators in the early twentieth century (see examples in Yanabu et al. 2010), Naruse took a methodological approach in analyzing linguistic issues of translation between English and Japanese. Having translated Eugene Nida's *Toward a Science of Translating* (1964) into Japanese in 1972, Naruse was not content with translation being discussed on the fringe of literary studies, and he declared that "translation theory is a science that theoretically describes effective methods of translation" (1978: 1).[3] This desire for a systematic study of translation did not, however, attract sustained interest and discussion in Japanese academia at that time.

During the 1980s, some Japanese researchers became acquainted with certain developments in TS outside Japan. For example, Fumiko Fujinami, at that time a graduate student of German studies, started studying on her own the functionalist translation theory that was then gaining ground in Germany. As early as in 1984, she published papers in Japan on the development of TS in the German context, and she went on to Heidelberg to study under Hans Vermeer from 1987 to 1989 (pers. comm., May 2011). In Japan, however, Fujinami worked almost in isolation, and her work did not become widely known beyond the academic circle of German studies. She explored opportunities to establish an academic association for translation research in Japan, but could not generate sufficient interest and support from other scholars (pers. comm., May 2011).

Around the same time, Daniel Gile, the pioneering France-based scholar of interpreting and translation, was conducting research in Japan, and this led to a special issue of the Canadian journal *Meta* in 1988. Guest-edited by Gile, this publication contained several articles written by interpreters, translators, and linguists in Japan, mainly dealing with linguistic issues of Japanese translation and the professional practice of translating. Through interactions with Gile, some of the authors presumably became aware of the emergence of TS outside of Japan. In his introduction and full article, however, Gile shared his view of contemporary translation research in Japan as follows: "Japanese translation practitioners and theoreticians . . . apparently have little motivation to write for non-Japanese readers, or indeed to look at translation as it is practiced elsewhere" (1988a: 5), and "few are truly scientific or academic . . . with hardly any reference to foreign publications . . . highly personal and contain numerous anecdotes from their authors' lives" (1988b: 115).

In 1990, a small group of Japanese interpreters started studying the interpreting theory and research of the West. The group was led by Masaomi Kondō, a conference interpreter/economics professor who had learned of and was inspired by interpreting research and graduate-level interpreter training outside Japan at a conference he attended in the United States in 1989 (Kondō 2009). The group also launched its own nonrefereed journal, *Tsūyaku riron kenkyū* (Interpreting Research), to publish interpreting-related papers in Japan. During the ten-year tenure of this quarterly journal, a total of four articles on translation were published: three on linguistic features in translation between English and Japanese, and one on Chinese discourses of translation. These studies were more methodological than most of the previous publications on translation, such as essays and didactic texts. For example, Mizuno (1999) applied some theories and concepts developed within TS, such as functionalist theory and "shifts" in translation. Nevertheless, due to the journal's explicit focus on interpreting research, these four papers on translation were simply overshadowed by those on interpreting, which totaled more than sixty over the same period.

According to Akira Mizuno (pers. comm., July 2011), who was one of the core members of the group, the development of interpreting research in Japan at that time can be linked to the explosive demand for and high visibility since the late 1980s of media interpreters, who have interpreted TV news reports of historical events such as the Tiananmen Square incident, the fall of the Berlin Wall, and the Gulf War. These interpreting phenomena attracted great attention from the Japanese public, and some academically oriented interpreters "hungered" for theoretical frameworks to better understand and articulate their work. Moreover, Kondō (pers. comm., July 2011) suggests that those who had started teaching interpreting at universities felt pressure to engage in research and to publish on interpreting and that the interpreting research group and its journal were able to address this new interest in and need for interpreting research. By contrast, according to Mizuno (pers. comm., July 2011), translation scholars— however few in number—had already been resorting to publishing outlets in the fields of language and literary studies and they might not have been motivated to go beyond those boundaries.

In the meantime, Itagaki (1995) independently argued that the study of translation should be viewed as a separate discipline, and he used the term *hon'yaku-gaku* as the name of this proposed discipline. Despite his aspiration and references to Dryden's "translation theory" as the "Bible" for translators in Japan (1995: 71), this book essentially did not go beyond impressionistic remarks based on Itagaki's own experiences as a translator. By contrast, Hirako (1999), a professor of linguistics and German philosophy, provided a much more systematic, theory-based discussion of translation. Although he does not seem to have been aware of the development of TS in the West and he primarily drew on linguistics and German philosophy, Hirako's view of translation as intercultural communication was a clear departure from earlier microlinguistic comparisons of source and target texts.

In short, since the 1970s, there have been some Japanese works that examined translation extensively as their main object of scholarly inquiry and attempted to cultivate a new, distinct academic field for studying translation in Japan. These activities were rather disjointed, however, and they did not constitute a cohesive force capable of developing into an institutional endeavor so as to promote research on Japanese translation or play an active part in the advancement of TS in the international arena. It was only after the turn of the millennium that TS as a discipline started taking shape in Japan.

Translation Studies (TS) in Japan

The emergence of any new field of study may be signaled by the formation of an academic organization, conferences, publication outlets or university departments, and programs dedicated to the discipline. This is exactly what has happened over the past several years in the case of TS in Japan: the establishment of an academic society to promote the discipline, the founding of graduate programs in translation and interpreting, the launch of a journal devoted to TS, and related activities. The following is a summary of such key developments that have led to the current state of TS as an emerging discipline in Japan.

First, an association related to TS was established. As mentioned earlier, an interpreting research group had been founded in Japan in 1990. A decade later this group reorganized itself into a formal academic association called Nihon Tsūyaku Gakkai (Japan Association for Interpretation Studies). In 2005 a handful of translation researchers led by Akira Mizuno formed a subgroup within this organization in order to advance the study of translation in Japan. The activities of this subgroup gained ground with the 2007 launch of a semi-peer-reviewed journal dedicated to TS, called *Hon'yaku kenkyū e no shōtai* (Invitation to Translation Studies). At the same time, there was an increase in the number of translation-related articles in the association's main journal, *Tsūyaku kenkyū* (Interpretation Studies). In 2008 the name of the association was changed to include translation, becoming Nihon Tsūyaku Hon'yaku Gakkai (Japan Association for Interpreting and Translation Studies (JAITS)), and the name of the main journal was changed to *Tsūyaku hon'yaku kenkyū* (Interpreting and Translation Studies). In the latest issue published in 2011, 7 of the 9 peer-reviewed articles were concerned with translation. As of November 2011, the association's members number over 360, and about 140 people attended the annual conference in Kobe in 2011. Of the 23 papers presented there, 14 (including 5 by graduate students) focused on translation, outnumbering the presentations on interpreting research. Two more study groups were established in western Japan in 2010. Kansai Tsūyaku Hon'yaku Riron oyobi Kyōju-hō Kenkyūkai (The Interpreting and Translation Studies Initiatives Kansai), led by Yasumasa Someya, meets every month for a discussant-led session on the latest research on translation and interpreting, and the Kansai Translation Studies Kenkyūkai (Kansai Translation Studies Research Group), led by Nana Sato-Rossberg, has been organizing panel discussions and calling for papers for publications. These are separate groups, operating independently. The former mainly focuses on linguistic, cognitive, and didactic issues in both translation and interpreting, while the latter mainly focuses on the cultural and philosophical aspects of translation.

Secondly, some graduate programs in professional training and research in translation and interpreting have been launched: at Rikkyo University in Tokyo and Kobe College (MA level only) in 2002. Although there have been doctoral dissertations in TS produced at Japanese universities without programs dedicated to the discipline (e.g. Ihara 2003; Sato-Rossberg 2007; Satō 2008), the steady sources of theses on translation in Japan have been Rikkyo and Kobe, along with the interpreting program at the Tokyo University of Foreign Studies, which was established in 2003. As discussed below, graduate students are major contributors to the recent growth of TS in Japan.

Thirdly, there have been some major publications that have laid a foundation for meta-discussion on TS in the Japanese context. For instance, Fujinami (2007) presented a view of translation as intercultural communication by applying functionalist theory to a systematic analysis of published Japanese translations. This was one of the first Japanese books to offer extensive theorizing on translation along with empirical data. In 2009 a Japanese translation of the second edition of Jeremy Munday's *Introducing Translation Studies* (2008) was published. This translation project was carried out by faculty and graduate students in TS at Rikkyo University. This effort was followed by a 2010 translation of Anthony Pym's *Exploring Translation Theories* (2010). While these two publications introduced concepts and Japanese translations of the metalanguage of TS as primarily developed in the West, another group of scholars published an anthology of key Japanese essays on translation that had originally been published between 1872 and 1944 (Yanabu et al. 2010). Each essay, written by a renowned translator or writer, is accompanied by a commentary by a contemporary translation scholar. Together these publications have helped set TS in Japan on a sounder initial footing.

Lastly, international exchanges in research on Japanese translation have increased rapidly in recent years, mainly through publications and conferences. There is a growing number of researchers who study and/or conduct research on Japanese translation in TS programs at universities in Europe, Australia, Korea, China, Canada, and the United States, for example. In addition to publications in English and/or the language of their institution, some of these researchers contribute to journals published in Japan. The research methodologies and theoretical frameworks they apply to discuss translational phenomena in the Japanese context serve as a useful reference for Japanese researchers who might not be as familiar with the development of the discipline outside

Japan. Papers by Japan-based translation scholars are still rare in international journals,[4] but *TTR*'s special issue on Japanese translation (2009) included four articles originating in Japan, providing international scholars with a glimpse of contemporary Japanese research on translation. An increasing number of Japanese translation researchers are also presenting papers outside of Japan, such as at conferences of the International Association for Translation and Intercultural Studies and the Asian Translation Traditions series. Within Japan, a major international conference organized by Ritsumeikan University and titled TS in the Japanese Context was held in Kyoto in 2010. This English-Japanese bilingual conference was attended by 160 scholars and students of Japanese translation from within Japan and abroad, and a wide range of topics was covered, from literary translation to community interpreting.

Who is doing what?

Let us now look at some of the works produced over the past decade in the field of TS in Japan. To maintain the focus on institutional identity, the object of examination here is those works that explicitly associate themselves with TS. In other words, the focus is on the 77 papers published in JAITS' two journals: 37 published from 2001 to 2010 in *Interpreting and Translation Studies* (known as *Interpretation Studies* from 2001 to 2007) and 40 published from 2007 to 2011 in *Invitation to Translation Studies*. Although a brief overview of the characteristics of these papers is provided, in line with the aim of this paper the main focus of discussion here is on the disciplinary sources of their theoretical and methodological underpinnings and the institutional backgrounds of the authors.

In terms of country of origin (the place where the article was written), 66 articles (86%) originated in Japan, 4 in Australia, 3 in Canada, 2 in the United Kingdom, and 1 each in Korea and Sweden. Most of the articles (92%) are written in Japanese, and the rest are in English. Forty-four articles (57%) address translation between Japanese and English, and the others deal with Chinese, French, Spanish, German, Italian, Korean, Mongolian, and Bosnian-Croatian-Serbian in combination with Japanese. The areas of research are spread over various categories, such as text analysis (19 articles), translation history (15), audiovisual translation (10), translator training (9), translation quality assessment (8), the translation process (7), and translation technology (5). A variety of research methods are applied. Historical/archival research is used most frequently, followed by case studies. There are some studies that draw on experiments, surveys, and corpora as well.

A total of 42 different authors contributed to these 2 journals during this timeframe. The most frequent contributor published 6 articles. One feature that might differ from translation journals elsewhere in the world is the high proportion of works by graduate students. Whereas university teachers contributed 30 articles (39%), graduate students contributed 41 articles (53%): 35 by doctoral students and 6 by master's students. This included 7 articles by graduate students affiliated with overseas universities (Australia and Canada). Other contributors included freelance translators and teachers at technical colleges and private vocational schools. Nine authors (21%) have relatively recent experience in studying abroad: they either completed in the past 10 years or are currently working on their masters and/or doctoral theses on translation at universities outside Japan: 5 in Australia, 2 in Spain, 1 each in the United Kingdom and Canada.

Most of the articles in these two journals explicitly lay out theoretical frameworks for their data analysis and argumentation. Of the concepts and theories developed within TS, the notion of translation norms is applied most frequently (11 articles), indicating the influence of Description Translation Studies in Japan. Several articles refer to functionalist theory, some binary concepts of equivalence, explicitation, polysystems theory, and translation universals. A number of articles adopt interdisciplinary approaches, drawing on theories and concepts from other disciplines, including various branches of linguistics (especially those in line with systemic functional grammar, cognitive linguistics, sociolinguistics, and linguistic anthropology), education (especially language teaching), literary studies, and sociology.

It might be useful to provide a list of works cited most frequently in the papers examined here, as this could indicate the most influential disciplinary sources of theoretical and methodological approaches applied to the study of translation in the Japanese context, at least within this particular community. Table 1.1 shows the seven publications cited most frequently. The "Number of articles" indicates how many articles cite each work, and the "Number of authors" indicates how many different authors cite that work.

The most cited publications are Toury (1995) and Munday (2008/2009). While Toury (1995) is generally cited by articles that purport to adopt a Descriptive Translation Studies approach and that apply the concept of norms in translation, various parts of Munday (2008/2009) and Baker (1992) are referred to as a general introduction of certain concepts and findings of existing translation

Table 1.1 Works most cited in translation-related articles in JAITS journals (2001–11)

Author	Year	Title	Number of articles	Number of authors
Toury, G.	1995	*Descriptive Translation Studies and Beyond*	16	12
Munday, J.	2001/2008/2009*	*Introducing Translation Studies*	16	12
Baker, M.	1992	*In Other Words*	11	10
Nida, E.	1964/1972**	*Toward a Science of Translating*	8	7
Venuti, L.	1995	*The Translator's Invisibility*	8	7
Blum-Kulka, S.	1986/2004	"Shifts of Cohesion and Coherence in Translation"	8	7
Halliday, M. A. K.	1994/2001***	*An Introduction to Functional Grammar*	8	6

   * "2009" refers to the Japanese translation of the second edition of Munday's book
  ** "1972" refers to the Japanese tr anslation
*** "2001" refers to the Japanese translation

research. Nida (1964/1972) and Venuti (1995) are mostly cited in discussions of binary categories of equivalence and translation methods (i.e. formal vs dynamic equivalence; domestication vs foreignization). Blum-Kulka (1986/2004) is drawn on to introduce the concept of explicitation, and Halliday (1994/2001) is mainly cited by studies that compare source and target texts. All of these publications are available in book form, and three are available in Japanese translation. Japanese authors did not make this most-cited list, indicating the greater influence of non-Japanese authors on contributors to these two journals. The most frequently cited publication originally written in Japanese is Mizuno (2007b), which applies Itamar Even-Zohar's polysystems theory to analyze literary translation in early modern Japan. It is referred to in six articles by five different authors.

Discussion

This examination of the institutional development of TS in Japan and publications within that community reveals some features characterizing the emerging discipline in this part of the world. First, although interest in translation as an object of academic inquiry has appeared sporadically since the

1970s, it did not amount to a collective endeavor to make it a distinct academic field until after the turn of the millennium. Since then scholarly activities concerning translation have rapidly gained momentum, leading to a nascent stage of TS in Japan. Secondly, unlike some other regions in the world where interpreting research is considered an autonomous subdiscipline within TS, the institutionalization of TS in Japan has sprung out of an organization that focuses on interpreting research. Thirdly, graduate students are playing a significant part in publications and conference presentations on TS in Japan. Finally, although linguistic orientations remain strong, many translation researchers in Japan are also receptive to applying theories, concepts, and methods developed by Western translation scholars to Japanese translational phenomena. These characteristics are all interconnected, and they can be analyzed together as follows, mainly in terms of three institutional and social factors: (1) a shift to emphasizing more practical aspects in language education at Japanese universities; (2) contacts with the international community of translation and interpreting researchers; and (3) a cultural environment in which there is a general interest in translation and well-established publishing channels for translation-related books.

Shift to a more practical orientation in higher education

Against the backdrop of increased global demand for mediation in communication across languages in commerce, government, and culture, there has been a growing number of university departments and programs around the world that are dedicated to teaching translation (see the Translator-Training Observatory by the Intercultural Studies Group). This development in higher education is one of the driving forces behind the institutionalization of TS. When a practice-oriented program is established, "research becomes a natural part" (Gile 2010: 258), since the program's credibility might suffer without research activity. Toury (2008: 404) notes that the institutional recognition of translation as an academic field drives people to engage more in research and leads to the production of more doctoral dissertations on translation. Translation teachers might also be motivated to promote distinct research and theorizing on translation so as to legitimize translator training in universities and make it independent from language or literary studies programs, as Pym (2010: 49–50; 2011: 54–6) suggests in the case of German functionalist theory, for example.

University programs dedicated to translation or interpreting did not exist in Japan until several years ago. Instead translator training has generally been in the hands of private companies, such as translation agencies and language schools.

This training takes the form of professional translators correcting students' translation assignments, along the lines of the traditional apprenticeship-type approach generally found in the teaching and learning of skills and crafts in Japan. It constitutes a segment of the huge language teaching market (estimated at over $8 billion[5]), to which translator-aspirants seem to resort (rather than to universities) when it comes to learning practical skills. This is because these private schools are generally believed to offer courses that are more relevant to market needs and to act as a gateway to the professional market.

The situation has, however, changed over the past decade. The prolonged economic difficulties in Japan have led to a general trend for Japanese universities to offer more practical courses so as to boost students' marketability in the depressed job market. According to Someya (2010: 73–4), the number of Japanese universities offering BA- and/or MA-level translation and/or interpreting courses increased fivefold from 1997 to over a hundred in 2005. Someya (2010: 74) suggests two major reasons for this trend: one is the expectation that translation and interpreting courses can compensate for some of the deficiencies in the current offerings of English programs at Japanese universities; the other is the "advertising" effect in recruiting new students by offering translation and interpreting courses, which are considered new and different from traditional English courses. The Japanese education ministry has also promoted an emphasis on practical aspects in the teaching of English in recent years. In 2000 a report by an advisory group to the ministry[6] acknowledged the importance of translation and interpreting in society and stressed the desirability of training professional interpreters and interpreting researchers in higher education and the desirability of advancing machine translation. In response to continual pleas from the business world for Japanese universities to train students in communication skills in English, in 2003 the ministry announced "the action plan to cultivate Japanese with English abilities" (Saitō 2007b: 209–13). Under this government-level initiative to promote practical aspects in English learning, several Japanese universities have received grants for interpreting and translation-related projects over the past several years. With such government endorsement for the teaching of translation and interpreting in higher education, the academic environment seems to have become more accommodating to the institutionalization of TS.

Since this is a recent development, there are not yet many experienced academics for teaching translation or conducting research on translation. On the other hand, more and more students are working on MA and PhD theses on translation in the new translation and interpreting programs, and they are generally encouraged or required to publish their papers. This alone can explain why graduate students' contributions account for more than half of the publications examined above.

International contacts

Besides the changes in the institutional environment surrounding Japanese universities, the development of TS in Japan has also been fostered through international contacts. As described above, the main force that drove the institutionalization of TS was the group of translation researchers within JAITS. The academic backgrounds of these members and early contributors of translation papers to the association's journals point to their international exposure, mainly via two avenues—through research on interpreting and through graduate studies outside Japan.

The reason that an organization for interpreting research preceded one for translation research can partly be explained, as alluded to earlier, by the extent of engagement with the community of translation and interpreting scholars outside Japan. As indicated earlier, during the 1980s and 1990s, Japanese translation scholars did not seem greatly interested in publishing in international journals or engaging with the international community of translation researchers. By contrast, Masaomi Kondō started a study group on interpreting research in 1990 because he was inspired by a conference he attended in the United States (Kondō 2009). As a member of AIIC, an international organization representing professional conference interpreters, Kondō had opportunities to interact with the international community of interpreting scholars. In the early 1990s members of this interpreting study group started presenting papers at international conferences and publishing in international journals. Their engagement with interpreting researchers from around the world no doubt exposed them to some developments in TS as well, since translation research and interpreting research are usually bundled together in conferences and journals. It is assumed that some of these interpreting researchers became aware of theories and methods used in translation research and started paying attention to translation issues as well.

The other aspect of international contacts is the fact that early contributors to journals on translation research in Japan were people who had studied or were studying in graduate programs in Australia and the United Kingdom. The theories and methods used in their papers on Japanese translation might have directed attention to the development of TS outside Japan. Since then, as indicated earlier, there has been a steady flow of contributions (one to two per issue) from researchers who have completed or are working on a doctoral dissertation in TS programs overseas. These researchers are also playing a part in disseminating information on the tradition of and perspectives on Japanese translation to the international community of translation scholars.

The founding statement of *Invitation to Translation Studies* (Mizuno 2007a) clearly indicates an awareness of the global development of TS and Japan's position in it. Mizuno (2007a: 1–2) explains that the purpose of this journal is to establish TS as a discipline in Japan, since in his view it lagged three decades behind Europe. He also mentions that the call for papers for *TTR*'s special issue on Japanese translation research was the catalyst for the launch of a journal dedicated to TS within Japan. Thus the global reach of TS indeed seems to have played an important role in the inception of the discipline in Japan.

Cultural infrastructure

Lastly, attention should be paid to the cultural infrastructure that has facilitated the recent publication of academic books related to TS in Japan. In addition to the anthology and two translated books mentioned earlier, Japanese translations of Antoine Berman's *L'épreuve de l'étranger* (1984) and Michaël Oustinoff's *La traduction* (2003) were published in 2008, as was an anthology of writings on translation by German philosophers and authors (translated and commented on by a Japanese scholar; Mitsugi 2008). In 2010 a Japanese translation of Cronin's *Translation and Globalization* (2003) was published. Further, a book consisting of selected papers from the above mentioned conference at Ritsumeikan University was published in 2011, edited by Nana Sato-Rossberg, the main organizer of the conference. Almost all of these books were released by well-respected commercial (rather than academic) publishers with significant experience in publishing translated books through the mainstream distribution system at bookstores and online in the Japanese publishing world. This might be rather unusual compared with some settings outside Japan, where books related to TS might not be so visible beyond the relevant academic communities.

The reason that these commercial publishers are interested in works related to TS might be found in Japan's *hon'yaku bunka* (translation culture or culture of translation). This term is primarily linked to the crucial role translation has played throughout the political, academic, and cultural history of Japan (e.g. Yanabu 1978; Sugimoto 1988), but it also reflects the ubiquity of translation[7] and general interest in translation (especially its professional aspects) in contemporary Japan. In addition to self-reflective essays by renowned translators, magazine-format career guidance books on how to become a translator abound, one of which recently included advertisements for over 100 translation programs, all run by translation companies or language schools (ALC 2011). It is possible that some publishers have found commercial value in more academically oriented writings on translation as something novel that goes beyond the popular discourse on translation and as textbooks for use in classes now that Japanese universities have started offering programs and courses related to TS.

Thus it is possible that this "translation-friendly" cultural environment played a supportive role when efforts to promote TS as a discipline commenced in Japan. Since all the literature in Table 1.1 is available in book form and some of it in Japanese translation, accessibility and visibility seem to be one of the key elements in non-Japanese writers reaching and being recognized by a greater number of Japanese researchers. With several essential scholarly books on translation[8] now readily available to the general public at online and onsite bookstores in Japan, the role these commercial publishers play in the promotion of TS should not be underestimated.

"Japanese Translation Studies"

Many of the works examined in this chapter and in the anthology edited by Yanabu and colleagues (2010) deal with translation in early twentieth-century Japan, when it played an important role in Japan's modernization and the evolution of Japanese literature. Yet despite their intense interest in investigating the Japanese translation tradition, none of these researchers seem to overemphasize "Japanese-ness" or argue for a separate "Japanese Translation Studies" to be developed based on traditional Japanese discourses on translation by suggesting the irrelevance of "Western" translation theories[9] to the Japanese context. Researchers of translation in Japan seem to be flexible and not fixated on any particular approach, whether it be "Western" or "non-Western." They apply theories and methods, regardless of origin, as they see fit in order to address their research questions.

The reason could be that Japan has a longstanding history, especially in scholarly work, of importing ideas and knowledge (from China up to the nineteenth century and from the West in modern times), translating them into Japanese, adapting them to Japanese situations, and refining them through discourse in Japanese. TS is no exception. Researchers examine available theories and methodologies, regardless of their origin, and apply them if they are helpful in resolving research problems. Moreover, a nationalistic orientation in academia does not seem to exist in Japan, at least in the field of TS at this time. There are no political circumstances that might prompt academics to debate "national" versus "foreign" scholarship or academic "regionalism" versus "globalism," unlike in China (Cheung 2011) and other areas (Simeoni 2007a), for example.

Looking ahead

This paper has described how TS is taking shape as a discipline in Japan and has analyzed the contextual factors that have contributed to its development. With its long and rich history of translation and the sheer volume and indispensable role of translation in contemporary Japan, Japan seems to offer a natural space for TS. The concept of investigating translation as an academic subject is gaining ground, as translation courses are taught at a growing number of Japanese universities and theories and research methods developed by Western translation scholars are being introduced more extensively. The general interest in translation and the well-established business of publishing translations provide a cultural infrastructure that facilitates publications related to TS. TS seems to have taken off in Japan in the past decade, but it is not certain if it can take advantage of the current momentum in the future. Ongoing meta-discussion on the evolving definition, scope, and methods of the discipline itself is needed to maintain disciplinary identity, and the following areas might also need to be addressed for the advancement of TS in Japan and beyond.

First, it is important to develop more translation programs in institutions of higher education so as to establish the status of TS firmly in Japan. The number of translation courses at universities is increasing, but most are taught as part of language programs with the primary purpose of enhancing students' language and intercultural communication skills (Naganuma 2008), and they do not amount to a major or degree in translation. A degree or major specifically in translation would increase the visibility of the discipline and might attract more students. Whether the emphasis is on practical training or on theory and research, such degree/major programs would lead to more research on translation because of the thesis requirement and pressure for faculty publications. For effective operation of translation programs, research on pedagogical issues such as curriculum, assessment, and thesis supervision should be promoted and shared with the international community of translation researchers.

Secondly, translation researchers in Japan should be encouraged to have more global engagement by submitting papers to international journals and conferences more actively. Issues have been raised about the use of English and Anglo-American academic discourse in TS (e.g. Cheung 2009; Snell-Hornby 2010), such as the disadvantageous position nonnative speakers are placed in and the limitations on the approaches and examples allowed. Although critical reflection on such practices might be necessary, the benefits of engaging with a wider research community are too great to ignore. As noted above, international contact was one of the driving forces for the initial development of TS in Japan. Opportunities to present research findings and exchange opinions from different perspectives can lead to new shared discoveries in understanding translational phenomena. As indicated in the significant number of contributions by graduate students, the initial effort to promote TS in Japan might have focused more on the broadening of the researcher base than on the quality of researchers' work. While the number of contributions by graduate students is a promising sign for the future, the relative dearth of articles by more experienced researchers is a concern. There is also a practice of Japanese scholars publishing mainly in their internal university journals, which are not necessarily refereed rigorously. If research is evaluated only by the standards of a small group in Japan and not exposed to or tested by a larger establishment with a rigorous refereeing process, it might end up as another example of the "Galapagos syndrome" (evolution in isolation)—a buzzword to describe the current decline of Japanese inventions. It is time for Japanese translation scholars to challenge and be challenged by global discussions in the field of TS. This discipline that studies the intercultural phenomenon of translation is meant to involve dialogue across cultures.

Lastly, translation researchers in Japan, or anywhere for that matter, should pay due attention to the current practice of translation. This is especially relevant when one of the thrusts for the development of the discipline at Japanese universities is the trend to emphasize practical aspects of language learning. Translation scholars are often accused of being out of touch with the professional realities of translating (e.g. Chesterman and Wagner 2002). By addressing current issues affecting the professional community, such as machine translation, translation tools, volunteer translation (which became especially visible during the recent earthquake crisis), and ethical issues, researchers might be able to present findings that can have a positive impact on the practice and social status of translators. Even in historical studies, researchers should be attentive to the relevance of their investigation to contemporary translators (Pym 1998: ix–xi). Socially meaningful research can only make a positive contribution to the advancement of the discipline.

Notes

1 See examples in the Doctoral Dissertation Bibliographic Database by the National Institute of Informatics in Japan. http://dbr.nii.ac.jp/infolib/meta_pub/ G0000016GAKUI1, accessed May 5, 2011.

2 In his most recent article Yanabu (2010: 18–22) does refer to TS in the West and points to Bible translation as the main reason that there is a long tradition of academic inquiry into translation in the West.

3 All quotes from Japanese texts are translated by the author unless otherwise stated.

4 For publications in 2010, for example, John Benjamins' Translation Studies Bibliography Database contains 19 entries on Chinese translation versus 4 entries on Japanese translation, none of which originated in Japan. www.benjamins.com/ online/tsb/, accessed May 5, 2011.

5 The estimate is based on market research conducted in 2009 (Yano Research Institute 2010).

6 The official report of the 22nd National Language Council. www.mext.go.jp/b_ menu/shingi/12/kokugo/toushin/001217.htm, accessed May 5, 2011.

7 The translation market in Japan was estimated to be worth over $2 billion in 2007, and the number of translation companies in Japan exceeded 1,000 in 2009 (Japan Translation Federation 2009). Nearly 5,500 translated books (about 7 percent of total book publications) were published in Japan in 2009 (Shuppan News 2010).

8 It should be noted that the narrow selection available could result in a skewed impression of the overall spectrum of TS.

9 See Pym (2011) on the vagueness of the term "Western translation theories."

References

ALC. 2011. *Hon'yaku jiten* [Translation guidebook]. Tokyo: Mukku.

Baker, M. 1992. *In Other Words*. London and New York: Routledge.

Berman, A. 1984. *L'épreuve de l'étranger*. Paris: Gallimard. Translated by S. Fujita as *Tasha to iu shiren* (Tokyo: Misuzu Shobō, 2008).

Blum-Kulka, S. 1986/2004. "Shifts of Cohesion and Coherence in Translation." In *The Translation Studies Reader*, edited by L. Venuti. London and New York: Routledge, pp. 298–314.

Chesterman, A. and E. Wagner. 2002. *Can Theory Help Translators?* Manchester: St. Jerome Publishing.

Cheung, M. P. Y. 2009. "Introduction. Chinese Discourses on Translation." *The Translator* 15(2): 223–38.

—. 2011. "The (Un)importance of Flagging Chineseness: Making Sense of a Recurrent Theme in Contemporary Chinese Discourses on Translation." *Translation Studies* 4(1): 42–57.

Cronin, M. 2003. *Translation and Globalization*. New York and London: Routledge. Translated by T. Furomoto et al. as *Hon'yaku to gurōbarizēshon: Shin hon'yaku kotohajime* (Osaka: Osaka Kyōiku Tosho, 2010).

Fujinami, F. 1984. "Doitsu ni hon'yaku-gaku" [Translation Studies in Germany]. *Gaikokugo gaikoku bungaku kenkyū* 8: 1–12.

—. 2007. *Hon'yaku kōi to ibunkakan komyunikēshon* [Translating and intercultural communication]. Tokyo: Shoraisha.

Gile, D. 1988a. "Introduction." *Meta* 33(1): 115–26.

—. 1988b. "Les publications japonaises sur la traduction: Un aperçu." *Meta* 33(1): 115–26.

—. 2010. "Why Translation Studies Matters: A Pragmatist's Viewpoint." In *Why Translation Studies Matters*, edited by G. Hansen, D. Gile, and N. P. Pokorn. Amsterdam and Philadelphia: John Benjamins, pp. 251–61.

Halliday, M. A. K. 1994. *An Introduction to Functional Grammar*. London: Edward Arnold. Translated by N. Yamaguchi and T. Kakehi as *Kinō bunpō gaisetsu* (Tokyo: Kuroshio Shuppan, 2001).

Halverson, S. 2010. "Translation." In *Handbook of Translation Studies*, edited by T. Gambier and L. van Doorslaer. Amsterdam and Philadelphia: John Benjamins, pp. 378–84.

Hermans, T. 2006. *Translating Others*. Manchester: St. Jerome Publishing.

—. 2007. *The Conferences of the Tongues*. Manchester: St. Jerome Publishing.

Hirako, Y. 1999. *Hon'yaku no genri* [The principle of translation]. Tokyo: Taishūkan shoten.

Hung, E. and J. Wakabayashi. 2005. *Asian Translation Traditions*. Manchester: St. Jerome Publishing.

Ihara, N. 2003. "Hon'yaku ni okeru wahō: Ika /dōka strategy no kanten kara" [Speech presentation in translation: From a perspective of foreignizing and domesticating strategy]. Doctoral dissertation, Kobe University.

Intercultural Studies Group. *Translator-Training Observatory*. http://isg.urv.es/tti/tti. htm, accessed May 5, 2011.

Itagaki, S. 1995. *Hon'yaku-gaku* [Translation studies]. Tokyo: Shinzansha.

Japan Translation Federation. 2009. *Hon'yaku hakusho 2008* [Translation white paper 2008]. Tokyo: Japan Translation Federation.

Kawamoto, K. and K. Inoue (eds). 1997. *Hon'yaku no hōhō* [Methods of translation]. Tokyo: Tokyo University Press.

Kondō, M. 2009. "Genesis of the Japan Association for Interpretation Studies (JAIS)." AIIC Webzine, Summer 2009. www.aiic.net/ViewPage.cfm/article2406.htm, accessed May 5, 2011.

Kondō, M. and J. Wakabayashi. 1998. "Japanese Tradition." In *Routledge Encyclopedia of Translation Studies*, edited by M. Baker. London and New York: Routledge, pp. 485–94.

Levy, I. 2011. *Translation in Modern Japan.* London and New York: Routledge.

Maruyama, M. and S. Katō. 1998. *Hon'yaku to nihon no kindai* [Translation and modern Japan]. Tokyo: Iwanami Shoten.

Mitsugi, M. (ed. and trans.). 2008. *Shisō toshite no hon'yaku: Gēte kara Ben'yamin, Burohho made* [Translation as philosophy: from Goethe to Benjamin, Broch]. Tokyo: Hakusuisha.

Mizuno, A. 1999. "Kinōteki hon'yaku riron e no joshō" [Prologue to functional translation theory]. *Interpreting Research* 15: 50–77.

—. 2007a. "Hajimeni" [Introduction]. *Invitation to Translation Studies in Japan* 1: 1–2.

—. 2007b. "Kindai nihon no bungakuteki tagen shisutemu to hon'yaku no isō" [Literary polysystems and positions of translation in modern Japan]. *Invitation to Translation Studies in Japan* 1: 3–43.

Morinaka, T. 2006. "Translation as Dissemination." In *Translation, Biopolitics, Colonial Difference,* edited by N. Sakai and J. Solomon. Hong Kong: Hong Kong University Press, pp. 39–53.

Munday, J. 2008. *Introducing Translation Studies,* 2nd edn. London and New York: Routledge. Translated by K. Torikai et al. as *Hon'yaku-gaku nyūmon* (Tokyo: Misuzu Shobō, 2009).

Naganuma, M. 2008. "Ankēto ni miru nihon no daigaku hon'yaku kyōiku no genjō" [The state of Japanese translator training at universities: A survey]. *Interpreting and Translation Studies* 8: 285–97.

Naruse, T. 1978. *Hon'yaku no shosō* [Aspects of translation]. Tokyo: Kaibunsha.

Nida, E. A. 1964. *Toward a Science of Translating.* Leiden: E. J. Brill. Translated by T. Naruse as *Hon'yaku-gaku josetsu* (Tokyo: Kaibunsha, 1972).

Oustinoff, M. 2003. *La traduction.* Paris: Presses Universitaires de France. Translated by Y. Hattori as *Hon'yaku: sono rekishi, riron, tenbō* (Tokyo: Hakusuisha, 2008).

Pöchhacker, F. 2004. *Introducing Interpreting Studies.* London and New York: Routledge.

Pym, A. 1998. *Methods in Translation History.* Manchester: St. Jerome Publishing.

— 2010. *Exploring Translation Theories.* London and New York: Routledge. Translated by K. Takeda as *Hon'yaku riron no tankyū* (Tokyo: Misuzu Shobō, 2010).

—. 2011. "Translation Theory as Historical Problem-Solving." *Intercultural Studies Review* 9: 49–61.

Pym, A., M. Shlesinger, and Z. Jettmarová (eds). 2006. *Sociocultural Aspects of Translating and Interpreting.* Amsterdam and Philadelphia: John Benjamins.

Saitō, Y. 2007a. *Hon'yaku no sahō* [The art of translation]. Tokyo: Tokyo University Press.

—. 2007b. *Nihonjin to eigo* [Japanese people and English]. Tokyo: Kenkyūsha.

Sakai, N. 1997. *Translation and Subjectivity.* Minneapolis and London: University of Minnesota Press.

Satō, M. 2008. "Eibungaku hon'yaku no 'hon'yaku kihan' ni kansuru ichi kōsatsu" [A study of norms in translations of English literature]. Doctoral dissertation, Hokkaido University.

Sato-Rossberg, N. 2007. "Chiri Mashiho no Ainu shin'yō-yaku ni okeru sōzō: bunka to performance o hon'yaku suru" [The creative translations of Ainu chanted-myths by Chiri Mashiho—Translating Ainu culture and performance]. Doctoral dissertation, Ritsumeikan University (published as *Translating Culture* from Sapporo-dō Press in 2011).

Sato-Rossberg, N. (ed.). 2011. *Toransurēshon sutadīzu* [Translation Studies]. Tokyo: Misuzu Shobō.

Shlesinger, M. 2004. "Doorstep Inter-subdisciplinarity and Beyond." In *Translation Research and Interpreting Research*, edited by C. Schäffner. Clevedon: Multilingual Matters, pp. 116–23.

Shuppan News. 2009. *Shuppan Nenkan* [Publishing yearbook]. Tokyo: Shuppan News.

Simeoni, D. 2007a. "Translation and Society: The Emergence of a Conceptual Relationship." In *Translation–Reflections, Refractions, Transformations*, edited by P. St-Pierre and P. C. Kar. Amsterdam and Philadelphia: John Benjamins, pp. 13–26.

—. 2007b. "Between Sociology and History: Method in Context and in Practice." In *Constructing a Sociology of Translation*, edited by M. Wolf and A. Fukari. Amsterdam and Philadelphia: John Benjamins, pp. 187–204.

—. 2008. "Norms and the State: The Geopolitics of Translation Theory." In *Beyond Descriptive Translation Studies*, edited by A. Pym, M. Shlesinger, and D. Simeoni. Amsterdam and Philadelphia: John Benjamins, pp. 329–42.

Snell-Hornby, M. 2010. "Is Translation Studies Going Anglo-Saxon? Critical Comments on the Globalization of a Discipline." In *Why Translation Studies Matters*, edited by G. Hansen, D. Gile, and N. P. Pokorn. Amsterdam and Philadelphia: John Benjamins, pp. 97–104.

Someya, Y. 2010. "The Teaching of Translation in the Context of College Education: Its Purpose and Rationale." *Gaikokugo kyōiku kenkyū* [Studies in foreign language teaching] 3: 73–102.

Sugimoto, T. 1988. "The Inception of Translation Culture in Japan." *Meta* 33(1): 25–31.

Teplova, N. 2009. "Presentation." *TTR* 22(1): 11–18.

Toury, G. 1995. *Descriptive Translation Studies and Beyond*. Amsterdam and Philadelphia: John Benjamins.

—. 2008. "Interview in Toronto." In *Beyond Descriptive Translation Studies*, edited by A. Pym, M. Shlesinger, and D. Simeoni. Amsterdam and Philadelphia: John Benjamins, pp. 399–413.

Tymoczko, M. 2007. *Enlarging Translation, Empowering Translators*. Manchester: St. Jerome Publishing.

—. 2009. "Why Translators Should Want to Internationalize Translation Studies." *The Translator* 15(2): 401–21.

Venuti, L. 1995. *The Translator's Invisibility*. London and New York: Routledge.

Wakabayashi, J. and R. Kothari (eds). 2009. *Decentering Translation Studies*. Amsterdam and Philadelphia: John Benjamins.

Wolf, M. and A. Fukari (eds). 2007. *Constructing a Sociology of Translation.* Amsterdam and Philadelphia: John Benjamins.

Yanabu, A. 1978. *Hon'yaku bunka o kangaeru* [Thoughts on translation culture]. Tokyo: Hōsei University Press.

—. 2009. "Translation in Japan: The Cassette Effect." *TTR* 22(1): 19–28.

—. 2010. "Nihon ni okeru hon'yaku" [Translation in Japan]. In *Nihon no hon'yaku-ron* [Japanese discourse on translation], edited by A. Yanabu, A. Mizuno, and M. Naganuma. Tokyo: Hōsei University Press, pp. 1–34.

—. 2011. "Selections by Yanabu Akira." Translated by I. Levy, T. Gaubatz, and A. Haag. In *Translation in Modern Japan*, edited by I. Levy. London and New York: Routledge, pp. 46–72.

Yanabu, A., A. Mizuno, and M. Naganuma (eds). 2010. *Nihon no hon'yaku-ron* [Japanese discourse on translation]. Tokyo: Hōsei University Press.

Yano Research Institute. 2010. *Gogaku bijinesu shijō ni kansuru chōsa kekka 2010* [Results of a survey on the language business market 2010]. www.yano.co.jp/press/pdf/631.pdf, accessed May 5, 2011.

2

Situating Translation Studies in Japan within a Broader Context

Judy Wakabayashi

Introduction

Here I would like to consider Translation Studies (TS) in Japan within its broader regional and intellectual context. Internationally, the academic discipline of TS is today most closely associated with the West (a problematic but convenient shorthand construct which, like "Asia," overlooks internal diversity and changes over time). This situation suggests a hierarchical relationship in which the West is positioned as the potential "bestower" of translation-related knowledge and thinking to countries perceived as "lagging" in this respect. It is understandable and commendable that a growing number of Japanese researchers are now eager to join the broader community of TS researchers, and they can undoubtedly gain much by introducing Euro-American concepts and analytical frameworks. Yet this should not be at the expense of local ideas and realities. Although in Japan TS is still a fledgling discipline, Japanese society has rich discourses on translation that trace at least as far back as the Confucian philosopher Sorai Ogyū (1666–1728) and the hereditary translator Ryōei Motoki (1735–94). And for nearly a millenium before that the Japanese had been implementing an intra-/intertextualizing practice known as *kanbun kundoku*[1] that is closely intertwined with the linguistic, orthographic, and cultural relations between China and Japan and that is hence not fully accounted for in theories based on very different realities.

My goal here is to question the relationship between the Western and Japanese[2] discourses on translation and to situate both within a broader international context, drawing particularly—and to make a deliberate political point—on lessons from another Asian "player" in TS, in the hope that recent debates in China might prove instructive. I will also add a few comments from an outsider's perspective on the current state and future direction of TS in Japan.

On transplanting paradigms

Let me start by reflecting a little on the importation of foreign paradigms. In the Edo period (1603–1868) the hereditary translators in Nagasaki and the scholars in the Edo capital who translated Dutch scientific works were enormously influential in introducing European knowledge. During Japan's centuries of national isolation they were faced not only with immense linguistic and translational difficulties, but also with the challenge of introducing new ways of thinking and new academic traditions. These imported ideas were not adopted unthinkingly, but were tested against existing ideas—perhaps most famously in the 1771 incident when some scholars were so impressed by how the dissection of a corpse confirmed the superior accuracy of a Dutch anatomical chart over Chinese works that they decided to introduce Western Learning by translating Dutch books. This critical attitude of empirically testing imported ideas is perhaps somewhat lacking in the adoption of TS in Japan today. Although one aspect of the oft-cited notion of Japan as a "translation culture" refers to its valorization of imported ideas, this should not mean wholesale acceptance without due reflection (and self-reflection). In his article "Traveling Theory" Edward Said (1998: 168–9) suggests that theories are "a response to a specific social and historical situation," so they are not automatically applicable in other contexts. He argues that the fact that the movement of theories "necessarily involves processes of representation and institutionalization different from those at the point of origin [. . .] complicates any account of the translation, transference, circulation, and commerce of theories and ideas." So considering the applicability of imported theories is not necessarily about championing national identity or "uniqueness." It is simply that historical circumstances in Japan have led to a translational trajectory and ideas on translation that differ somewhat from those in Europe, and these differences need to be acknowledged and taken into account—even as present-day circumstances mean that there is a growing convergence both in practice and ideas. This stance is not about blindly asserting "Japaneseness," but about recognizing those practices and discourse elements that are relevant and valuable in Japan and that might even offer insights beyond that context. This does not imply uncritical acceptance or "defense" of traditional ideas or practices, but nor should it mean unthinking espousal of imported ideas or practices.

Many translation scholars in Japan today seem to be importing TS as an established edifice, without full awareness of the debates that occurred in the process of constructing this edifice and without full consideration of its relevance to the Japanese context. Euro-American theories might indeed be a good fit for many aspects of translation in Japan, but this needs to be verified. As Kim (2009: 416) warns, "It is quite easy to get induced to reconstruct Asian realities consistent with the logic of the dominant Western paradigms." There are also facets of the Japanese situation (e.g. the practice of *kanbun kundoku*; the effect of the interplay among the different Japanese scripts[3]) that are *not* adequately covered by current Euro-American theories. Although it is undoubtedly beneficial for Japanese researchers to become familiar with TS in the West and to draw on these ideas for intellectual stimulation, evaluating their applicability[4] to the Japanese context is also essential. Without such a critical consciousness, it is easy for theories that have gained authority elsewhere to be reduced to dogma when they travel (Said 1998: 179), rather than taking on a fully transformative potential in their new home—a transformation that might eventually lead to alternative or more refined forms of these ideas in their point of origin.[5]

Certainly, it is easier to focus on issues already explored elsewhere than to formulate original agendas and new paradigms. And revamping Euro-American theories for the Japanese context might indeed lead to new insights modulated for local circumstances. Yet in terms of TS as an *international* discipline, such an approach is less likely to result in fundamental epistemic change or new perspectives. And in the meantime Euro-American scholarship will have moved on, leaving Japan always trying to catch up, always intellectually dependent or imitative.

Japanese translation scholars can, however, occupy strategic ground if they focus on the Japanese context—not just by applying imported ideas to this local context, but also productively critiquing these ideas from a Japanese vantage point, tapping into existing Japanese conceptual bases more fully, and developing new perspectives in line with Japanese realities, values, and concerns. This does not mean that Japanese researchers should restrict themselves solely to studying Japanese contexts of translation, which would merely be replacing one form of ethnocentrism with another, or that they are unqualified to discuss ideas and practices that are not specific to Japan. It is simply that they have an advantage when they explore Japanese circumstances and ideas of translation. Nakayama (1984: 236) has suggested that those outside of Western scholarship can put this position to good use:

> Criticism that comes from within the Western academic tradition cannot help but be parochial. The task of independent evaluation is best entrusted to a judge who stands outside the tradition. [...] Let us gradually take up the works of Western scholars that are so much a part of our scholarly lives and write our assessment of them, preferably in a Western language. Should this

happen on a significant scale, Western scholars will be forced to take note of how their work is being received in Japan, and Japan will begin to serve as a vehicle and reminder of the need for objective judgment.

The fact that Japanese researchers know far more about Western scholarship on translation than vice versa gives Japanese scholars the benefit of a broader perspective.

The provincial nature of Euro-American ideas on translation has often gone unnoticed in the past, and their presumed universality and universal applicability remain unsubstantiated.[6] Although imported ideas provide a ready-made theoretical foundation and Euro-American thinking is now a part of Japanese thinking in all walks of life, these imported concepts might be inadequate accounts of translation as practiced and conceived in Japan over time (just as some ideas and practices originating in Japan might lack broader relevance). Adapting Kruger (2008: 62), we could say that the challenge is "to develop an indigenous, contextually appropriate . . . methodology and approach . . . that draws on international 'best practices', but does not reproduce them. In this way we can assimilate 'best practices', but adapt these to local knowledge."[7]

Chinese debates on the relationship with Euro-American Translation Studies

One alternative to using the "West" as the reference point is to compare Japan's situation with that of its Asian neighbors. Specifically, I would suggest that recent debates in China about the relationship between local discourses on translation and ideas imported from the West have implications for Japanese researchers. TS in Japan can be usefully considered not only in bilateral terms vis-à-vis the West, but also through triangulation with contemporary China, which is ahead of Japan in explicitly considering the relationship between local and imported ideas on translation. This does not mean replacing the Westcentric focus with an Asiacentric one, but supplementing and complementing the current discourse so as to achieve greater balance.

Since the mid-1980s the alleged "backwardness" of traditional Chinese ideas on translation, which have been described as impressionistic and focused on prescriptivism and translation criticism (Cheung 2011: 51), has led to an enthusiasm for "Westernized Translation Studies" among many Chinese scholars, based on the belief that these new and different ideas are the way to modernize Chinese discourses and establish a more scientific academic discipline of translation. This greater familiarity with Euro-American discourses has "yielded fruitful results" in China (Sun and Zheng 2008: 71), and in the past few years it is likewise starting to offer new insights in Japan.

Yet we cannot simply *assume* the validity or explanatory power of Western-derived theories, concepts and methods in non-Western contexts, or their superiority over home-grown counterparts. Their legitimacy and relevance must be tested in these new contexts, and adjustments (possibly including rejection) made if necessary. And in fact, not all Chinese translation scholars have accepted imported ideas without critique or modification. Since the mid-1990s, the situation in China has moved on from the initial enthusiasm for Euro-American ideas on translation. Today there is a debate between mainstream "progressives," who continue to advocate familiarity with Western ideas in the name of "paradigm shift," and "conservatives," who are concerned about what they regard as uncritical and excessive acceptance of Euro-American theories and who advocate the elaboration of theories with "Chinese characteristics." The point here is not which view is "right"; my argument is that thinking through the relationship between existing and imported discourses is a healthy and necessary step as TS emerges as an academic discipline in new contexts and engages with its counterparts elsewhere. I have seen no signs of similar "writing back" in Japan, partly perhaps because these imported ideas have not yet had as much impact there. As they grow in influence, however, it might be worth looking toward the Chinese response to this encounter between different paradigms[8] so as to minimize or preempt any unwarranted future backlash and so as to be alert to the importance of merit rather than origin. This is not about flagging Japaneseness or clinging to tradition or sheltering in a cultural ghetto (Cheung 2011: 51), but about relevance and "fit" in a different context and what might be gained by examining local realities in the light of imported insights (and vice versa).

One aspect of the reaction in China, which has witnessed increasing Sinocentrism since the late 1980s (Guo 2009: 253), involves criticism of views that equate Euro-American Translation Studies with progress and modernity. Sun and Zheng (2008: 64) challenge the assumption that "the only important developments are those leading towards modernity, as defined by the Western experience." There are alternative (non-Western) modernities—as well as alternatives to modernity. Sun and Zheng (2008: 68) also argue that tradition and modernity are not mutually exclusive and that a critical attitude toward Western ideas does not necessarily mean "the petrification of tradition" (69). Nor is the Westernization of local discourses the only possible future path for non-Western scholars of translation. As noted above, Japan might also expand its thinking on translation by looking to its Asian neighbors such as Korea, with which it shares much in terms of cultural and historical background and which is also ahead of Japan in terms of its engagement with TS in the West.

Another aspect of the backlash against Western TS in China involves (re)valorizing traditional ideas and calling for the revitalization or (re)construction of a theory or theories of translation with distinctive Chinese characteristics.[9] Whether motivated by nativism, nationalism, or a reasoned rejection of claims to culturally "neutral" universalism, calls for local theories imply that these theories are difficult to internationalize. At the same time, such calls project cultural confidence[10] (a necessary but potentially dangerous attribute) vis-à-vis Euro-American theorizing. Sun and Zheng (2008: 72) conclude that

> Chinese characteristics should not be pursued for their own sake or simply restricted to the level of language transfer. If there are any Chinese characteristics, they are to be manifested in the distinctive perspectives or methodologies informed by our specific culture. All in all, distinctive Chinese characteristics are an inevitable reality rather than a desirable goal.

The positive aspect of this backlash in China is that it has led to a more considered weighing up of the relationship between Chinese and Western ideas on translation. Tang (2007: 369) argues that

> Chinese scholars cannot afford to adopt an isolationist strategy to defend themselves against the dominance of Western metalanguages because discursive cultural nationalism can only induce the "narrowing down" of a recently broadened horizon, which will do more harm than good to Chinese Translation Studies.

Culture-specific claims and universalizing (homogenizing) claims both carry the risk of bias and essentialism. As is often the case with polar opposites,[11] the debate tends to neglect the possibility of an alternative in which the best elements of both approaches might engage in a productive fashion somewhere between—or beyond—the two extremes. Chan (2001: 229) argues that in order to be "reciprocal and constructive," mediation between the worldviews of the East and West "must be selective, discriminatory, progressive and multi-dimensional." She adds that "with our own tradition, we need consolidation, re-reading. With the West, we need positive engagement, not containment" (2001: 239). Chinese scholars are now emerging who not only bring Western insights to bear on translation in China, but also Chinese insights to bear on Western ideas. In these ways ideas on translation are transformed and evolve.

Tang (2007: 370) suggests that a dialogue between Chinese and Western scholars can be achieved more easily if Chinese scholars become familiar with Western metalanguages, theoretical frameworks, and modes of academic writing and presentation. This does not, however, exonerate Western scholars from making some attempt to learn about non-Western ideas. Chang (2009: 313) notes cautiously that "the position of Chinese translation studies has become less peripheral, but it remains to be seen whether it will become a source of repertoire transfer." The questions of how to project a Chinese voice in the international arena and whether and how to establish a "Chinese theory of translation" have not been fully resolved (Guo 2009: 248), but the first step is to raise such questions—and that is what I am advocating for Japanese scholars.

Implications for Japan

Such debates about the relationship between the local and Euro-American discourses of translation have been virtually nonexistent in Japan, perhaps because it feels less threatened than China by Westernization and because it has not recently undergone an experience such as the aftermath of the Cultural Revolution that led to "dissatisfaction with established repertoires" (Chang 2009: 310) and a "sense of self-insufficiency" (318) since the late 1970s.

While relative isolation allows ideas to develop in autonomous directions, the downside is that the potential for intellectual stimulation from outside is not fully tapped. Although some Japanese find foreign theories overly theoretical and "burdensome" (Konishi 1994: 8), the belatedness of the Japanese uptake of ideas from TS has not been because of overt rejection of foreign ideas or necessarily because of the strength and validity of Japanese ideas. Rather, it was largely due to a lack of familiarity with contemporary developments in TS. In the past decade this has begun to change rapidly, and this is a welcome development. Nevertheless, embracing Euro-American theories and methodologies uncritically would mean that Japanese discourses become derivative and lose much of their potential to contribute something new to the discipline. Still in the stage of assimilating imported ideas, most Japanese translation researchers have yet to transform these ideas critically or give them new meanings that would help "translate" the discipline.[12]

An overemphasis on Euro-American ideas also risks distancing Japanese scholars from their own traditions of thinking about translation, although existing ideas are likely to continue (and to continue evolving). In addition to

Japanese ideas and concepts pertaining specifically to translation, it would be worth revisiting and excavating the philosophical, religious and intellectual traditions and the literary and aesthetic theories of Japan's past in search of ideas on, for example, the relationship between word and meaning and/or language and the world that might be relevant as incipient "theories" of translation[13] (e.g. the rather controversial concept of *kotodama*, the spiritual power of words), although such ideas need to be situated in their historical context and not romanticized.[14] And of course existing ideas might overlap with imported ideas, perhaps pointing to fundamental similarities in translation across languages and cultures, although apparent resemblances to Western ideas can be misleading. For instance, the standard "equivalents" of *chokuyaku*, *iyaku*, and *hon'yakuchō*—that is, *literal translation, free translation*, and *translationese*—fail to convey the exact meaning and associations of these Japanese concepts (see Wakabayashi 2009: 184–9).

Other elements in Japanese writing on translation reflect different emphases from contemporary Euro-American discourses. Examples include the focus on "translation words" (i.e. interest in the social consequences of equivalents coined to express key imported concepts), the longstanding interest in the sociopolitical implications of translated texts,[15] the predominant source orientation and the acceptance of translational language, the focus on micro-level critiques of mistranslations, historical writing of an outstanding descriptive and empirical (but not necessarily analytical) nature, the emphasis on professional translation (in addition to literary translation), the large body of writing on field-specific translation, the relatively longstanding interest in subtitling, and the didactic, commercial, and pragmatic nature of many contemporary works. Although Ueda (2007: 252) rightly points out that a work does not need "to overtly claim a certain theoretical framework ... for it to display its theoretical engagement," the theoretical engagement of most contemporary Japanese writing on translation is indisputably less overt than in Euro-American scholarship, and this contributes to the impression that Japanese writing is "less scholarly."

A sense of difference can easily lead to essentialism (enshrining or reifying differences), and calls for protecting and fostering local perspectives can degenerate into an inward-looking, conservative, and unproductive anxiety over national or cultural identity. Moreover, an excessive focus on the culture-specific might reinstate the very hierarchy it is intended to dislodge, and it might lack broader relevance or theorizability. A related argument is that universal commonalities in translation render culture-specific theories unnecessary. Although this remains to be demonstrated, we should not allow the urge for local distinctiveness to blind us to genuine similarities.

Rather than an outright rejection of imported ideas (which would itself constitute a form of provincialism) or even a fusion or harmonization of the local and the imported, a more productive approach could be likened to chamber music, whereby the different instruments contribute to the "conversation of friends" while retaining their distinctive characteristics and each taking the lead at different times as appropriate. Japanese scholars can do more than passively absorb, emulate, or even creatively elaborate on Euro-American ideas and conceptual tools. Contributing to an expanded ontology of TS requires drawing on Japan's *own* sources of intellectual tradition and contemporary thinking so as to generate new perspectives that will contribute to the international stock of ideas on translation. I hope we will see a reappraisal whereby traditional Japanese ideas about translation might, paradoxically, be regarded as "new" and where "new traditions" will also be invented in Japan.

The current and future state of TS in Japan from an outside perspective

I would like to conclude with some observations on the state of TS in Japan, although I am aware of the sensitivities involved in such comments coming from someone who is not Japanese. Elsewhere I have highlighted some of the valuable features of Japanese discourses on translation,[16] but here the focus is on certain problematic aspects or underdeveloped areas that have come to my attention in the years I have been researching translation in the Japanese context. Although there is a growing community of Japanese researchers with an interest in translation, including a handful trained at universities in the West or integrated into Western academia in some way, TS in Japan has not yet achieved full status as a formal discipline.[17] On the international scene, Japanese scholarship on translation remains on the periphery. Although developments in the past few years mean that both of these situations are changing rapidly and the future holds considerable promise, it would be misleading to claim that TS in Japan is on a footing comparable to that in Europe.

One indicator of evolution and formalization as an academic discipline— that is, recognition as a distinct scholarly field—is the existence of degrees in translation (rather than translation courses as part of language or literature degrees). Again China is ahead of Japan in this respect.[18] A 2007 survey of translator training at Japanese universities shows that translation is still taught in individual courses (not degree programs),[19] mainly as an undergraduate elective and primarily aiming at language education or intercultural communication training, rather than professional translator training. Translator training in Japan remains heavily influenced by commercial schools, with the 2011 issue of the *Hon'yaku jiten* (Translation almanac) listing 281 courses offered at 82 schools (a notable decline or consolidation from the previous year, when there were 402 courses at 84 schools). Although the number of translation classes at universities now *seems* to outweigh those at vocational establishments, commercial institutions remain the focus of the translator training scene in Japan in terms of visibility and student numbers.[20] These schools have their merits, but they are primarily profit-oriented businesses, and the instructors generally lack the interest and expertise to examine translation from an academic perspective. An encouraging sign is the introduction of translation-related courses in some graduate programs (at Rikkyo University, Kobe College, and Aoyama Gakuin University). One practical step that might be considered in order to educate researchers (as distinct from training professional translators) is a summer school in translation research—similar to those held in Europe and Hong Kong, but combining ideas from the "international" discipline of TS with Japanese translation realities and perspectives. Although logistically not easy, this could help fast-track the acquisition of Euro-American research methodologies and ideas on translation, as well as explicitly address their relationship to existing Japanese approaches, and it could act as a breeding ground for a new generation of translation scholars in Japan and help round out the knowledge of those already in the field. "Train the trainer" courses would be another useful step, as translation pedagogy (as distinct from translator training) is still in its infancy in Japan, and this might be a way of fostering interaction between vocational and academic institutions that have translation courses.

Another parameter of a mature discipline is the existence of its own academic association. The establishment in 2005 of the Special Interest Group for Translation Studies within The Japan Association for Interpretation Studies was a welcome move in this direction.[21] The next step might be to make this interest group an academic association in its own right, stepping out from the shadow of its sister discipline (a situation that is the reverse of the relationship more typical in the West). I applaud the work of Akira Mizuno, Nana Sato-Rossberg, and Kumiko Torikai, among others, in helping to bridge the gap between Western and Japanese translation and interpreting research and in doing so much to foster up-and-coming researchers, who are among those starting to present some interesting and valuable work not just in Japan but also in international arenas.

I would also encourage Japanese translation researchers to publish more in peer-reviewed academic journals where the refereeing is anonymous, independent and "blind," including in venues other than university bulletins. Articles that appear in the latter "in-house" publications cannot be easily ordered from overseas, and they do not receive full academic recognition, thereby failing to elevate the status of TS in Japan. Moreover, since writing solely for Japanese audiences deprives most non-Japanese scholars of insights from a Japanese perspective, I hope that Japanese writers will also contribute more to journals outside of Japan—and that these journals will in turn be open to different rhetorical conventions, such as different ways of developing a topic.

A related step is for Japanese researchers to continue familiarizing themselves with the main ideas on translation elsewhere so that they are equipped to determine whether these fully encapsulate the Japanese experience. I hope to see more Japanese not only studying TS abroad and incorporating this knowledge into a consideration of translation in Japan, but also becoming more active on the international scene so as to not just learn from non-Japanese scholars but also educate them about translation in the Japanese context. This is starting to happen. As Cheung (2011: 52) emphasizes, "understanding is a prerequisite for . . . the exchange of views on equal terms."

Perhaps as important as a dialogue between Japanese and non-Japanese scholars is a debate *within* Japan among different views on translation. Have there been no "turns" in the Japanese discourse? Of course, one "turn" is Japanese researchers' growing interest in Euro-American Translation Studies, and a related "turn" is the incipient development of TS as a discipline in Japan, but are there no new *local* ideas worth noting? Do the informal and essayistic remarks of "star" translators such as Motoyuki Shibata and Naoki Yanase[22] represent the most innovative thinking in Japan today? This is not to imply any criticism of their writings, which have played a role in keeping translation in the spotlight among the Japanese public, but simply to suggest the desirability of supplementing them with more systematic and formalized ideas and writing on translation. Academic studies of translation have in fact long existed in Japan, although they have typically been grounded in other disciplines such as literary studies, historical linguistics, or philosophy. There is a need for a more encompassing and inclusive discourse in Japan, where currently there is a division into writing by those with a familiarity with Euro-American Translation Studies, other academic writing on translation, and the commercial/professional discourse.

One practical step toward bringing Japanese and non-Japanese discourses into dialogue is, ironically, translation. As Japanese history has amply demonstrated, making knowledge available through translated texts adds to the common intellectual weal. Translating Japanese works on translation into other languages would present some challenges, in part because non-Japanese readers generally lack familiarity with the relevant historical background and Japanese rhetorical conventions. Moreover, works focusing on Japanese translation *practice* have little applicability outside of Japan. Nevertheless, translating selected works into European languages (and, ideally, other Asian languages) is a project worth undertaking.

Conversely, translating influential non-Japanese works into Japanese will make these ideas more broadly available to Japanese readers who have difficulty reading these works in the original. Recent translations include a 2009 team translation of Jeremy Munday's *Introducing Translation Studies* and Kayoko Takeda's 2010 translation of Anthony Pym's *Exploring Translation Theories*. Such introductions of a range of theories (rather than just the ideas of individual theorists) are encouraging to see. The fact that relatively few European-language works on translation are available in Japanese means, however, that the spectrum of ideas on which to draw is narrowed and the works that *are* available take on a disproportionate weight. Another work that might usefully be translated is Mark Shuttleworth's *Dictionary of Translation Studies*. Compiling an original Japanese dictionary of translation terminology (both indigenous and imported) would be an even more worthwhile project that would help clarify the concepts and definitions of Japanese terms relating to translational practices and thinking.

One question that arises in such endeavors, however, is the translatability of vocabulary and concepts of translation. One of the markers of a mature discipline is having its own terminology, but the vocabulary and concepts of translation are deeply rooted in local contexts and traditions. For instance, Nana Satō-Rossberg[23] has pointed out that the term *hon'yaku-gaku* (literally, the study of translation) does not map perfectly onto *Translation Studies* and that these two terms need to be distinguished carefully, depending on the context. In his numerous writings Akira Yanabu[24] has repeatedly highlighted the problems that arose in the past when Japanese translators assigned fine-sounding but often misleading labels to imported European concepts and how the resulting discrepancies distorted the interpretation of these concepts, which then took on a new life of their own. It is important not to repeat this mistake when translating the terminology of our *own* discipline. With the introduction of Euro-American Translation Studies in the past few years there has been something of a proliferation of Japanese "equivalents" for terms in this field. Although I am not the best judge of these renditions, some seem to resemble the "translation words" so criticized by Yanabu.

Some translation-related equivalents currently in use in Japan seem awkward or incorrect,[25] or they fail to make adequate distinctions.[26] Once terms become accepted, it is difficult to dislodge them, so I would urge Japanese scholars to give careful consideration to finding and standardizing accurate and meaningful equivalents, aiming at understandable renditions that might also enter the public discourse. Conversely, it is important to exercise caution when writing about Japanese concepts of translation in other languages.

In order for ideas or practices of translation originating in Japan to hold their own against ideas and practices elsewhere and potentially gain broader relevance, they first need to be spelt out explicitly and given a more prominent position within Japan itself. One useful step toward clearer self-definition is the compilation of key Japanese writings on translation, and the publication of an anthology covering 29 works from the Meiji period (1868–1912) to World War II (Yanabu et al. 2010) is a welcome recent development, with plans afoot for additional volumes. Much of value has been written in Japan over the years, but it is largely scattered and not always easily accessible. Compiling seminal writings into a single volume or series, with translations into modern Japanese where necessary and with commentaries or scholarly introductions contextualizing each piece will not only improve access to these ideas and offer a better understanding of Japanese views as a whole and of their development over time, but also enhance the status of TS in Japan as a discipline with its own canonical works and introductory overviews. Alongside imported theories, which have held the spotlight for the last few years, Japanese ideas on translation should be taught systematically in Japanese classes on translation as an object for self-reflection. A further valuable step would be an explicit book-length comparison of local and Western thinking on translation.

In relation to the question of how to revitalize the traditional Chinese discourse on translation without falling into the trap of cultural essentialism, Cheung (2011) discusses four possible approaches:

1. "Total immersion in the theoretical text through careful reading of primary material and extensive reading of secondary material of the time." (Cheung 2011: 48)
2. Conducting "in-depth research on previously unavailable material . . ., or . . . understudied primary material in order to fill gaps in knowledge or remove blind spots in existing scholarship." (Cheung 2011: 49)
3. Rereading traditional ideas via modern (Western) interpretive and analytical frameworks and presenting the findings "in a mode of discourse

and with a logic that is understandable to researchers from the West" (Cheung 2011: 49). She cautions, however, that this approach "is problematic if it is justified on the grounds of a 'lack' or a 'weakness' in those discourses," which would reflect "a teleological view of modernization predicated on the master narrative of progress." (Cheung 2011: 50). Hence she suggests using "the concept of difference as existing in varying degrees of inseparability from the concept of similarity, so that it is always possible to say there is difference in similarity and similarity in difference." (Cheung 2011: 50)

4. Using "translation and editorial commentary, as well as other paratextual apparatuses, to create a discursive space for intercultural dialogues" (Cheung 2011: 50). The points of comparison between the local and Western discourses are "intended to facilitate further explorations in a dialogic, fully collaborative mode" (Cheung 2011: 50)—in other words, engagement, rather than a monologue on either side.

All these approaches are well worth considering in the Japanese context.

Conclusion

Although here I have aired some criticisms of the state of the discipline in Japan, I would like to reiterate my conviction that Japanese discourses on translation contain much of significance that needs to be valued by Japanese researchers and that could also be of interest to researchers elsewhere. Conversely, there is much that Japan can learn from contemporary TS in the West—for example, the analytical, critical, and ideologically oriented aspects, as opposed to a more "archaeological," descriptive, and practical approach. And Japan's new outward orientation should not overlook its Asian neighbors. Not only might fresh insights and perspectives be revealed by delineating "Japanese" ideas and praxis more sharply vis-à-vis those in other Asian cultures, but it is also ideologically important for Japan to acknowledge its regional context, rather than always positioning itself vis-à-vis the West.

The challenge I offer is for Japanese scholars to become both more *familiar* with and *independent* of TS elsewhere. This apparent contradiction can be resolved in the form of a considered independence based on thorough familiarity and critical engagement. Then, rather than seeking to "catch up," Japanese researchers who wish to move the field forward can be "forever looking ahead—scanning the horizon and thinking about where to go next"

(Nakayama 1984: 226). I have great hopes for the developments that are starting to emerge in Japan and that I fully anticipate will proliferate and mature in the coming years as Japan cultivates its own modern discipline of TS, drawing fully on local and imported discourses.

Notes

1   See Wakabayashi (1998: 58–60) for a brief discussion of this practice of accessing Chinese texts through reordering and Japanese glosses. *Kanbun kundoku* allows Chinese texts to be interpreted in Japanese, and for centuries it was used in Japan instead of translation.

2   Commenting on the practice of classifying translation theories by "nationality," Chang (2009: 317, n. 7) rightly points out that this "seems to be academically untenable, since a body of theories thus grouped together may not function as a system vis-à-vis another one. It may also not be advisable to give an account of the work of a theorist . . . in isolation from that of another one belonging to another nation." Regarding theorists of Japanese ethnicity as "merely" Japanese robs them of possible broader relevance. For convenience, however, here I group the ideas of "Japanese" writers (whether defined by ethnicity, cultural identity or language of writing) together under the rubric of Japanese discourses, using the plural form to suggest the internal diversity.

3   Another area where there is a potential lack of fit relates to the fact that for Asians "meaning and understanding are heavily dependent upon the subtlety, and even silence, of language and the sensitivity of language users" (Shi-xu 2009: 387). This raises the issue of how this affects translation between high-context Asian languages and languages used in low-context cultures—a question that has not been fully addressed in Euro-American discourses on translation.

4   Ueda (2007: 252) rightly criticizes the notion of "'applying'" theories, however, arguing that "The word 'using' posits theory to be an abstract and ahistorical apparatus that exists out there, waiting to be 'used' to derive a given interpretation. In such a scheme, the analyzing subject stands independently of the theory he 'uses.'"

5   In a later article Said (2000) recognized the possibility for theories to be revitalized in a new context—not by being duplicated but by being modified and given different emphases, resulting in a hybrid version of the theory.

6   In an instance of a non-Western gaze showing Western ideas in a different light, Phukan (2003: 29–30) comments that the Indian repudiation of a universal theory of translation "serves as a challenge to the hegemony of theory over practice, *another peculiar feature of the West.*" (emphasis added).

7   As Kim (2009: 416) points out, however, such an approach still constitutes a rather limited move: "The paradigm, to use Kuhn's (1970) term, is not simply the current theory, but the entire worldview in which it exists, and all of the implications which come with it. While modifying theories is the fabric of scientific progress, this position still falls under working within the Western paradigm."

8   Chang (2009: 315–16) suggests three causes for the clash between the Chinese and Western traditions: (1) Traditional Chinese scholarship has a utilitarian focus ("learning should bring immediate benefits to society") and it values "insight and daring hypotheses more than in-depth analysis and substantiation," so "there is hardly any place there for methodology and theorization"; (2) cohesion and "conformity to dominant norms are prioritized over individual rights, competition and independent thinking"; and (3) "the conflict between internationalism and nationalism." See Cheung (2011) for a full discussion of "Chineseness" in contemporary Chinese discourses on translation.

9   Some of these characteristics are listed in Tan (2009: 287–8) and Zhu (2004: 332–3). Tan (2009: 292–5) identifies five features of the "Chineseness" of Chinese translation theory—pragmatism, reliance on cultural heritage (i.e. use of traditional cultural concepts to theorize about translation), preoccupation with *xin* (faithfulness), intuitive (rather than analytical) thinking, and terseness. Some of these—particularly pragmatism and intuitive thinking—resonate strongly with the Japanese situation.

10 The support among some scholars of Chinese origin for postcolonial ideas that value the local has been interpreted in a negative light by certain observers as a way of supporting existing power structures in Chinese culture and an excuse for not challenging them—in other words, as a way of reinforcing old prejudices and hierarchies in a new singularizing guise that suppresses dissent. See Cheung (2011: 44).

11 Shi-xu (2009: 386) argues that "the tendency to view the universe in binary, oppositional terms is contrary to the worldview and ways of thinking of Asians [...] for Asians, such an approach is over-simplistic at best and will only lead researchers to overlooking complexities in, interconnections between and dynamics of things or peoples or indeed cultures."

12 One example of recent interaction is how Nozaki (2004) is critical of French ideas on translation in relation to the Japanese context. In a welcome instance of productive "negotiation" between the Japanese and "international" discourses, Miki Satō's excellent doctoral dissertation (2008) modifies Toury's concept of translation norms so as to better fit the Japanese context. Unfortunately, both of these works are currently available only in Japanese, thereby limiting their impact beyond Japan.

13 In the Chinese context, Sun and Zheng (2008: 78) note that some scholars have demonstrated the power of "impressionistic" terms from Chinese aesthetics, such

as *shen* (spirit), *qi* (ether), and *xing* (form), in explaining the relationship between translators and the Other.

14 Adapting the warning by Niranjana (1992: 180), we might also caution against unfounded attempts to show that Asian discourses on translation are already modern and hence worthy of the West's attention or are validated only in relation to Western thinking.

15 Despite this interest and numerous works on translation in relation to Japanese society and culture, Japanese writing on translation has not taken a "cultural turn" similar to that which has occurred in the West (and China) since the 1980s. The implications of postcolonial, deconstructionist, feminist, and sociological theories of translation—particularly the more overtly ideological aspects—have barely been explored in the Japanese context.

16 For instance, in a paper presented at the IATIS conference in Melbourne in 2009, titled "A Lopsided Conversation: The Japanese Discourse within 'International' Translation Studies."

17 This is suggested, for instance, by the fact that Translation Studies is not listed in the Research Fields List of the Kaken Database of Grants-in-Aid for Scientific Research, a government-supported database that includes the humanities. (Nor, however, does the National Endowment for the Humanities in the United States include "Translation Studies" in its list of project fields—likewise indicating the poor standing of this discipline in that country.)

18 The first translation department in mainland China was established in 1997 and the first graduate degree program in 2004, and 110 doctoral degree students of translation had graduated from 14 universities by the end of 2004 (Tan 2008: 591). In Hong Kong the first translation program dates back to 1972, and there are strong offerings in translation at the undergraduate and graduate levels.

19 This survey by the Special Interest Group for Translation Studies (Hon'yaku kenkyū bunkakai) lists 95 university courses, most of which were established after 2001. *Hon'yaku kenkyū e no shōtai* (*Invitation to Translation Studies*, vol. 3: 9) states that as of 2009 there were nearly 200 Japanese universities with translation classes, numbering over 500 classes in total.

20 For instance, between 20,000 and 30,000 students have taken the on-site and correspondence classes offered since 1974 by a corporate (not government-accredited) "university" now known as Babel University Professional School of Translation, and as of June 2010, 83 students had completed its "Master of Science in Translation" by correspondence (established in 2003) (interview with Vice Chancellor Tomoki Hotta in June 2010).

21 This occurred a decade after the establishment of the Translation Research and Teaching Committee of the Chinese Translators Association in 1995. In Korea, the 1999 formation of an association of academics with an interest in translation

immediately attracted over 300 members. In 2008, The Japan Association for Interpretation Studies changed its name to Nihon Tsūyaku Hon'yaku Gakkai (Japan Association for Interpreting and Translation Studies) so as to include translation.

22   Shibata is a professor of American literature at the University of Tokyo and is well known as a translator of contemporary writers such as Paul Auster, Stuart Dybek, and Steven Millhauser. Yanase is best known for his playful and inventive rendition of James Joyce's *Finnegans Wake*. He has also translated many other challenging authors, including Lewis Carroll and Douglas R. Hofstadter. Their essays and interviews often appear in non-academic media venues in Japan.

23   Personal communication.

24   Representative works by Yanabu include *Hon'yakugo seiritsu jijō* (Translation words: Formation and background), Iwanami Shinsho, 1982; *Hon'yaku to wa nanika— Nihongo to hon'yaku bunka* (What is translation? The Japanese language and the culture of translation), Hōsei Daigaku Shuppankyoku, 1976; and *Hon'yaku gakumon hihan* (Criticism of translation academia), Nihon Hon'yakusha Sentā, 1983.

25   For example, the rendition of *atomistic approach* as *genshiron-teki hōhō* and *global knowledge* as *sekai no chishiki*.

26   For example, the rendition of both *coherence* and *cohesion*—two different concepts—as *matomari* (and sometimes as *kessokusei*).

References

Chan, E. K. 2001. "Back to the Future: The Future Development of Translation Studies in Hong Kong." In *Translation in Hong Kong: Past, Present and Future*, edited by S. Chan. Hong Kong: Chinese University Press, pp. 227–44.

Chang, N. F. 2009. "Repertoire Transfer and Resistance: The Westernization of Translation Studies in China." *The Translator* 15(2): 305–25.

Cheung, M. 2011. "The (Un)importance of Flagging Chineseness: Making Sense of a Recurrent Theme in Contemporary Chinese Discourses on Translation." *Translation Studies* 4(1): 41–57.

Guo, Y. 2009. "Theorizing the Politics of Translation in a Global Era: A Chinese Perspective." *The Translator* 15(2): 239–59.

Kim, M. 2009. "Cultural Bias in Communication Science: Challenges of Overcoming Ethnocentric Paradigms in Asia." *Asian Journal of Communication* 19(4): 412–21.

Konishi, J. 1994. "Japanese Literature in East Asia." *The Japan Foundation Newsletter* 22(1): 7–8.

Kruger, H. 2008. "Training Editors in Universities: Considerations, Challenges and Strategies." In *Translator and Interpreter Training: Issues, Methods and Debates*, edited by J. Kearns. London and New York: Continuum, pp. 39–65.

Munday, J. 2008. *Introducing Translation Studies*, 2nd edn. London and New York: Routledge. Translated by K. Torikai et al. as *Hon'yaku-gaku nyūmon* (Tokyo: Misuzu Shobō, 2009).

Nakayama, S. 1984. *Academic and Scientific Traditions in China, Japan, and the West.* Tokyo: University of Tokyo Press.

Niranjana, T. 1992. *Siting Translation: History, Post-Structuralism, and the Colonial Context.* Berkeley: University of California Press.

Nozaki, K. 2004. "Hon'yaku riron to hon'yaku no hazama de—Furansu bungaku no baai" [The gap between translation theory and translation—In the case of French literature]. *Kokubungaku kaishaku to kyōzai no kenkyū* [Japanese Literature: Studies of Interpretation and Educational Material] 49(10): pp. 113–19.

Phukan, S. 2003. "Towards an Indian Theory of Translation." *Wasafiri* 40: 27–30.

Pym, A. 2010. *Exploring Translation Theories.* London and New York: Routledge. Translated by K. Takeda as *Hon'yaku riron no tankyū* (Tokyo: Misuzu Shobō, 2010).

Said, E. W. 1998. "Traveling Theory." In *Imported: A Reading Seminar*, edited by R. Ganahl, pp. 157–81. New York: *Semiotext(e)*. Originally appeared in *Raritan* (1982), 1(3): 41–67.

—. 2000. "Traveling Theory Reconsidered." In *Reflections on Exile and Other Essays.* Cambridge: Harvard University Press, pp. 436–52. Originally appeared in *The World, the Text, and the Critic*, 1994: pp. 226–47.

Satō, M. 2008. "Eibungaku hon'yaku no 'hon'yaku kihan' ni kansuru hitokōsatsu" [A consideration of "translation norms" in translations of English literature]. Doctoral dissertation, Hokkaido University.

Shi-xu. 2009. "Asian Discourse Studies: Foundations and Directions." *Asian Journal of Communication* 19(4): 384–97.

Shuttleworth, M. 1997. *Dictionary of Translation Studies.* Manchester: St. Jerome Publishing.

Sun, H. and Z. Zheng. 2008. "Chinese Scholars and International Translation Studies." *Translation Watch Quarterly* 4(1): 62–79.

Tan, Z. 2008. "Towards a Whole-person Translator Education Approach in Translation Teaching on University Degree Programmes." *Meta* 53(3): 589–608.

—. 2009. "The 'Chineseness' vs. 'Non-Chineseness' of Chinese Translation Theory: An Ethnoconvergent Perspective." *The Translator* 15(2): 283–304.

Tang, J. 2007. "The Metalanguage of Translation: A Chinese Perspective." *Target* 19(2): 359–74.

Ueda, A. 2007. "Review of Murakami Fuminobu's *Postmodern, Feminist and Postcolonial Currents in Contemporary Japanese Culture* (2005)." *Journal of Japanese Studies* 33(1): 251–5.

Wakabayashi, J. 1998. "Marginal Forms of Translation in Japan: Variations from the Norm." In *Unity in Diversity? Current Trends in Translation Studies*, edited by L. Bowker, M. Cronin, D. Kenny, and J. Pearson. Manchester: St. Jerome Publishing, pp. 57–63.

—. 2009. "An Etymological Exploration of Japanese Views on 'Translation.'" In *Decentering Translation Studies: India and Beyond*, edited by J. Wakabayashi and R. Kothari. Amsterdam: John Benjamins, pp. 175–94.

Yanabu, A., A. Mizuno, and M. Naganuma (eds). 2010. *Nihon no hon'yakuron: Ansorojī to kaidai* [Japanese discourse on translation: An anthology with commentary]. Tokyo: Hōsei Daigaku Shuppankyoku.

Zhu, C. 2004. "Translation Studies in China or Chinese-Related Translation Studies: Defining Chinese Translation Studies." *Babel* 50(4): 332–45.

3

A Nagasaki Translator of Chinese and the Making of a New Literary Genre

Emiko Okayama

Introduction

Translation history is an important part of Translation Studies (TS). According to Anthony Pym (1998: 10), however, translation history in the West has been essentially a "history of translation theory," which he regards as a limitation. Pym maintains that too little attention has been paid to translators themselves and the contexts in which they have operated, so he proposed that translation history research focus on these two points. Since then there has been a move away from the preoccupation with theory to a more holistic approach that deals with the following questions: who translates, what is translated, when is it translated, why is it translated, and how? Studies of these five features are by no means new. However, Pym's (2008: 45) argument is that by studying the first three (who, what, and when), the last two (why and how) will reveal their significance more clearly. The present paper is an attempt to focus on one influential Japanese translator of Chinese and the context in which he operated in early modern Japan. I will examine all five of Pym's questions in relation to this particular translator, Kanzan Okajima (1674–1728).

In Japan, translation history is most often regarded as having started in the Meiji period (1868–1912), when broad contact with the West began, so the focus tends to be on translations from European languages. This ignores the long history of contact with Chinese culture and the practice of *kanbun kundoku* (Japanese reading of Chinese texts, which constitutes an unusual kind of translation, as explained below). Yet as Kaganoi (2002: 83) observes, the solid foundation in reading texts written in Classical Chinese and the training in *kanbun kundoku* subsequently enabled the Japanese to translate vast amounts of information from the West and facilitated a relatively smooth transition from a feudal to a modern society. In addition, the encounters with spoken Chinese and with Dutch[1] in the Edo period (1603–1868), although much more restricted in scale, introduced phoneticism[2] as a major intellectual concern (Sakai 1991: 252) and prepared the Japanese to cope with the influx of European languages in the Meiji period. Therefore an understanding of the nature of Edo-period translations not only enhances our understanding of Meiji-period translation but also allows us to capture the transition as continuity in translation practice, rather than a discontinuity between the early modern and modern periods.

Referring to Pym's (2008) conceptual framework, my chapter focuses on Kanzan Okajima, a pre-Meiji *tōtsūji* (the term used for professional translators[3] of Chinese in Edo Japan, most of whom were based in the port city of Nagasaki) and his professional context as an example of an intercultural existence before the arrival of large-scale Western influences. The purpose is to identify the role that Kanzan (as he is usually known) played in the formation of a new literary genre, *yomihon*, through his translations of Chinese vernacular novels. These novels were based on the spoken language, which was very distinct from Classical Chinese, the written standard, and they were also more popular than works written in Classical Chinese. Here I draw attention to the process of transforming Ming and Ch'ing novels into *yomihon*, highlighting several related factors such as the status of Classical Chinese as the most prestigious form of writing in Japan, the established use of *kanbun kundoku* among Japanese intellectuals, and the extension of *kanbun kundoku* to texts written in vernacular Chinese.

Yomihon is a literary genre that first emerged in Kamigata (the Kyoto/Osaka area) in the late eighteenth century and then in Edo (present-day Tokyo) in the early nineteenth century. Akinari Ueda (1724–1809) was the most notable writer of *yomihon* during the former period, and Bakin Takizawa (1767–1848) the most notable during the latter period. As the name indicates, *yomihon* (literally, "reading books") were a new type of fiction in which the text assumed greater importance than in the picture stories popular throughout the eighteenth century. Historical facts were also significant in *yomihon*, which project a fantasy world born out of historical events. *Yomihon* incorporated various sources from Japanese and Chinese fiction, with Chinese vernacular novels constituting the major inspirational sources. These vernacular novels originated in the south of China and were written in the language spoken in southern China, which could not be understood by Japanese intellectuals, who were traditionally educated in Classical Chinese. So the transfer process from Chinese vernacular novels to *yomihon* followed four stages that were mostly but not necessarily sequential, as described below: *wakoku* (annotation of the original Chinese novel with *kunten* diacritical, syntactic and punctuation markers[4]) → translation → adaptation → *yomihon*. In a time when there were few opportunities for direct personal contacts with Chinese people, only a small number of translators had training in spoken Chinese and were able to deal with the first stage. Kanzan Okajima was one of them.

Existing studies of Kanzan Okajima

Studies of Kanzan can be classified according to how the authors of these studies view him—that is, as a scholar of Chinese vernacular novels, a scholar of spoken Chinese, or a translator. Early twentieth-century studies (e.g. Aoki 1927 and Ishizaki 1940) tended to view Kanzan as a literary figure. They identified the connection between Edo novels and Chinese vernacular novels such as *Shui-hu zhuan* (Water margin) and acknowledged Kanzan as the person who initiated the process of receiving these novels into Japanese literature. Takashima (2006) has summarized the history of reception of *Shui-hu zhuan* in Japan between the Edo and postwar periods. Quoting Kanzan's contemporaries' views of Kanzan, Takashima portrays him as an outsider to the Edo intellectual scene, while acknowledging that his translation was highly competent.

In the postwar period, reevaluation of Kanzan as a scholar of spoken Chinese triggered a string of studies on his dictionaries and textbooks of spoken Chinese (e.g. Torii 1957, Nagasawa 1959–76). However, these approaches were bibliographic and lacked detailed analysis of the content. The development of intercultural studies since the 1990s brought a new wave of multilingual scholars who have carried out text analyses from both Chinese and Japanese viewpoints. Okada (2006) examined Kanzan's dictionaries of spoken Chinese to identify their characteristics and described their terminology and their influence on Japanese writing. Wakaki's extensive studies (2004, 2008, and 2009) are invaluable in terms of elucidating Kanzan's profile and the contents of his dictionaries. Okumura's approach (2007: 356) was to focus on Kanzan as a language scholar and teacher and to analyze his four dictionaries from a terminological viewpoint. She points out that the spoken Chinese used by Kanzan can be characterized as lying between the Chinese practiced by the professional translators of Chinese and that practiced by intellectuals in Edo and Kyoto.

As is evident from the above, most studies on Kanzan are from the perspective of Chinese studies, rather than TS or Japanese studies. By contrast, this paper views Kanzan not only as a translator of written texts but also as a multidiscursive mediator (Pym 2008: 33)—that is, it examines how his multiple skills and movements enabled him to connect to diverse networks of people and events to form a creative space. The term *tsūji* (professional translator or interpreter), from which *tōtsūji* (professional translator of Chinese) derives, is a combination of *tsū* (transfer) and *ji* (things)—that is, *tsūji* were people who convey matters, implying that they were intercultural mediators in a broad sense. This suggests that the roles of translators in eighteenth-century Japan were more diverse than those of contemporary translators. This paper also stresses the introduction of Chinese vernacular novels as Kanzan's creative contribution to the emergence of the *yomihon* genre, in contrast to the common view of the translator's role as secondary and derivative.

Pym's principles and Arida's model

Pym (1998: 5–10) notes that most publications on translation history since the 1960s have been concerned primarily with the history of translation theories and translated texts. He considers this a narrow and dehumanizing view and argues that translation history research should be extended to cover a much wider field that includes the actions, agents, and effects of translation, as well as other causally related phenomena. To achieve this, he proposes the following principles (Pym 2008): "First Principle, study translators, then texts" (30); "Second Principle, look for professional intercultures" (37). Thus this approach focuses on translators and the context in which they work as a preliminary stage of investigation. "Professional interculture" is a term used for translator communities to distinguish them from the general interculture. A professional interculture tends to consist of members who have professional skills, adopt secondary positions rather than being main players with respect to cross-cultural communication, are transitory, and move through professional networks (Pym 2008: 37–42). In this shifting interculture, translators take on several roles by choice or necessity, and consequently they form multiple allegiances in several domains, such as science, literature, and religion. Furthermore, each allegiance might develop a powerful network of translators, writers, philosophers, political leaders, and so on, which stimulates the creativity of the members of the network.

Capturing the full picture of this process is not easy, since it involves constant transformation. Although Pym (1998: 93) suggests that it is necessary to employ both the spatial and temporal axes, by his own admission his transfer models do not illustrate the process clearly (1998: 93–6). Hence this paper also employs

Ayssar Arida's interference model (2002), which is based on quantum theory,[5] in order to supplement Pym's framework. Arida's application of quantum theory to urban studies—especially the model of an "event" and an "event horizon" to visualize the duality of activities and environment—presents a useful avenue for exploring the relationship between translators' movements and social interaction. An event can be a thing or a happening, and it is "a source of waves that spread over [a] territory" (Arida 2002: 150). The territory that is affected by the event and filled with outward-moving probability waves is an "event horizon." When multiple event horizons intersect, their waves overlap and interference occurs, creating modified wave patterns that are qualitatively and quantitatively different. Such intersections of event horizons are peripheries and intercultures where cultures meet and activities intensify, resulting in the emergence of a new event or events. These start to generate new waves that in turn interfere with the waves of the original events (i.e. the source of the new waves). This process repeats itself to trigger chain reactions of events and transform the whole system (Arida 2002: 211).

Arida's concepts of an "event" and "event horizon" visualize the duality of activities and environment such as interactions of people, information, and cultures. They present a useful analogical model by which to explain the relationship between translators' physical movements and their social interactions. Event waves originating in the south of China and in the Japanese cultural centres of Kyoto, Osaka, and Edo intersected in Nagasaki, which was the only port open for trade with China and Holland between 1639 and 1854 and which subsequently became an intercultural centre (see Figure 3.1). The secondary waves emanating from Nagasaki then rippled back to the original Japanese "central-centres" to drain Nagasaki of its cultural density and values. Translators with mobility and memory are able to rise above the overlaps of event horizons, "carrying away the consciousness of the effect of one event outside its spatial event horizon and confronting it with the effect of the other event" (Arida 2002: 210). Although operating in two quite different areas of study, Pym and Arida describe a similar process and reinforce each other.

Pym's criticism of translation history based on theories and texts is not a rejection of theories and texts. His argument is that without knowledge of the context—translators as the medium of theories and translated texts, and the social background of the time—a sound understanding of translations is not possible. Therefore, identifying translators' movements and the structures of the networks to which they belonged is a necessary step before engaging in text analysis.

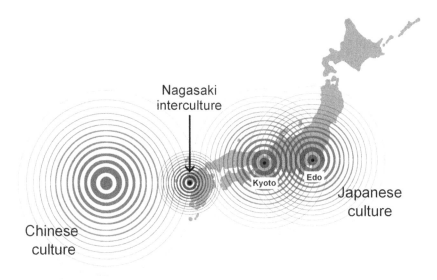

Figure 3.1 Nagasaki as an interculture

Cultural situation in the mid-Edo period

To appreciate how Kanzan's moves from Nagasaki to Kyoto, Osaka, and Edo contributed to the cultural scene, we must first understand the situation of Chinese studies in Japan in the mid-Edo period. The Japanese had been reading Chinese texts since ancient times. As Classical Chinese was the preferred language for official and intellectual works in Japan for many centuries, it acquired cultural cachet as a more prestigious form of writing than the indigenous forms. Nevertheless, reading Classical Chinese was not a straightforward matter, due to the considerable linguistic differences between Chinese and Japanese. Hence the Japanese developed a method of reading Classical Chinese texts by adding *kunten* markers. These diacritical, syntactic, and punctuation markers are inserted between the Chinese characters without disturbing the original Chinese text.[6] Readers follow the markers in order to read the text in Japanese word order, and they assign each Chinese character its Japanese reading (pronunciation). This method is called *kanbun kundoku*, which literally means "Chinese writing, Japanese reading." Although this technique had been in use among elite readers for centuries, it became available to the wider public for the first time in the Edo period (Katō 2006: 189). The growth of a readership among samurai, merchants, and wealthy farmers greatly fueled the importation of Chinese classics through Nagasaki and, in turn, enabled the publishing industry to flourish. Chinese works permeated intellectual arenas and became a foundation for creative activities, even more than in pre-Edo times.

The eighteenth century was one of the peaks for the use of Classical Chinese in Japan. It was also a time when considerable interest emerged in spoken Chinese among many intellectuals as a reaction to the study of Classical Chinese. This was triggered by a number of earlier events: the arrival of political refugees from China between the 1620s and 1650s; the arrival of monks from the Huang Po (J: Ōbaku) sect of Zen Buddhism, starting with Yinyuan (known in Japan as Ingen) in 1654; and the promotion of *Shushigaku* (Neo-Confucian philosophy founded in China by Chu Hsi) to the status of official doctrine to the ruling class from 1691.

The Ming dynasty was replaced by the Ch'ing dynasty in 1644, and the resulting political unrest pushed many educated Chinese to escape to Japan. These were cultured people who brought artistic skills with them. Most of the hereditary families of professional translators/interpreters in Nagasaki were migrants who had left China between the end of the Ming dynasty and the beginning of the Ch'ing dynasty (Hayashi 2000: 6).

Ingen arrived in Nagasaki after repeated requests from a group of prominent resident Chinese, and in 1661 he founded Manpukuji temple in Kyoto, sponsored by shogun Ietsuna Tokugawa. Ingen and his successors brought with them southern Chinese culture, which differed from the Classical Chinese culture of northern China. The impact of the Ōbaku sect went far beyond religion, as it was influential in the rapid spread of new forms and styles in painting, calligraphy, tea ceremony, pottery, architecture, landscape, and so on among the ruling class and wealthy merchants and farmers. Among them, the shogunal advisor Yoshiyasu Yanagisawa (1657–1714) was a keen believer, and he invited Ōbaku monks to his residence whenever they visited Edo. Kanzan Okajima was employed by Yanagisawa and taught him spoken Chinese for a while. Kanzan's relationship with the Ōbaku sect continued until his death, and he acted as a medium between Ōbaku monks and influential figures, including Yanagisawa and other prominent scholars.

Chu Hsi (1130–1200) had presented a new interpretation of Classical Chinese philosophy based on the *Four Books* (*Analects of Confucius*, the *Mencius*, the *Great Learning*, and the *Doctrine of the Mean*). In Japan these classics were read by means of *kanbun kundoku*. In 1691 this branch of Neo-Confucianism (*Shushigaku*) was promoted to official status in Japan, which then triggered a reactionary movement that valued reading the original texts, rather than Chu Hsi's commentaries. This movement, known as *Kogaku* (studies of the classics), included the Confucian philosophers Jinsai Itō (1627–1705) and his son Tōgai (1670–1736) in Kyoto and Sorai Ogyū (1666–1728) in Edo. Although *kanbun kundoku* was an ingenious way of accessing Chinese texts, it created a gap between the original Chinese and the marked-up text. In addition, writing in Classical Chinese reflected neither everyday speech nor the changes occurring in speech in China. These gaps between Chinese and Japanese and between written and spoken Chinese were precisely what *Kogaku* scholars highlighted in their criticism of *kanbun kundoku* as being unfaithful to the original text. Sorai (as he is usually known) went furthest, advocating the study of spoken Chinese as a foreign language.

These three events originating in southern China were separate matters until their waves met in the early eighteenth century, when the boom in learning spoken Chinese reached its peak in Japan. Each event involved an encounter with spoken Chinese, which made the Japanese, who had long been familiar only with Classical Chinese as a written language (one that had become the standard language of officialdom), realize for the first time in many centuries that Chinese was in fact a foreign language.

A multidiscursive translator

Kanzan Okajima and spoken Chinese

Kanzan Okajima was born in Nagasaki in 1674, and in his teens he started learning spoken Chinese at a private language academy run by the most prominent teacher of spoken Chinese in Nagasaki at the time. Kanzan became a professional translator of Chinese at the age of 20 and eventually came to be regarded as the best Japanese speaker of Chinese in the Edo period. In an essay titled *Shundai zatsuwa* (1748), the Confucian scholar Kyūsō Muro described Kanzan as a keen scholar and fluent in spoken Chinese.

There were two types of professional translators of Chinese in Nagasaki during the Edo period: official translators—highly paid hereditary translators whose total number at any one time was limited to nine—and privately employed translators who had to find jobs by themselves. Income records for 1708 show that the highest-ranking official translators earned the equivalent of approximately 35 million yen by today's standards, while the lowest-ranked apprentice interpreters earned only 500 thousand yen[7] (Hayashi 2000: 61). Gen'ichirō Fukuchi, a writer who spent some time in Nagasaki at the end of the Edo period, commented that "*Tōtsūji* and *Oranda tsūji* [translators of Dutch] enjoyed a luxurious life style" (quoted in Hayashi 2000: 88).[8] By contrast, the income of privately employed translators, who were a lower rank than apprentice official interpreters, must have been meagre. Since Kanzan was not born into a hereditary family of official translators, he was not eligible to become an official translator and hence had a low income. The year Kanzan became an apprentice (1687) and the following year were peak years in trade with China,[9] so there were 200–300 translators/interpreters of Chinese working in Nagasaki. This ever-increasing trade with China had no doubt influenced Kanzan's initial career choice. In 1688, however, a law was passed to scale the trade back to 70 ships per year in order to reduce the outflow of silver, and the law came into effect in 1689. Chinese visitors were also moved to the Chinese compound in Nagasaki in 1689. This would have caused a loss of work for private translators, who were dependent on the visiting Chinese traders. In his resignation from the position of privately employed translator in 1701, Kanzan cited his inability to support himself on his income as a reason for seeking his fortune elsewhere.

The language skills and knowledge of Ming and Ch'ing culture that the Nagasaki translators of Chinese cultivated were called *Kiyō no gaku* (Nagasaki-style studies), by which was meant the study of spoken Chinese. To learn *Kiyō no gaku*, one had to travel to Nagasaki. Since the Chinese compound was not open to the public, the population of Chinese speakers was limited to the Chinese translators and a small number of people who had access to Chinese monks or scholars in Nagasaki. Although the intellectuals in the central cities looked down on these translators' Chinese, which largely consisted of the vocabularies of trade, commerce, and administration, the intellectuals nevertheless felt it necessary to study spoken Chinese so as to advance their understanding of Confucian teachings and other Chinese philosophies (Okumura 2007: 284). Thus the demand for spoken Chinese was growing in Kyoto and Edo at the same time that Kanzan was reconsidering his future in Nagasaki, so his plan to seek his fortune elsewhere was not entirely reckless. Through his contact with visitors to Nagasaki he must have sensed the demand for spoken Chinese in the central cities.

After leaving Nagasaki in 1704, Kanzan moved between several cities where he taught, translated Chinese vernacular novels, published numerous textbooks, and nurtured many talented speakers of Chinese. He mixed with daimyo and high-ranking samurai; with leading Confucian scholars such as Tōgai Itō, Sorai Ogyū, and Shundai Dazai; with Ōbaku monks such as Daichō Shaku; and with leading publishers in Kyoto, Osaka, and Edo. These were part of Kanzan's network of people. Translators often participate in more than one form of professional activity, and Kanzan too was no "mere" translator. He was an interpreter, literary commentator, language teacher, textbook writer, and Confucian scholar. With these broad abilities, he made allegiances with people of various ages, from different places, in different professions, and of different status. The rich and powerful were willing to pay Kanzan because of his specialized skills, which in turn enabled him to move from client to client and place to place as opportunities arose. The following sections will examine Kanzan's various activities in more detail.

Kanzan's translations of Chinese vernacular novels

Tsūzoku kōmin eiretsuden (1705), *Chūgi suikoden* (the first five volumes were published in 1728 and the second five volumes in 1759), and *Tsūzoku chūgi suikoden* (1757–90) are regarded as Kanzan's translations of Chinese vernacular novels.

Chūgi suikoden (1728), a translation of the epic novel *Shui-hu zhuan*, was published two weeks after Kanzan's death, and it consisted of only the first ten of the original hundred chapters. The important feature of this work is that it was the first *wakoku* translation of *Shui-hu zhuan*. As noted earlier, *wakoku* was a technique traditionally used by the Japanese to read Chinese classics, and it involved directly adding *kunten* marks to the original texts. While the practice of *wakoku* for texts written in Classical Chinese had a centuries-old tradition and numerous precedents, *wakoku* renditions of Chinese vernacular novels were almost unheard of before Kanzan's *Chūgi suikoden*. Adding *kunten* to vernacular Chinese was a highly skilled task that required competence in both Classical and vernacular Chinese. In *wakoku* the Japanese word order is indicated by "return markers" and word function is indicated by *okurigana* (conjugation and grammatical markers), with the meaning of words occasionally being given in the katakana syllabary on the left-hand side of the vertically written characters. In Kanzan's time only a handful of scholars and translators of Chinese were able to do this. The way Kanzan inserted these marks demonstrates a profound understanding of the text (Takashima 2006: 75). Classical Chinese is a compact written language in which each character represents a word and there are few grammatical markers, but vernacular Chinese novels were based on spoken Chinese and contained compound words, words indicating grammatical function and words from the vernacular language, and their rambling style did not lend itself to *wakoku*. Therefore Kanzan was totally dependent on his knowledge and original interpretation of Chinese vernacular novels. To indicate compound words he made use of a dash-like marker (e.g. 三一下, 喝一道, 目一今) without which Japanese readers would not have been able to identify the word breaks. Kanzan's *wakoku* enabled people who were not familiar with Chinese vernacular novels but who were used to reading Chinese classics with *kunten* markers to read these vernacular novels with relative ease and satisfy their thirst for new novels.

Tsūzoku chūgi suikoden (1757–90) was published posthumously in three installments over 34 years. *Tsūzoku* was an Edo-period term for translation, referring specifically to rendering Chinese works in readable Japanese. The back of the cover of this work says it was translated and edited by Kanzan Okajima. It is not a *wakoku* (a form that retains the original Chinese text format), but a *kanbun kundoku*-style rendition written out in Japanese word order and using a mixture of Chinese characters and katakana. Compared with Kanzan's earlier *kanbun kundoku*-style translation, this work contains numerous omissions and additions, which has led some scholars to doubt whether it was Kanzan's work. It is possible, however, that a number of people edited his completed translation after his death and then published it. This could explain some inconsistencies. For example, the difference between Chapters One in *Chūgi suikoden* and *Tsūzoku chūgi suikoden* is that the latter does not contain the poems and scene descriptions of the former, although the main texts are almost identical. This suggests that someone might have deleted these parts to make the text more succinct. The important point here, however, is that it was published as Kanzan's translation, indicating the long-lasting value of his name as an authority in translating Chinese vernacular novels, even three decades after his death.

Translating a vernacular novel into the formal *kanbun kundoku* style (rather than vernacular Japanese) might appear strange to modern Japanese readers, but this was a familiar style for intellectuals of the time, who looked down on vernacular Japanese as writing for women and children. In spite of the questions surrounding the translation, *Tsūzoku chūgi suikoden* became the most influential version of *Shui-hu zhuan* in Japan for the next two centuries. The second half of the eighteenth century witnessed an explosion of adaptations of this work—for example, Ayatari Takebe's Heian-style *Honchō suikoden* (1773), Chinen Itami's Muromachi period drama *Onna suikoden* (1783), and Kyōden Santō's *Chūshingura* parody titled *Chūshin suikoden*. Often far removed from the original, these stories nevertheless built upon themes borrowed from *Shui-hu zhuan* (*Suikoden*), as their titles indicate.

In the nineteenth century, Bakin Takizawa transformed adaptations of *Shui-hu zhuan* into a more substantial novel titled *Nansō satomi hakkenden* (1814–42; hereafter referred to as *Hakkenden*), but his earlier works had already exhibited the influence of *Shui-hu zhuan*. His first *yomihon* novel, *Tsūzoku Takao senjimon* (1796), had been an amalgamation of *Shui-hu zhuan* and a kabuki play titled *Meiboku sendai hagi*. At this stage, Bakin (as he is usually known) did not own a full 100-volume *Shui-hu zhuan*. Takashima (2006: 286) suggests that Bakin consulted Kanzan's *wakoku* "translation" and the shorter 70-volume *Shui-hu zhuan*, which was easier to acquire. Bakin had also published the first ten volumes of *Shinpen suiko gaden* (1805–7) in a style that mixed Chinese characters (kanji) and hiragana, with hiragana annotations for the kanji and accompanied by Hokusai Katsushika's illustrations. This was heavily based on Kanzan's *Chūgi suikoden* and *Tsūzoku chūgi suikoden,* with the kanji parts left almost untouched while incorporating some of the poems and scene descriptions, which were marked with indentation in *Chūgi suikoden* but absent in *Tsūzoku chūgi suikoden*. The important characteristic of *Shinpen suiko gaden* is its Japanese-style writing (*wabun*), which distinguishes it from the *kanbun kundoku* style of *Tsūzoku chūgi suikoden*. Takashima (2006:191) attributes Bakin's innovation to the *furigana* (hiragana annotations) he added to the kanji in *Shinpen suiko gaden*: "Bakin maintained the original kanji, but added *furigana* annotations to increase the comprehension of the text by less educated Japanese." In other words, this work had a dual system whereby Chinese characters represented the original Chinese and the hiragana annotations represented the Japanese meaning. In addition, Bakin published his critical views of *Shui-hu zhuan* as *Yaku Suikoden* (1805) and *Kinseitan o najiru* (1817).

Thus before writing *Hakkenden*, Bakin had produced a number of translations, adaptations, and criticisms of *Shui-hu zhuan*, as if he needed to go through these steps in order to create his own original novel. *Hakkenden* is a 106-volume epic based roughly on *Shui-hu zhuan* and other Chinese and Japanese novels, but the setting, characters, time, and underlying theme were all transformed to suit the Japanese environment. It is considered by many to be the best *yomihon* ever. Along with *Hakkenden*, Bakin also wrote *Keisei suikoden* (1825–35) in the *gōkan* genre (picture stories accompanied by hiragana writing), with the gender of the characters reversed. In terms of the storyline, this is a faithful adaptation of *Shui-hu zhuan* but in hiragana instead of kanji and using the seven–five syllable rhythm so familiar to Japanese readers. At this point the Chinese vernacular novel *Shui-hu zhuan* had been transformed into a uniquely Japanese picture story read by women and children in Japan.

The transition from Chinese vernacular novel to *yomihon*—from Kanzan's *wakoku* in 1728 to Bakin's *Hakkenden* in 1814—took almost a century. It is known that Bakin's collections included Kanzan's translations, and without Kanzan's *wakoku* and *tsūzoku* it would have been difficult for the subsequent translations and adaptations to materialize, and *Hakkenden* might not have been written. Japanese readers found Chinese popular novels highly entertaining and were fascinated by aspects of Chinese culture in them that were absent in the Chinese classics. Although Kanzan's translations are largely forgotten today, it is clear that they played a key role in literary creation and deserve greater attention. Equally important is the fact that his translations of Chinese vernacular novels and his lectures on the subject imparted the "conception of the [Chinese] vernacular novel as a means of expressing original thoughts" (Pastreich 2002: 11–12) and emotions and that they encouraged Japanese writers to do the same.

Kanzan's dictionaries and textbooks of spoken Chinese

Kanzan's translation activities also stimulated scholars at the two leading academies of Chinese and Confucian studies, Tōgai Itō's Kogidō in Kyoto and Sorai Ogyū's Ken'en in Edo. Both academies introduced the reading of vernacular Chinese as part of their curricula. Kanzan was involved in both academies at different times of his life. As previously noted, he was active in more than translation and he wrote a number of dictionaries and textbooks, some of which were used in these academies. For instance, *Jikai binran* (a dictionary) was published in seven volumes in Osaka in 1725. *Tōyaku binran* (another dictionary) appeared in five volumes in Kyoto in 1726, and *Tōwa binyō* (also a dictionary) was published in Kyoto in six volumes in the same year.

The most famous of all is *Tōwa sanyō*, a language primer that was first published in Edo in 1716 in five volumes; a sixth volume appeared two years later. This was the first work of its kind in which vocabulary and expressions were systematically arranged so that learners could progress from simpler exercises to more complex ones. It also has katakana annotations for Chinese characters, with tonal indicators and punctuation marks. However, the Chinese tones are indicated only in the sixth volume, which contains two short Nagasaki-based stories in the vernacular and are regarded as Kanzan originals. Each story was written in two different styles, as shown in the following examples (written horizontally for convenience, rather than vertically as in the originals): first, with the Chinese pronunciation along the right-hand side in katakana (A), in vernacular Chinese (B); second, with the Japanese pronunciation along the right-hand side in katakana (C), in *kundoku*-style translation written in a mixture of Chinese characters and katakana (D).

A. リイテヨンヤンチウジンヱ丶•ナイフウキヤアテツウ•ルウヲイチヨンソ
    ウキン•

B. 李－徳－容楊－州人也 乃富－家嫡－子 而為衆所敬[10]

C. リトクヨウ　ヤウシウ　スナハ　フウキ　チヤクシ　シヨニン　ウヤマ

D. 李－徳－容ハ楊州ノ人ナリ。　乃チ富－貴ノ人ノ嫡－子ニテ。　諸一人
    コレヲ敬ヒケル。[11]

Translation: Ri Tokuyō is from Yōshū. He is the son of a rich family. People
    admire him.

This format is similar to that used in Kanzan's translation into Chinese of the fourteenth-century Japanese war epic *Taiheiki* as *Taiheiki engi* (1720), which contains both *wakoku* and *kundoku* versions. This format allowed readers to learn vernacular Chinese as a foreign language in Chinese pronunciation without changing the word order and while consulting the Japanese *kundoku* "translation" to ensure comprehension. This was the practice advocated by Sorai Ogyū, and it could be said that Kanzan implemented Sorai's idea.

Kanzan's dictionaries and textbooks were widely used at academies and by individual learners of spoken Chinese, and along with his translations they contributed to the increase in speakers of Chinese and fans of Chinese vernacular novels. These dictionaries and textbooks contain not only vernacular expressions but also expressions that appear in Classical Chinese texts, and Kanzan's *Suikoden* translations took the form of *wakoku* (*Chūgi suikoden*) and *kanbun kundoku* (*Tsūzoku chūgi suikoden*). These facts suggest that his target audience was the educated class, who were familiar with Classical Chinese. As Wakaki (2004:12) points out, we must bear in mind that the boom in spoken Chinese came on the back of the popularity of *tsūzoku mono* (Japanese translations and adaptations of Chinese vernacular novels). The increased opportunities for learning spoken Chinese and the growing population of speakers and readers of vernacular Chinese also acted as catalysts for this boom.

Translators and the transfer of culture

Nagasaki, where translators of Chinese formed a professional interculture, was an intersection and an intercultural city where foreign and Japanese cultures met. This intercultural space was not, however, entirely open to the rest of Japan.

Nagasaki was under the direct jurisdiction of the Tokugawa shogunate, and travel between Nagasaki and the rest of Japan was tightly monitored. During their stay in Nagasaki, Chinese traders and visitors were confined to the Chinese compound, to which the only Japanese citizens with free access were courtesans. Furthermore, the positions of the official translators were hereditary, and language skills were passed on from father to son within select Chinese families. Guarded by many layers of visible and invisible barriers, the speaking of Chinese was thus largely confined to a small professional interculture in Nagasaki until Kanzan moved to Kamigata and Edo in the early eighteenth century.[12] If Nagasaki was a stationary and closed interculture, the person of Kanzan was a movable and open interculture, and his mobility allowed him to make contact with various events and people and in turn to become an active and effective medium of transfer.

Starting in the mid-seventeenth century, studies of Classical Chinese in Japan had witnessed unprecedented growth in the publishing industry. Along with the promotion of Neo-Confucian philosophy to the shogunate's official doctrine, the reaction of the *Kogaku* movement and the popularity of Ōbaku Buddhism among prominent samurai and merchants, this laid the ground for the emerging interest in speaking Chinese. These multiple "event horizons" originating from a particular event or person spread, interfered with each other, transformed and were transformed like ripples on water, triggering new events at their intersections. Kanzan's moves to Kyoto and Edo were like pebbles thrown into the overlapping event horizons, from which spread new waves of spoken Chinese and Chinese vernacular novels, undergoing numerous interactions with waves from other event horizons so as to finally emerge as the *yomihon* genre.

In other words, lacking any one of these interacting event horizons, the results might have been very different. This is demonstrated by the experience of Dōei Hayashi, who moved from Nagasaki to Edo in search of opportunities 50 years before Kanzan started teaching spoken Chinese at the Ken'en academy in Edo. Dōei was the eldest son of an influential resident Chinese in Nagasaki. He moved to Edo at the age of 21 (1662), but within 2 years returned to Nagasaki in disappointment. Ingen had opened the Manpukuji temple only the previous year, and neither Sorai nor Tōgai were yet born. Soon after Dōei's return, he was nominated for the position of junior interpreter, then promoted to senior interpreter in 1675, and he remained in Nagasaki for the rest of his life. Although Dōei was known for his mastery of spoken Chinese and Chinese poetry as well as his intellect, his cultural influence did not reach beyond the confines of Nagasaki. It is ironic that Kanzan, who struggled to survive as a low-ranking private translator, became an effective agent of literary transfer, while Dōei, who was born into a comfortably-off family and climbed to the top of the ranks of official interpreters, remained inside a closed interculture as a relatively unknown regional figure, even though the two men might have been equally talented. This indicates the importance of translators' mobility as intercultural agents, at least in Edo Japan. This does not mean, however, that Kanzan was simply in the right place at the right time; rather, he had multiple skills and the flexibility to seize the moment and belong to versatile networks. He had both practical Chinese skills and the essential knowledge of Classical Chinese; he had contacts with publishers in both Edo and Kamigata; he worked for a daimyo and for influential samurai; he mixed with the shogun's Neo-Confucian scholars (Kyūsō Muro and Hōkō Hayashi) and *Kogaku* scholars (Sorai Ogyū and Tōgai Itō); and he maintained a close relationship with Ōbaku monks throughout his life. Unlike Dōei, Kanzan was a versatile and multidiscursive translator in the full sense of the term.

Conclusion

By tracing Kanzan's footsteps, this paper has highlighted the literary transfer process in which Kanzan's translations played a key role—from Chinese vernacular novels to *wakoku*, then to translation, on to adaptation, and finally to *yomihon*. Kanzan's movements and the growth of interest in spoken Chinese in the cities to which he moved together boosted the popularity of Chinese vernacular novels and the number of learners of spoken Chinese. Some of these learners started writing annotated guides to Chinese vernacular novels, which further promoted these novels and initiated Japanese adaptations, laying the ground for the emergence of *yomihon* as a literary genre.

Kanzan's contributions can be summarized as follows: the introduction of a new literary genre, the Chinese vernacular novel, into the literary scene that was stagnating after a century of isolation following Japan's closure to the outside world in 1639; enabling Japanese readers of Classical Chinese to read Chinese vernacular novels by means of the *wakoku* technique, which was formerly used only for Classical Chinese texts; and making spoken Chinese, which had been monopolized by the translators of Chinese in Nagasaki, accessible to the interested public in Kyoto, Osaka, and Edo. The growth in the number of speakers of Chinese meant an increased readership for Kanzan's translations and textbooks as well as an increase in publications related to spoken Chinese, and these three factors subsequently reinforced each other.

In line with Pym's two principles, this paper has observed Kanzan's movements against the background of national seclusion in eighteenth-century Japan and demonstrated the interacting waves of personal and social dimensions and the intricate networks of people contributing to the transfer of information and cultural activities. Arida's event and event horizon model has helped explain such interactions. Kanzan moved among these networks as an intercultural agent playing several roles, including writer, teacher, diplomats' assistant, story-teller, and translator. He was an active and effective agent, "precisely because he did more than translate," as Pym (2008: 10) writes in a different context.

This paper also highlights the distinctively Japanese form of translation known as *wakoku*. This raises questions about the interpretation of the relationship between source and target languages as a dichotomy. *Wakoku* maintains the visual appearance of the source text, but is read in the target language. In other words, it can be both source and target text. This process does not fit easily into Western translation theories and practice. Both *wakoku* and *kundoku* (the written-out form) require a good understanding of the original Chinese text and the Japanese language and are therefore close to translation. Scholars remain divided, however, on whether to regard these practices as translation (see Wakabayashi 1998 and 2005 and Kornicki 2010). This question calls for more investigation from a TS perspective and further development of conceptual frameworks suitable for the East Asian kanji cultural sphere consisting of China, Japan, Korea, and Vietnam.

Notes

1   The Dutch were the only Europeans allowed a presence in Japan after the country was closed to the outside world in the seventeenth century. This presence consisted of a small trading base in the harbour of Nagasaki.

2   Phoneticism broadly means "the phonetic representation of sounds." Sakai (1991: 252) uses the term as an antonym of ideography and states that "phoneticism requires that a graphic inscription be related to the sounds *univocally*." This was a new concept to the eighteenth-century Japanese.

3   Although "translators" is used for *tsūji* here, it should be remembered that the work of the *tsūji* covered interpreting, translating, and some other related tasks.

4   *Kunten* consist of *kaeriten* (return markers) placed on the bottom left side of a character, *okurigana* (conjugation and grammatical markers), and punctuation marks on the bottom right side. *Kunten* were later applied not only to texts imported from China but also to those written by Japanese in Classical Chinese.

5   Quantum theory is a landmark approach that recognizes "non-local, holistic properties that transcend time and space, and link all elements of human, artificial, and natural space into patterns of dynamic interference" (Arida 1998). In the quantum universe, things do not exist as binary oppositions such as nature/man-made, parts/whole, space/time, past/future, but exist as dynamic and complementary dualities. The theory has already been adapted successfully as a model for mental processes (Penrose 1994), psychological and social behavior (Zohar 1990), enterprise management (MG Taylor Corporation 1997) and urban studies (Arida 2002).

6   This practice resulted in preserving in their original forms many Chinese texts that were long lost in China (Katō 2006: 201).

7   These figures would be about 430 thousand and 5 thousand US $ 430,000 and 5,000 dollars, respectively (exchange rate as of June 3, 2011).

8   All English translations in this paper are by the author.

9   137 ships visited Nagasaki in 1687 and 194 in 1688.

10 *Tōwa san'yō*, Vol. 6:16. *Kunten* and tonal markers have been deleted here because of the difficulty of representing them in horizontal text.

11 *Tōwa san'yō*, Vol. 6: 22. The character 人 has no kana annotation.

12 The fact that Kanzan had to wait for three years after his resignation before moving to Kyoto reflects the restrictions on movement in and out of Nagasaki, although movement between Kamigata and Edo was relatively easy (Wakaki and Etchu, personal correspondences, 2010).

References

Aoki, M. 1927. *Shina bungei ronshū* [Papers on Chinese literature]. Tokyo: Kōbundō shobō.

Arida, A. 1998. "Quantum Environments: Urban Design in the Post-Cartesian Paradigm," http://quantumcity.com/publication/quantum-environments-urban-design-in-the-post-cartesian-paradigm-thesis-conclusions/, accessed March 24, 2010.

—. 2002. *Quantum City*. Oxford: Architectural Press.

Etchu, T. 2010. Director, Nagasaki History and Culture Society (personal correspondence).

Hayashi, R. 2000. *Nagasaki tōtsūji: Ōtsūji Hayashi Dōei to sono shūhen* [Chinese translator of Nagasaki: Dōei Hayashi and his times]. Tokyo: Yoshikawa Kōbunkan.

Ishizaki, M. 1940. *Kinsei nihon ni okeru Shina zokugo bungakushi* [History of vernacular Chinese literature in premodern Japan]. Kyoto: Kōbundō Shobō.

Kaganoi, S. 2002. *Nihongo wa shinka suru* [Evolution of the Japanese language]. Tokyo: NHK Books.

Katō, T. 2006. *Kanbun no soyō: Dare ga nihon bunka o tsukutta ka?* [Kanbun and its contribution to Japanese culture]. Tokyo: Kōbunsha.

Kornicki, P. 2010. "A Note on Sino-Japanese: A Question of Terminology." *Sino-Japanese Studies* 17: 28–44.

MG Taylor Corporation. 1997. "A Model for Releasing Group Genius." www.MGTaylor. co./MGTaylor/glasbead/axioms.htm, accessed March 22, 2010.

Nagasawa, K. (ed.). 1959–76. *Tōwa jisho ruishū* [Dictionary of vernacular Chinese], vols 1–20. Tokyo: Kyūko Shoin.

Okada, K. 2006. *Edo igengo sesshoku: Rango, tōwa to kindai nihongo* [Edo intercultures: Dutch, vernacular Chinese and modern Japanese]. Tokyo: Kasama Shoin.

Okumura, K. 2007. *Edo jidai no tōwa ni kansuru kiso kenkyū* [Preliminary research on vernacular Chinese in the Edo period]. Osaka: Kansai Daigaku Shuppanbu.

Pastreich, E. 2002. "The Projection of Quotidian Japan on the Chinese Vernacular: The Case of Sawada Issai's 'Vernacular Tale of the Chivalrous Courtesan.'" Harvard University, Edwin O. Reischauer Institute of Japanese Studies: *Occasional Papers in Japanese Studies* 1: 1–21.

Penrose, R. 1994. *Shadows of the Mind: A Search for the Missing Science of Consciousness.* Oxford: Oxford University Press.

Pym, A. 1998. *Method in Translation History.* Manchester: St. Jerome Publishing.

—. 2008. "Humanizing Translation History." *Hermes* 42: 23–48. www.tinet.cat/~apym/on-line/research_methods/2008_Hermes.pdf, accessed March 24, 2010.

Sakai, N. 1991. *Voices of the Past: The Status of Language in Eighteenth-Century Japanese Discourse.* Ithaca: Cornell University Press.

Takashima, T. 2006. *Suikoden to nihonjin* [*Shuhuzhuan* and the Japanese]. Tokyo: Chikuma Bunko.

Torii, H. 1957. "Nihon ni okeru chūgokugogaku isan no seiri ni tsuite: goi shiryō o chūshin to shite" [The legacy of Chinese studies in Japan: A focus on vocabulary]. *Chūgokugogaku* 61: 78–81.

Wakabayashi, J. 1998. "Marginal Forms of Translation in Japan: Variations from the Norm." In *Unity in Diversity?: Current Trends in Translation Studies*, edited by L. Bowker, M. Cronin, D. Kenny, and J. Pearson. Manchester: St. Jerome Publishing, pp. 57–63.

—. 2005. "The Reconceptualization of Translation from Chinese in 18th-Century Japan." In *Translation and Cultural Change: Studies in History, Norms and Image-Projection*, edited by E. Hung. Amsterdam and Philadelphia: John Benjamins, pp. 122–45.

Wakaki, T. 2004. "Tōwa jisho, Tonkingo jisho, Chōsengo jisho" [Dictionaries of vernacular Chinese, Vietnamese, and Korean]. In *Jisho yōho: Nagasaki de jisho o yomu* [Reading dictionaries in Nagasaki], edited by N. Sonoda and T. Wakaki. Fukuoka: Kyushu Daigaku Shuppankai, pp. 3–16.

—. 2008. "Tōwagaku no shisō, Okajima Kanzan" [Reflections on studies of vernacular Chinese]. Hōsō Daigaku Nagasaki Gakushū Sentā, seminar handout (unpublished).

—. 2009. "Ri Tokuyō: zenkō niwa mukui ga aru hanashi" [Ri Tokuyō: The story of a good deed rewarded]. In *Karabune ōrai: Nihon o sodateta hito, fune, machi, kokoro* [Chinese trading in Nagasaki: People, ships, town and sensibilities], edited by Higashi Ajia chiikikan kōryū kenkyūkai. Fukuoka: Chūgoku Shoten, pp. 265–88.

Zohar, D. 1990. *The Quantum Self: Human Nature and Consciousness Defined by the New Physics*. New York: Bloomsbury.

4

Assimilation or Resistance?
Yukichi Fukuzawa's Digestive Translation of the West

Akiko Uchiyama

Introduction

Yukichi Fukuzawa (1835–1901) was a renowned intellectual and educator in the nineteenth century, when Japan underwent major social transition in the wake of the overthrow of the shogunate and the restoration of the Meiji emperor to the throne during the Meiji Restoration of 1868. The first half of Fukuzawa's life was lived in the feudal society of the Edo period (1603–1868), and the second half was lived in the modern nation that emerged during the Meiji period (1868–1912). As a scholar who contributed to Japan's modernization by introducing Western[1] thinking and as the founder of the prestigious Keio University in Tokyo, he is remembered today as one of the most important Meiji figures—to the extent that his portrait features on 10,000-yen notes.

It is no surprise then that numerous studies have been conducted on Fukuzawa, but he has been less discussed in the context of translation—as a translator per se or from a Translation Studies (TS) perspective. Since he was a prominent scholar of Western Learning, the connection between Fukuzawa and Western texts has mainly been investigated in terms of Western influences on his thinking.[2] Some studies of these influences emphasize how he did not simply translate, stressing instead his creativity and originality.[3] Although there are some researchers (e.g. Yanabu 1982, 2010) who study Fukuzawa's translation work, they often concentrate on the linguistic aspects. What I attempt here is to focus on the social and cultural aspects of translation to study Fukuzawa's work. I will examine how he translated Western texts and digested Western thinking and how he encountered the West as Japan went through a period of social turmoil. The analysis will adopt a postcolonial perspective—more specifically, the Brazilian discourse of "cannibalistic" translation—based on the premise that Fukuzawa's translations reflected the contemporaneous relationship between Japan and the West. His "cannibalistic" translation will be discussed in terms of absorbing Western culture in order to resist domination by that same culture.

Japan as the "colonized"

It is appropriate here to outline the relationship between Japan and the West in Fukuzawa's time in order to explain the relevance of a postcolonial perspective to the study of Fukuzawa. Japan had been closed for more than two centuries by a series of isolation orders issued to protect the country from outside influences. The Dutch were the only Westerners allowed to continue trading, but their presence was confined to an island off Kyushu. Then in 1853 Commodore Matthew Perry arrived in Japan to persuade it to open its ports for trade and diplomatic relations with the United States. Japan's isolation was brought to an end by the Kanagawa Treaty concluded in 1854.

This was the first instance of Japan entering into an unequal treaty with a Western nation and it was followed by treaties with such countries as Britain, France, Russia, and Holland. Meiji diplomacy subsequently exerted its utmost efforts to rectify such treaties. There were two main sources of inequality: Japan did not have tariff autonomy, and foreigners from the signatory countries were given extraterritoriality (consular jurisdiction). The former resulted in Japan having low import duties and high export duties, and the latter made foreigners on Japanese lands immune from Japanese law. Needless to say, these unequal treaties were forced upon Japan by Western nations through the implied threat of their military power. The Japanese lack of familiarity with international laws and treaties was also a contributing factor. On the West's part, the relationship with Japan was motivated by economic gain, one of the key driving forces behind Western colonial expansion. Even without formal political or military colonization, Japan was therefore in some sense entangled in the web of the Western colonial project.

The Meiji Restoration of 1868 facilitated the opening up of the country and brought increased contact with Western nations that were about to embark on full-scale territorial expansion. The Japanese became aware of Europe's technological superiority and feared that Japan might face actual colonization unless it caught up with the industrialized West. In this respect, the surrounding situation was not encouraging. In neighboring China—the country that Japan had admired for so long—the Opium War (1840–2) had already triggered "semi-colonization" by Britain and subsequently by other Western nations such as United States and France, and the Japanese feared a similar or worse fate.

Yet such an outcome did not materialize. Maruyama and Katō (1998: 8–9) point out two factors that helped Japan escape colonization: one is that Japan responded quickly to the presence of Western powers in Asia by modernizing; the other is that the Western nations were busy warring among themselves and the United States was preoccupied with its Civil War, so there was little leeway for paying much attention to Japan. Japan's quick response by modernizing was an important factor in its survival as an independent nation. "Pre-modern" Japan endeavored to catch up with the "modern" West by eagerly introducing Western knowledge and technology—military technology, medicine, railways, government system, international law, and so on. This was partly because the West was perceived as a "superior" civilization and partly as a means of survival. Radical changes in social and political systems were implemented, modeled after Western systems. This eager adoption of Western civilization was closely associated with the fear of colonization. Moreover, as Komori (2001: 7–8) explains, emulating Western systems and internalizing Western ideas inherently involves "self-colonization" on the part of Japan. Given these circumstantial and psychological factors, it is valid to include Meiji Japan in broad postcolonial debates.

Fukuzawa as an agenda-driven translator

Here I will briefly portray Fukuzawa as a translator so as to highlight the importance of translation in the study of this key figure. As a young man, he studied what was known as *rangaku* (Dutch Learning), the only established form of Western studies at the time. His training largely involved translation from Dutch into Japanese, and Fukuzawa (1958a: 4) later recounted that he was greatly influenced by his teacher Kōan Ogata's translation philosophy, which focused on ease of reading. Fukuzawa subsequently also studied English, as he regarded it as an increasingly important language.

By the end of the Edo period, Fukuzawa had been abroad three times, something that was highly unusual in Japan at that time. In 1860, as a personal steward to the ship's captain, he sailed to the United States aboard a government mission; he was an official translator for the first Japanese embassy to Europe in 1862; and he persuaded the head of a government mission to the United States in 1867 to include him in his party. On returning from his first trip to the United States, Fukuzawa obtained a position as a translator of official documents at the then Foreign Ministry. After the Meiji Restoration, he remained an independent scholar, choosing not to work for the new government. Sales of his books[4] allowed him to support himself, and his early works as a writer were mainly translations. His translation *Seiyō jijō* (Things Western; 3 volumes, 1866–70) was a case in point. This was one of the so-called Three Books of Meiji, the Meiji bestsellers that played an important part in the context of Japan's modernization.[5] Using his experience in Western countries and the knowledge gained from Western literature, Fukuzawa endeavored to introduce Western civilization to Japanese society. Translation occupied a significant place in his life and work and is thus an important medium for the study of Fukuzawa.

I start the examination of Fukuzawa's translation work with *Gakumon no susume* (*An Encouragement of Learning*; 17 sections, 1872–6). Today this is arguably the most popular work of Fukuzawa's own writing. Although it is not a translation, Fukuzawa indicates multiple Western sources that he partly drew on to write this book:

> In this work, I have expressed the general meaning of learning, sometimes by quoting literally and *sometimes by making paraphrases of Western sources*, and by citing matters which should be known by everyone in respect to both material and immaterial areas of learning. (1969: 10; emphasis added)

Hence it is valid to analyze certain parts of *Gakumon no susume* as translation in the broad sense of rewriting, drawing on André Lefevere's (1992) concept of translation as a form of rewriting. Moreover, some parts bear sufficient resemblance to the source text to be regarded as conventional translation.

Here I analyze a section that demonstrates Fukuzawa's humorous and sometimes satirical writing. He begins Section Eight by saying: "In the work entitled *Moral Science* by the American named Wayland, there is a discussion of the freedom of the human mind and body" (1969: 49). The book Fukuzawa refers to is *The Elements of Moral Science* by Francis Wayland, and he outlines Wayland's discussions on personal liberty by "translating" the English text. Wayland explains the importance of personal liberty as follows:

> It seems almost trifling to argue a point which is, in its nature, so evident, upon inspection. If, however, any additional proof be required, the following considerations will readily suggest themselves. It is asserted that every individual has an equal and ultimate right with every other individual to the use of his body, his mind, and all the other means of happiness with

which God has endowed him. But suppose it otherwise. Suppose that one individual has a right to the body or mind or means of happiness of another. That is, suppose that A has a right to use the body of B according to his, that is, A's *will*. Now, if this be true, it is true universally; hence, A has the control over the body of B, and B has control over the body of C, C of that of D, etc., and Z again over the body of A; that is, every separate will has the right of control over some other body or intellect besides his own, and has no right of control over its own body or intellect. Whether such is the constitution of human nature, or, if it be not, whether it would be an improvement upon the present constitution, may be easily decided. (1865: 203)

Fukuzawa expanded on this by doubling the length and adding explanation. He replaces the letters of the A to Z sequence with specific titles or positions of people. In his version, the full circle of control begins with the emperor, goes down through the shogun, daimyos, vassals, stewards, attendants, foot soldiers to peasants, and then comes back to the emperor. This approach greatly enhances the practical visualization and understanding of the argument. Fukuzawa's rhetoric was particularly effective in the early years of the Meiji period, when the strict hierarchy of the four classes (samurai, farmers, craftsmen, and merchants) persisted even after the government adopted a policy of equality in 1869.

Fukuzawa (1969: 51) also supplements Wayland's argument with examples and explanations as to how to control somebody else's actions:

The peasants are as much human beings as the emperor. Therefore what if the peasants do not hesitate to treat the emperor at will according to their own pleasure? For example, suppose they tell the emperor to stop when he wants to visit some place; they tell him to go back when he wants to go to his villa. Or suppose that the emperor's daily life was controlled by the arbitrary directives of the peasants, who deprive him of his fine clothes and substitute boiled barley for his delicious foods.

Fukuzawa's explanation goes on to present an absurd supposition that "Confucius led his pupils to do robbery and Śākyamuni carried a gun and went out hunting," and he declares "The results would be incongruous indeed! They would be strange, and unimaginable." Although such additions do not seem to resemble translation in the conventional sense, the resulting text is at least an adaptation. It might be classified as translation in the sense that it generally follows the logic (main points) of the original, even though it adds a witty twist. The chain of control comically depicted in the strict hierarchical system seems to emphasize the absurdity of controlling someone.

This illustration of control over somebody seems a little verbose, as Itō (1969: 33) points out, so it is useful to consider why Fukuzawa expanded the argument to this extent. He loathed the feudal hierarchy, which directly inflicted a sense of indignity on him.[6] His argument here is that people need to break free from the hierarchical values bolstering this system. In *Gakumon no susume*, Fukuzawa criticizes people in whom the feudal hierarchy had fostered a lack of independence and who, in turn, contributed to maintaining the hierarchical system. Beyond personal independence he envisaged the ultimate goal of true national independence, which is essentially underpinned by personal independence. The heading of Section Three, "National Independence through Personal Independence" (1969: 16), is the essence of this book. Fukuzawa felt it was vital to prepare people ideologically for personal liberty and independence, and this awareness stemmed from his concern for Japan's precarious position vis-à-vis the Western nations that were advancing eastward. This sense of urgency might be why he recounted the chain of control at such great length. In this respect, his translation was driven by his own agenda. Fukuzawa's rhetoric can also be understood in relation to his often bold argument style—that is, he lays great emphasis on what he feels important and, conversely, discards what he thinks less relevant to his point. This is also reflected in his translations.

Fukuzawa's understanding of civilization as reflected in his translations

Next I examine some of Fukuzawa's translations that deal with the concept of civilization, as his understanding of this is particularly important because of its link to the relationship between Japan and the West. The following example is taken from a supplement to *Seiyō jijō* (1868). As Fukuzawa himself explains, this supplementary volume (the second of a total of three volumes) is mostly a conventional translation of the main source book, *Political Economy, for Use in Schools, and for Private Instruction* (1852), edited and published by William and Robert Chambers. The author remained unknown for a long time, until Albert Craig ascertained in 1984 that it was written by John Hill Burton, a Scotsman who was qualified as a lawyer but earned a living as a writer.[7]

Yoshida's observation (2000: 64–5) is a useful place to begin the examination of Fukuzawa's understanding of civilization. Yoshida points out that the dynamic vector of progressing civilization in Fukuzawa's translation differs from the original work's static framework of barbarous versus civilized states. Yoshida contrasts the original "In the state of civilization" (1852/1999: 6) with Fukuzawa's translation: "as society advances towards civilization" (Fukuzawa 1868/1958b: 395, here back-translated into English).[8] Yoshida also refers to the following sentence in *Political Economy*:

> In our own country, which is called civilized, there are many things which belong properly to a low state of society. (1852/1999: 7)

This is translated by Fukuzawa as follows:

> After all, even in Britain, which calls itself civilized, enlightenment has not permeated everywhere. (Fukuzawa 1868/1958b: 397, back-translated into English)

Yoshida argues that Britain was without doubt a civilized country for Burton even if it contained "low state" elements and that Burton probably did not imagine that such a civilized country would progress further. By contrast, Fukuzawa was imbued with a mission to lead Japan to a civilized state like that of European countries. Therefore, concludes Yoshida, he emphasized the dynamic vector— that is, that Britain had room for further improvement—when translating "there are many things which belong properly to a low state of society."

Yoshida's observation on the dynamic translation versus the static original is convincing. Dynamism is indeed evident in Fukuzawa's translation, and it is also linked to his fluid writing style, unlike that of the original.[9] The static nuance is also evident in the following sentence in *Political Economy*: "there are certain localities which may be said to be still harbourages of barbarism, though surrounded by all the appearances of the civilised state" (1852/1999: 7). This static impression is partly caused by the writing style of the original. As the title clearly indicates, *Political Economy, for Use in Schools and for Private Instruction* is a textbook. The writing is descriptive and has a matter-of-fact tone, which contrasts with Fukuzawa's dynamic and fluid text. Nevertheless, Yoshida's argument that Burton probably did not imagine that civilized Britain would progress further is perhaps an overstatement, because in discussing Britain, Burton does refer to "the progress of civilisation" and to the state where "civilisation advances." Britain's civilization was static or steady only in the sense that it was thought to be at the forefront of the linear development of civilization. By contrast, Japan's civilization was dynamic in the sense that it was being urged to catch up with Western civilization on the path of development. Japan's development toward civilization was an urgent goal for Fukuzawa, who rhetorically emphasizes the point he is making.

The dynamic vector of progressing civilization is also seen in *Bunmeiron no gairyaku* (*An Outline of a Theory of Civilization*; 1875), which is one of Fukuzawa's major works. Fukuzawa (1897/1958a: 60) himself makes a distinction between *Bunmeiron no gairyaku* and his previous works, including translations, which he describes as "peddling" civilization piecemeal in order to introduce novel things and ideas from the West and to abolish Japan's rigid old customs. This book is more philosophical and is neither a translation nor a simple transfer of Western information. Nevertheless, Fukuzawa acknowledges the Western sources to which he referred in order to formulate his ideas: "I have generally paraphrased rather than directly translated Western sources in order to apply their content to the Japanese context" (1973: 3). The known Western source books for this work are *General History of Civilization in Europe*[10] by François Guizot, *History of Civilization in England* by Henry Thomas Buckle, and *Considerations on Representative Government, On Liberty*, and *Principles of Political Economy* by J. S. Mill. Fukuzawa refers to all these authors in *Bunmeiron no gairyaku* by briefly introducing their ideas in those books to develop his argument.

The following example from Chapter Three, "The Essence of Civilization," cites Guizot's text. Here Fukuzawa again emphasizes the dynamic progress of civilization by translating "Civilization is properly a relative term. It refers to a certain state of mankind as distinguished from barbarism," (Guizot 1870: 18) as "Now civilization is a relative thing, and it has no limits. It is a gradual progression from the primitive level." (Fukuzawa 1973: 35). Here he adds an explanation to the first sentence—that is, that civilization has no limits. While the source text refers to civilization as "a certain state" in the second sentence, Fukuzawa's translation describes it as "a gradual progression." In the following paragraph Guizot (1870: 18) actually does state that civilization "is susceptible to continual progress," so Fukuzawa's translation might reflect that part. His emphasis on progression does, however, seem to be stronger than the tone of *General History of Civilization in Europe*. In the part that follows these two sentences, Fukuzawa also emphasizes progression by repeatedly using the word *iyoiyo* (more), whereas the source text does not use the comparative degree.

These emphases, especially the part stating that civilization "has no limits," can also be regarded as a warning against blind admiration of Western civilization. Fukuzawa regards civilization as an "open-ended process" (1973: 15) and takes the view that Western civilization is still to progress further. This view is reflected in the following statements in *Bunmeiron no gairyaku*: "although we call the nations of the West civilized, they can correctly be honored with this designation only in modern history" (1973: 14–15); "present-day Europe can only be called the highest level that human intelligence has been able to attain at this juncture in history" (1973: 15). The reservations "only in modern history" and "only . . . at this juncture in history" indicate that Western civilization is to progress still further. Although Fukuzawa posits Western civilization as Japan's goal, it is only because it was relatively advanced at that particular time in history. For Fukuzawa, Western civilization as a goal did not mean blind admiration; it was more likely a practical choice in order for Japan to move forward.

The following analysis also concerns the progress of civilization, but in this example Fukuzawa manipulates the argument of the original. The example is taken from *Sekai kunizukushi* (Nations around the world; 1869), a geography book targeting children and the general public. This work introduces such information as geographical features, population, and social affairs in nations around the world. Fukuzawa (1869/1959a: 585) notes that *Sekai kunizukushi* is an abridged translation, drawing on a number of geography and history books published in the United States and Britain. The main source book is *A System of Modern Geography* by S. Augustus Mitchell, and the correspondence between some parts of *Sekai kunizukushi* and the source text is evident. Before we move on to the analysis, it is worth noting that the fact that *Sekai kunizukushi* is a geography book is itself relevant to the progress of civilization in Fukuzawa's time. As explained by Katō and Maeda (1989: 353), understanding world geography was directly linked to understanding the progress of civilization, and Meiji scholars tried to show the goal toward which Japan should strive.

Let us now examine how Fukuzawa's manipulations reflect his understanding of civilization, as evidenced by the illustrations depicting the states of civilization. Under the heading of "The States of Society," Mitchell (1865: 35–8) divides the human social condition into five states—"the Savage, Barbarous, Half-Civilized, Civilized, and Enlightened"—and describes how people live in each state. Four illustrations depicting the savage, barbarous, half-civilized, and enlightened states accompany the text. Fukuzawa translated "The States of Society," but he did not put these illustrations beside the translation. Instead he moved them to the section on Europe, whose civilization is depicted as what Japan should emulate. There Fukuzawa (1869/1959a: 610–12) explains that in the old days the now-civilized Europe was in a chaotic and ignorant state and that it went through the feudal period before forming the present political regime. He adds that these illustrations, copied from a Western geography book, give a general idea about society.

I have argued elsewhere (2009: 71) that this manipulation emphasizes that Europe has gone through gradual stages to achieve its level of civilization. The notion that Europe was once at the chaotic stage was important for Japan, which Fukuzawa believed should strive toward Western civilization. The important point here is that Fukuzawa moved these illustrations away from the racially implied "The States of Society." Mitchell explains that "some of the natives of Central Africa, of New Guinea, and Australia" are in the savage state (1865: 35); "The Tartars, the Arabs, and some North African tribes" are in the barbarous state (36); "China, Japan,[11] Turkey, and Persia are the principal countries" of the half-civilized state (38); and "The best examples of enlightened nations are the United States, England, France, and Germany" (38). The illustrations are in accordance with these descriptions. I have also observed (2009: 70) Mitchell's racially connected and confined description of progress in the section titled "The Races of Mankind"—for example, the Caucasian race "are the most improved and intelligent of the human family, and seem capable of attaining the highest degree of progress and civilization," and the Mongolian race are "limited in genius and slow in progress" (Mitchell 1865: 33). Here Fukuzawa's movement of the illustrations appears to break the racial confinement that might work against the Mongoloid Japanese achieving high-level civilization. In this sense Fukuzawa questions the racial implication and confinement presented by Mitchell and manipulates the information in the original to suit his purpose.

This attitude toward the original text can be related to Fukuzawa's later observation in *Bunmeiron no gairyaku*:

> Civilization is the only purpose and goal in mankind, but there are many roads to it. Reasonable progress will come only through a long process of trial and error. Therefore men's ideas should not be turned exclusively in one direction. It is necessary to experiment on a broad front, for experimentation is the soul of progress. (1973: 44)

Here Fukuzawa appears to question the nineteenth-century notion of linear development of civilization, with the Caucasian race leading the progress, even though he believed in the general direction of this progress. He could have developed this observation of "many roads" to civilization into a more open, dynamic, and perhaps "inclusive" theory of civilization (as opposed to the racially "exclusive" connotations of progress in some Western texts). Although this potential theory of civilization does not seem to have eventuated, I would argue that Fukuzawa's "manipulative" translation that questions the ideas presented in the original was instrumental in developing his understanding of civilization.

Fukuzawa and cannibalist translation

Translation in postcolonial contexts is sometimes discussed in the negative sense of how translation has been used to facilitate colonization, helping to mould cross-cultural relations into unequal power relations. By contrast, Fukuzawa's translation work seems to have constituted a positive means for him to implement his ideas and goals in strengthening Japan against possible colonization. In this sense, his translations can be likened to the Brazilian discourse surrounding cannibalism as a metaphor for translation. This discourse uses a digestive metaphor for translation itself, portraying it in a "positive" (or active) sense as a means of digesting foreign influences. The cannibalism metaphor in the cultural discourse in Brazil is associated in particular with the modernist Oswald de Andrade's "Manifesto antropófago," which was published in 1928 during the Anthropophagous Movement of the 1920s. Vieira (1999: 98) explains the metaphor as follows:

> Cannibalism is a metaphor actually drawn from the natives' ritual whereby feeding from someone or drinking someone's blood, as they did to their totemic "tapir," was a means of absorbing the other's strength, a pointer to the very project of the Anthropophagy group: not to deny foreign influences or nourishment, but to absorb and transform them by the addition of autochthonous input.

Although absorbing foreign influences suggests assimilation, it is not unreserved assimilation; instead it involves transformation of the foreign matter, adding autochthonous elements. Vieira (1999: 98) also explains the metaphor "as an irreverent verbal weapon" against colonial repression so that Brazil could be liberated from mental colonialism by making use of the anthropophagic ritual suppressed by the Jesuits. Here is a twist, foregrounding the demeaned ritual of anthropophagy and using it as a weapon of resistance. This also involves seeking out the identity of Brazilian culture. This metaphor has been adopted in the translation projects of the poet brothers Augusto and Haroldo de Campos, who initiated the concrete poetry movement in Brazil in the 1950s. They did not really intend to develop a translation theory as such, but practiced and discussed translation in relation to their own literary production. Haroldo de Campos (1986: 44) discusses de Andrade's anthropophagy as follows:

> Oswald's "Anthropophagy" . . . is the thought of critical devoration of the universal cultural heritage, formulated not from the insipid, resigned

perspective of the "noble savge [sic]" . . . but from the point of view of the
"bad savage," devourer of whites—the cannibal. The latter view does not
involve a submission (an indoctrination), but a transculturation, or, better,
a "transvalorization": a critical view of History as a negative function (in
Nietzsche's sense of the term), capable of appropriation and of expropriation,
de-hierarchization, deconstruction. Any past which is an "other" for us
deserves to be negated. We could say that it deserves to be eaten, devoured.
With this clarification and specification: the cannibal was a polemicist . . . but
he was also an "anthologist": he devoured only the enemies he considered
strong, to take from them marrow and protein to fortify and renew his own
natural energies.

The critical devouring of "the universal cultural heritage," involving
"transculturation" or "transvalorization," has significant bearing on Haroldo de
Campos' translation work, or rather "transcreation," as he terms it. Put simply as
a framework,[12] the anthropophagic metaphor for translation involves colonized
people devouring their colonizers' texts in order to create "new" works in the
target language by absorbing, altering, and appropriating the original. Barbosa
and Wyler (1998: 332) explain this concisely:

> It expresses the experience of a colonized people who devour what is offered
> to them by their colonizers but do not swallow it whole: quite the opposite,
> they spit out what is noxious to them, but what they keep they make wholly
> theirs by altering and changing it to suit their nutritional needs.

This explanation corresponds to the "anthologist" role of the cannibal described
above by Haroldo de Campos.

Interestingly, Fukuzawa (1973: 3) uses a similar digestive metaphor in
explaining how he drew on Western books:

> When quoting Western works and directly translating source materials, I
> have cited authors and editions used. But when I state the main ideas of an
> author or paraphrase the gist of the contents of another's work, I have not
> felt it necessary to record each and every item. These sources have become
> like food already digested within me. The food has been assimilated into my
> own body.

Digestion suggests some change in the "body" of the translator. The translator
absorbs nourishment from the original, discarding the residue, in order to
create something "new" in the target language. This involves alteration and
appropriation of the original to suit the "nutritional needs" of the translator

(and the Japanese people), to serve his purposes. Fukuzawa also uses a digestive metaphor when he describes bad translation in his article "Chojutsu no setsu" (On writing; 1878): "there are quite a few translators who gnaw at words and phrases of the source texts, swallow them as smatterings and spit them out while undigested" (1878/1962: 639–40). This kind of digestive metaphor in Japan is not original to Fukuzawa. For example, the secondary meaning of the Japanese word *kamikudaku* (to masticate) is to make a difficult concept understood easily—a process akin to translation. This kind of digestion/understanding metaphor is commonly used in Japanese speech, as elsewhere. It is nonetheless interesting that Fukuzawa used the metaphor to describe the translation process and likened his source texts to food taken into his body.

Also of interest is the fact that scholars researching Fukuzawa often use the digestive metaphor when they discuss his translation work. Saucier (2002: 342), for example, comments that it is perhaps more accurate to say that in *Seiyō jijō*, Fukuzawa expressed in Japanese what he "*soshaku shita*" from Western sources, rather than translating them. The verb she uses, *soshaku suru*, literally means "to masticate," and its secondary meaning is to think through the meaning of things and texts. Itō (1969: 23) has observed that the thoughts in the source texts have been completely absorbed into Fukuzawa's own flesh and blood. Similarly, in relation to Fukuzawa's famous statement that "heaven does not create one man above or below another man" (1969: 1), Nishikawa (2002: 243) comments that the idea of innate human rights became flesh and blood inside Fukuzawa. Tōyama (1970: 86) also uses the word *shōka* (digestion) to describe Fukuzawa's understanding of Western thought. Although the digestive metaphor in the sense of understanding is not unusual in the Japanese language, it is the frequent use of this metaphor that makes it characteristic of Fukuzawa's translation work.

As we discussed above, Fukuzawa's translations often consist of an abridged translation and adaptation, usually based on more than one Western source. Information from various sources was digested in his "body" before being reproduced in the Japanese language. And even in what is deemed conventional translation, Fukuzawa in some way took an "appropriative" approach, emphasizing what he thought was more important for Japan's "nutritional needs." Consequently, he was an "anthologist," selecting what was nutritious for Japanese society. Autochthonous elements are incorporated, while foreign elements are often adapted to the Japanese context. He was also a "polemicist," questioning the ideas presented in the originals.

In addition to this shared digestive framework, Fukuzawa's translation approach also shows some resemblance to the notion of cannibalistic translation

in spirit. Kawano's explanation (1995: 5) of the transformation that occurred in the Meiji period is germane to investigating this further. He argues that the Meiji transformation was a process of resistance against and assimilation into the West. Kawano uses the terms *teikō* and *dōka* to describe this process. While *teikō* can be reasonably rendered as "resistance," translating *dōka* as "assimilation" is somewhat problematic owing to the complexity of what is entailed by "assimilation." Assimilation can be described as a process by which one is incorporated into a host culture, which implies that one resides in or is surrounded by the host culture. In this sense, assimilation more aptly represents, for example, the process whereby a colonized culture is assimilated into a colonizer culture or a minority culture is assimilated into a majority host culture. I use the term "assimilation" in a somewhat loose sense, suggesting that Japanese culture has been significantly influenced by Western culture, resulting in radical social change largely based on Western systems.

We can now return to Kawano's further explanation (1995: 5) where he refers to the process of "resistance" and "assimilation":

> This self-contradictory and paradoxical process of resistance and assimilation subtly and intricately defined the thoughts and behaviors of the Tokugawa shogunate, supporters of the Emperor, the Meiji government and public opinion leaders. People in the time of the Meiji Restoration either adopted or abandoned such contradictory notions as opening up or excluding foreigners, Westernization or nationalism, civil rights or state power, and independence or invasion; furthermore, on the whole they succeeded in balancing these incompatible elements.

These Japanese, including Fukuzawa, achieved a difficult balance. Fukuzawa certainly embraced Western civilization, but this attitude was in part driven by the fear of Japan's possible colonization by Western nations. This fear was pressing and shared by many.

The notion of simultaneous "assimilation" and "resistance" is reflected in Fukuzawa's translation work. At the risk of oversimplification, we can say that for Fukuzawa translation involved learning from the West and disseminating Western knowledge and culture among the Japanese people, with the goal of turning Japan into a developed nation. Such a purpose inevitably entails assimilation, absorbing and incorporating Western culture. However, Fukuzawa proposed advancing toward civilization precisely for the purpose of preserving Japan's national polity—that is, to protect Japan's independence. What he meant by independence was "putting our people into contact with foreign countries, making them maintain their dynamic spirit through a thousand trials, and turning them into a house that can withstand gales and downpours" (1973: 194–5)—not returning to the isolation of the past, a time when Japanese people did not have direct contact with the West, just like a house that had never been subjected to violent weather. Thus Fukuzawa envisaged the goal of resisting Western dominance while being subject to contact with the West. This is not unreserved assimilation, but rather a deliberate process envisaged as leading to the development of Japanese civilization so as to eventually put the country on an equal footing with the West. Fukuzawa's promotion of Western civilization is thus purposeful, aiming at assimilation leading to resistance and beyond.

This assimilation leading to resistance is coupled with a cannibalistic dehierarchization in the light of absorbing foreign influences so as to resist those very same influences. Of course, Japan did not go through a physical colonization process like that of Brazil, where the foreign influences exist as colonial legacies. In Brazil, these influences are to be negated and devoured by a "cannibal." Fukuzawa's translations do not partake of that aggressiveness of the cannibal, and foreign influences are voluntarily introduced through his translations. Nevertheless, the two digestive translation processes have something in common—something that might be called resistance from within.

Before closing this section, it is important to mention another critical difference between these two translation approaches. Japan mainly introduced foreign ideas in the Japanese language, in the form of translation, whereas Brazilian "cannibal" translation comes out in Portuguese, the language of the colonizer. This difference is also linked to the framework of assimilation. When Fukuzawa says of his drawing on Western sources that the "food has been assimilated into"[13] his own body, what is suggested is assimilation of the Western sources into the target language/culture. This assimilation is in the opposite direction from that discussed above, whereby a minor or colonized culture is assimilated into a host or colonizing culture. Assimilation can occur in both directions: the target culture being assimilated into the (dominant) source culture, or the source culture being assimilated into the target culture. In the case of Fukuzawa's translations, foreign elements were assimilated into the translator's body, then transformed and appropriated for his purposes before reception by the readers of the translation. What the readers received was a translation (digestion or appropriation) of the West, which was in some sense assimilated into Japanese culture. Fukuzawa's cannibalistic translation approach was supported by the sound fabric of Japanese society, maintaining Japan's identity while nourishing it with Western elements.

Conclusion

Yukichi Fukuzawa was a prominent Meiji scholar of Western Learning who contributed to Japan's modernization. He was also a skilful translator who translated many Western texts when Japan started to have increasing contact with Western nations and faced the possibility of being colonized. His work as a translator in a time of radical social change makes him an important subject in TS in the sociocultural context, especially in the context of postcolonial translation. Fukuzawa conducted "cannibalistic" translation in a metaphorical sense, absorbing Western elements as his nutrients. He appropriated the originals to suit his purposes and adapted the foreign elements to the Japanese context. He was selective of the Western texts and the portions he translated, absorbing what he thought was nutritious for him and Japanese society and discarding what he regarded as unnecessary or perhaps noxious. He sometimes questioned the ideas in the original and manipulated the information to suit his argument.

Fukuzawa's translation work was largely driven by his goal of introducing Western civilization to Japan, a goal that was underpinned by his ultimate aim of placing Japan on an equal footing with Western nations so as to resist their dominance. This framework of absorbing Western culture in order to resist it is associated with cannibalistic dehierarchization, although Fukuzawa was not an aggressive "cannibal" devouring the dominant culture. He actively absorbed Western culture, and the contradictory framework of simultaneous "assimilation" and "resistance" was somehow balanced in his translations. This is supported by the very nature of translation, which simultaneously involves different languages and cultures. The critical difference from Brazilian "cannibalistic" translation is that Fukuzawa translated Western texts into his own language, with foreign elements "assimilated" into his body; this indicates a fundamental Japanese fabric into which Western culture was "assimilated." Fukuzawa exhibited a form of "post-colonial translation" in the sense that he actively attempted to negotiate a pseudocolonial cultural space when Japan encountered the West.

Notes

1   For the sake of the argument in this paper, the terms "Western" and "the West" are used here to refer to what people in Japan at that time were deemed to have understood as "Western" and "the West"—generally referring to the United States and European nations with which Japan started to have contact in the mid-nineteenth century.

2　Masao Maruyama's *Bunmeiron no gairyaku o yomu* (Reading *Bunmeiron no gairyaku*, 1986) and Toshimitsu Anzai's *Fukuzawa Yukichi to seiō shisō* (Yukichi Fukuzawa and Western thought, 1995) are examples of this approach.

3　For example, Masao Itō's "Fukuzawa no moraru to Uērando no *Shūshinron*" (Fukuzawa's morals and Wayland's *The Elements of Moral Science*, 1969).

4　Fukuzawa (1958a: 26), for example, notes that the first volume of *Seiyō jijō* (Things Western) sold no fewer than 150,000 copies, and if pirate copies were included, it must have had a circulation of between 200,000 and 250,000 copies.

5　The other two books, both translations, were *Yochi shiryaku* (Brief description of world geography; 1870–7) by Masao Uchida and *Saigoku risshihen* (Success stories in the West; 1870–1) by Keiu (Masanao) Nakamura.

6　In his autobiography, Fukuzawa expresses his revolt against the feudal system in which "the distinction between high and low were clearly defined" even among children (2007: 18). He even states that "the feudal system is my father's mortal enemy which I am honor-bound to destroy" (2007: 6).

7　Nevertheless, the book is conventionally listed under the name of the Chambers.

8　English translations from Japanese are mine unless otherwise stated in the references.

9　This dynamism and fluidity is supported by Fukuzawa's plain and easy-to-read writing style, rather than the formal Sino-Japanese style preferred by intellectuals at the time. His interest in the art of speech could also be a contributing factor.

10　Fukuzawa read an English translation of the French original, *Histoire de la civilisation en Europe*.

11　In *Sekai kunizukushi,* Fukuzawa omitted this mention of Japan.

12　In this paper, the metaphor of anthropophagous translation is discussed somewhat superficially as a framework, rather than being analyzed as a poetics of translation.

13　It is important to note that this is an English translation and Fukuzawa did not use the word "assimilated." His original text (1959b: 6) says: *sono mono wa gaibutsu naredomo, hitotabi ware ni toreba onozukara waga shinnai no mono tarazaru o ezu* (Although these matters are foreign, once they are taken into my body, they are incorporated into my body). The expression "assimilated" conveys this meaning.

References

Andrade, O. de. 1991. "Cannibalist Manifesto" (Manifesto Antropófago). In L. Bary, "Oswald de Andrade's 'Cannibalist Manifesto.'" *Latin American Literary Review* 19(38): 38–47.

Anzai, T. 1995. *Fukuzawa Yukichi to seiō shisō: shizen-hō, kōri-shugi, shinka-ron* [Yukichi Fukuzawa and Western thought: natural law, utilitarianism, and evolutionism]. Nagoya: Nagoya Daigaku Shuppankai.

Barbosa, H. G. and L. Wyler. 1998. "Brazilian tradition." In *Routledge Encyclopedia of Translation Studies*, edited by M. Baker. London and New York: Routledge, pp. 326–33.

Buckle, H. T. 1872. *History of Civilization in England*, 2 vols. New York: D. Appleton and Company.

Campos, H. de. 1986. "The Rule of Anthropophagy: Europe Under the Sign of Devoration." Translated by M. T. Wolff. *Latin American Literary Review* 14(27): 42–60.

Chambers, W. and R. (eds). 1852/1999. *Political Economy, for Use in Schools, and for Private Instruction*. Bristol: Thoemmes Press; Tokyo: Kyokuto Shoten.

Craig, A. M. 1984. "John Hill Burton and Fukuzawa Yukichi." *Kindai Nihon kenkyū* [Journal for the study of modern Japan] 1: 218–38.

Fukuzawa, Y. 1958a. "Fukuzawa zenshū shogen" [Introduction to the collected works of Yukichi Fukuzawa]. In *Fukuzawa Yukichi zenshū* [The collected works of Yukichi Fukuzawa] (Vol. 1). Tokyo: Iwanami Shoten, pp. 1–65.

—. 1958b. *Seiyō jijō* [Things Western]. In *Fukuzawa Yukichi zenshū* [The collected works of Yukichi Fukuzawa] (Vol. 1). Tokyo: Iwanami Shoten, pp. 275–608.

—. 1959a. *Sekai kunizukushi* [Nations around the world]. In *Fukuzawa Yukichi zenshū* [The collected works of Yukichi Fukuzawa] (Vol. 2). Tokyo: Iwanami Shoten. Originally published in 1869, pp. 579–668.

—. 1959b. *Bunmeiron no gairyaku* [An outline of a Theory of Civilization]. In *Fukuzawa Yukichi zenshū* [The collected works of Yukichi Fukuzawa] (Vol. 4). Tokyo: Iwanami Shoten, pp. 1–212.

—. 1962. "Chojutsu no setsu" [On writing]. In *Fukuzawa Yukichi zenshū* [The collected works of Yukichi Fukuzawa] (Vol. 19). Tokyo: Iwanami Shoten, pp. 639–41.

—. 1969. *An Encouragement of Learning* [*Gakumon no susume*]. Translated by D. A. Dilworth and U. Hirano. Tokyo: Sophia University.

—. 1973. *An Outline of a Theory of Civilization* [*Bunmeiron no gairyaku*]. Translated by D. A. Dilworth and G. C. Hurst. Tokyo: Sophia University.

—. 2007. *The Autobiography of Yukichi Fukuzawa* [*Fukuō jiden*]. Translated by E. Kiyooka. New York: Columbia University Press.

Guizot, F. 1870. *General History of Civilization in Europe, from the Fall of the Roman Empire to the French Revolution*. New York: D. Appleton and Company.

Itō, M. 1969. "Fukuzawa no moraru to Wayland no *Shūshin-ron*" [Fukuzawa's morals and Wayland's *The Elements of Moral Science*]. In M. Itō, *Fukuzawa Yukichi ronkō* [On Yukichi Fukuzawa]. Tokyo: Yoshikawa Kōbunkan, pp. 1–77.

Katō, S. and A. Maeda. (eds). 1989. *Buntai* [Writing style]. *Nihon kindai shisō taikei 16* [Modern Japanese thought 16]. Tokyo: Iwanami Shoten.

Kawano, K. 1995. *Nihon no kindai to chishiki-jin* [Japan's modernity and intellectuals]. Tokyo: Iwanami Shoten.

Komori, Y. 2001. *Posutokoroniaru* [Postcolonial]. Tokyo: Iwanami Shoten.

Lefevere, A. 1992. *Translation, Rewriting, and the Manipulation of Literary Fame*. London and New York: Routledge.

Maruyama, M. 1986. *Bunmeiron no gairyaku o yomu* [Reading *Bunmeiron no gairyaku*]. Tokyo: Iwanami Shoten.

Maruyama, M. and S. Katō. 1998. *Hon'yaku to Nihon no kindai* [Translation and Japan's modernity]. Tokyo: Iwanami Shoten.

Mill, J. S. 1861. *Considerations on Representative Government*. London: Parker, Son, and Bourn.

—. 1865. *On Liberty*. London: Longmans, Green, and Co.

—. 1884. *Principles of Political Economy*. New York: D. Appleton and Company.

Mitchell, S. A. 1865. *A System of Modern Geography: Physical, Political, and Descriptive*. Philadelphia: E. H. Butler & Co.

Nishikawa, S. 2002. "Kaisetsu" [Afterword]. In Y. Fukuzawa, *Fukuzawa Yukichi chosakushū* [The works of Yukichi Fukuzawa] (Vol. 3). Tokyo: Keio Gijuku Daigaku Shuppankai, pp. 241–68.

Saucier, M. 2002. "Kaisetsu" [Afterword]. In Y. Fukuzawa, *Fukuzawa Yukichi chosakushū* [The works of Yukichi Fukuzawa] (Vol. 1). Tokyo: Keio Gijuku Daigaku Shuppankai, pp. 341–51.

Tōyama, S. 1970. *Fukuzawa Yukichi—Shisō to seiji to no kanren* [Yukichi Fukuzawa: His thoughts concerning politics]. Tokyo: Tokyo Daigaku Shuppankai.

Uchiyama, A. 2009. "Translation as Representation: Fukuzawa Yukichi's Representation of the 'Others.'" In *Agents of Translation*, edited by J. Milton and P. Bandia. Amsterdam and Philadelphia: John Benjamins, pp. 63–83.

Vieira, E. R. P. 1999. "Liberating Calibans: Readings of *Antropofagia* and Harold de Campos' Poetics of Transcreation." In *Post-colonial Translation: Theory and Practice*, edited by S. Bassnett and H. Trivedi. London and New York: Routledge, pp. 95–113.

Wayland, F. 1865. *The Elements of Moral Science*. New York and Chicago: Sheldon and Company.

Yanabu, A. 1982. *Hon'yaku-go seiritsu jijō* [Formation of translation words]. Tokyo: Iwanami Shoten.

—. 2010. "Kaidai 8: Fukuzawa Yukichi 'Fukuzawa zenshū shogen'" [Commentary 8: On the introduction to the collected works of Yukichi Fukuzawa]. In *Nihon no hon'yaku-ron: Ansorojī to kaidai* [Japanese discourse on translation: An anthology with commentary], edited by A. Yanabu, A. Mizuno, and M. Naganuma. Tokyo: Hōsei Daigaku Shuppankyoku, pp. 108–14.

Yoshida, T. 2000. "*Kaitai shinsho* kara *Seiyō jijō* e—kotoba o tsukuri, kuni o tsukutta rangaku·eigaku-ki no hon'yaku" [From *Kaitai shinsho* to *Seiyō jijō*: translations that formed language and the country in the time of Dutch and English Learning]. In *Hon'yaku to Nihon bunka* [Translation and Japanese culture], edited by T. Haga. Tokyo: Kokusai Bunka Kōryū Suishin Kyōkai, pp. 50–66.

5

Stylistic Norms in the Early Meiji Period: From Chinese Influences to European Influences

Akira Mizuno

Stylistic norms in translation

This paper explores changes in the stylistic norms of translations produced in the early and mid-Meiji period (i.e. 1868–98) in Japan. Although the issue of style[1] in translation has already been dealt with by such authors as Catford (1965), Nida and Taber (1969), and more recently Boase-Beier (2006), their main concerns were, respectively, translatability, the classification of stylistic features, and style as the result of a cognitive state, not stylistic "norms." Popović (1970) covered style shifts, but showed interest only in literary norms. Somekh (1981) and Nord (1991) discussed stylistic norms, but concerned themselves primarily with stylistic shifts between the source and target languages. Unlike those studies, this paper focuses on changes within the stylistic norms of a single language—that is, the target language—as manifested in translations. In this, I shall be following the analysis of "translational stylistics" proposed by Malmkjær (2003).

Stylistic norms could be regarded as belonging to the textual-linguistic norms that govern the selection of material for formulating the target text (TT) (Toury 1995: 59), although Toury does not specifically mention stylistic norms. Toury also indicates that translation norms are unstable and changing entities with complex structures, and he suggests the possibility of the parallel existence of three types of competing norms: the mainstream norm, remnants of previous norms, and the rudiments of new norms (Toury 1995: 62–3). This was the case in early Meiji Japan (especially with regard to stylistic norms), but with certain qualifications. It is not necessarily the case that one norm prevails over others as a result of competition among norms. Rather, it is possible that internal forces or necessities prompt gradual changes in norms, changes that occur with few or no overt conflicts. I would argue that the mainstream stylistic norm in the early Meiji period shifted over the course of a few decades (though the issue of when a *variant* of a norm becomes a *different* norm requires further discussion). This argument is similar to that in Kayyal (2008), one of the few papers—either within or outside of Japan—that have dealt with changes in stylistic norms.

Kanbun kundoku style as the mainstream style

In the early Meiji period a variety of styles of written Japanese existed side by side. There have been many classifications of these styles of writing, such as those by Satō (1891), Ikuta (ca. 1907), Ōtsuki (1907), Yamamoto (1964), and Seko (1968). For example, Morioka (1991a: 17) lists the following styles: *kanbun* (texts written in Chinese, which had long been used by Japanese intellectuals as a prestigious form of writing), *kanbun kundoku* style (Chinese texts rearranged in Japanese syntactical order and with Japanese inflectional suffixes added), *wakan setchū* style (an eclectic mixture of Japanese and Chinese based on *kanbun kundoku* style), *wabun* (Classical Japanese) style, *zokubun* (vernacular) style, and others. The consensus, however, is that *kanbun kundoku* style occupied the mainstream position (Ōtsuki 1907; Takano 1991). This was so not only in original writing, but also in the language used in translations (Hayashi 1976; Morioka 1991b). This is evident by examining translations of nonfiction works by the "Enlightenment" thinkers[2] of the time, such as those by Masanao Nakamura and Rinshō Mitsukuri, although in translations of literature, other styles such as Classical Japanese style and the vernacular style were used by some translators. It should be noted that in the early Meiji period translations of nonfiction works were more numerous and more influential than translations of literary works, because Japan's needs at that time were for knowledge about Western society.

Takano (1991: 401–2) observes that although *kanbun kundoku* style was the mainstream style throughout the Meiji period, it gradually gave way to other styles that incorporated European-influenced phraseology. The reason Tanaka gives for this development is that writers sought a wide range of expressions that would accommodate a variety of thinking as Japanese society underwent fundamental changes in the course of modernization. To this I would add two other factors: (a) the influence of movements calling for reform of the Japanese language and for *genbun itchi* (literally, unification of the spoken and written languages, meaning vernacularization of the written language), and, above all, (b) the impact of translations.

The origins of *kanbun kundoku* style

Before analyzing the changes that occurred to *kanbun kundoku* style, we need to present a brief exploration of *kanbun kundoku* (literally, reading Chinese in Japanese),[3] from which *kanbun kundoku* style derived. The factors that constitute *kanbun kundoku* style are also potential analytical criteria.

Until the twentieth century, the act of reading Chinese texts in Japan usually involved applying a predetermined Japanese reading (i.e. the Japanese word having the same meaning as the Chinese) to a particular Chinese character or phrase. The readings were fixed, so a particular Chinese character or phrase came to trigger a particular reading for Japanese readers. Since around the seventh century, Japanese people have also annotated Chinese texts with various diacritics, including character- and phrase-inverters, in order to indicate how to read Chinese texts according to Japanese word order. Other diacritical marks were used to add Japanese grammatical inflections written in kana (the two phonetic syllabaries). This process not only constituted "pre-print translation" (Semizu 2006: 293), but also a *mental* translation that did not result in a physically separate TT. Sometimes a Chinese text thus annotated was rewritten in Japanese word order, but whether this rewriting process occurred on paper or only in the mind, it was called *kanbun kundoku*.

Kanbun kundoku constituted a kind of extremely literal translation of Chinese texts, forcing almost word-for-word translation (Tsukishima 1963: 44). As Meldrum (2009: 46) notes, "Early translation in Japan, therefore, can be viewed as source-language oriented." From this method developed a written style known as *kanbun kundokutai* (*kanbun kundoku* style), which produced expressions that had not existed in Japanese before the introduction of Classical Chinese works (Yamada 1935: 33). In short, the early development of written Japanese was mediated by this literal translation method and Chinese-derived expressions. During and toward the end of the Edo period (1603–1868), when European languages were introduced, the *kanbun kundoku* method used with Chinese was transformed into *ōbun kundoku* (literally, reading Indo-European languages as Japanese) via the study of Dutch, the main European language present in Edo Japan, and later via the study of English (Morioka 1999: 19). This practice of *ōbun kundoku*, whereby European words were assigned their word-for-word Japanese equivalent and numbers were used to indicate Japanese word order, paved the way for *ōbunmyaku* (literally, European-influenced style, meaning texts whose style had strong European overtones) in the Meiji period.

Characteristics of *kanbun kundoku* style

In order to analyze the characteristics of and changes in *kanbun kundoku* style as used in translations in the early Meiji period, we need a means to determine the extent of difference between original writings in *kanbun kundoku* style and translations in this style. This first entails specifying the characteristics of *kanbun kundoku* style because, as Takano (1991) points out, many who have written about *kanbun kundoku* style have only an impressionistic view and no definition of the style. On the basis of the works of Tsukishima (1955: 281) and Kaji (2010: 123), I have identified seven characteristics that can act as criteria for evaluating the degree of adherence to *kanbun kundoku* style: expressions specific to *kanbun kundoku*; a more restricted range of auxiliary verbs than in non-Chinese-influenced Japanese; fewer honorifics; fewer conjugations of auxiliary verbs and postpositional particles; more restricted vocabulary for emotional expressions and euphemisms; abundant use of kanji (Chinese character) compounds; and greater use of present forms than past or present perfect forms except when required by the context. The term *kanbun kundoku* style simply means a style that has the above characteristics and is subject to Japanese grammatical rules (Shirafuji 1982: 129).

The first two criteria need additional explanation. Specific phraseology derived from the practice of *kanbun kundoku* involves expressions that did not previously exist in the Japanese language. They were originally a kind of translationese (Meldrum 2009: 46) that was produced by routinized literal translation of Chinese expressions, but they were gradually incorporated into Japanese to the extent that they could no longer be distinguished from nontranslated Japanese. These expressions have been compiled by Yamada (1935), Tsukishima (1963), and Takano (1991), and they include such phrases as *iwaku* (say), *atawazu* (impossible), *nansurezo* (why), *shikōshite* (and then), *subekaraku—beshi* (as a matter of course—must), *ani* (never), and *katsute* (until now).

Typical auxiliary verbs used in *kanbun kundoku* style are *ki, tari*, and *ri* (past and perfect); *mu* (future); *zu* (negation); *ru* and *raru* (passive); *shimu* (causative); *beshi* (conjecture and possibility); *nari* (assertive); and *gotoshi* (situation). Other auxiliary verbs (e.g. *keri, tsu*, and *nu*) and conjugations of auxiliary verbs (e.g. *kari* and *keri*) are rarely used in *kanbun kundoku* style, so if a translated text uses such auxiliary verbs and their conjugations, it indicates a departure or deviation from the norms of *kanbun kundoku* style. The same is true for the use of honorifics and emotional expressions. In other words, the further a translated text departs from these criteria, the more it deviates from the norms of *kanbun kundoku* style.

Characteristics of *ōbunmyaku* style

For the purposes of the analysis in the latter part of this chapter, we also need to explore the characteristics of *ōbunmyaku* (European-influenced style). This infiltrated *kanbun kundoku* style through translations governed by source-oriented initial translation norms. Kisaka (1987: 124) defines *ōbunmyaku* as the expressions and styles brought into the Japanese language by literal translations of European texts, deviating from domestic conventions and retaining the foreignness intact. As we will see below, it was this European-influenced style that contributed greatly to the eclipse of *kanbun kundoku* style. As the source languages of translations in the Meiji period were predominantly European languages, source-oriented translations incorporated some linguistic features of those languages into the language of translations. Kisaka (1988: 363) also argues that these literal renditions made up for what were perceived as deficiencies in the Japanese language and were eventually incorporated into Japanese.

Kisaka (1987: 124) enumerates ten grammatical forms that are the markers of European-influenced style (i.e. these forms were not previously part of the Japanese language): explicit use of personal pronouns as the subject or object; use of *sore* (*it*) as a third-person singular neutral pronoun; use of *sore* as an impersonal *it*; expressions that mimic relative clauses; use of inanimate subjects with transitive verbs; use of inanimate subjects with the passive voice; use of generic subjects (*wareware* [*we*], *anata* [*you*]); literal translations of the *it-that* cleft construction; inversions; and causative constructions using literal translations of verbs such as *have, make,* and *give.* Morioka (1991b: 430–44) proposes a more elaborate categorization, but it is not greatly different from that of Kisaka. They both concentrate on grammatical categories but fail to include reflexive pronouns and various tenses, which undoubtedly constitute aspects of European-influenced style. We should also add rhetorical devices such as simile, metaphor, and personification. Furthermore, a literal rendering inevitably entails the transfer of construals (Langacker 2002: 5–15)—that is, the bringing into the target language of source language situations that are construed differently from in the target language—so the transfer of construals should be added to the list of characteristics of European-influenced style.

Ōbunmyaku not only changed the language and style of translations, but also transformed the Japanese language itself. It was *ōbunmyaku* that made the greatest impact on and determined the direction of the modern Japanese language (Seko 1968: 10). After the second decade of the Meiji period the vernacularized style freely incorporated European-derived expressions, and their proportion increased with the passing of time (Matsumura 1977: 212). Thus the Japanese language was transformed into a mixture of Classical Japanese style, the Chinese-influenced *kanbun kundoku* style, and the European-influenced *ōbunmyaku* style.

Stylistic norms in the first decade of the Meiji period

During most of the first decade of the Meiji period (i.e. 1868–77), translations were mainly produced by Enlightenment thinkers, bureaucrats, and politicians. It was not until around the end of this decade that a substantial number of translations of literary works began to appear. First I will examine nonfiction translations of Enlightenment works and analyze the styles of written Japanese used in these translations. For reasons of space, I shall restrict myself to the discussion of three high-profile translations.

Saigoku risshihen (Success stories in Western countries) by Masanao Nakamura (1870)

This famous translation of Samuel Smiles' *Self-Help* (1859) was one of the earliest translations of the Meiji period.

Source text (ST):

"Heaven helps those who help themselves" is a well-tried maxim, embodying in a small compass the results of vast human experience. The spirit of self-help is the root of all genuine growth in the individual; and, exhibited in the lives of many, it constitutes the true source of national vigor and strength. Help from without is often enfeebling in its effects, but help from within invariably invigorates. Whatever is done FOR men or classes, to a certain extent takes away the stimulus and necessity of doing for themselves; and where men are subjected to over-guidance and over-government, the inevitable tendency is to render them comparatively helpless.

Target text (TT):

Ten wa mizukara o tasukuru mono o tasuku to ieru kotowaza wa kakuzen (shikato)
[[heaven-T [themselves-ACC help those]-ACC help]-ACC say] proverb]-T surely (certainly)

keiken (tameshi kokoromi) shi⌈taru⌉ kakugen nari. Wazuka ni ikku no naka ni
experienced (tried)   do-PAST maxim] is Only one-phrase-G inside

amaneku jinji-seibai no   jikken (tameshi) o hōzō (kometearu) se⌈ri⌉. Mizukara o
broadly human-experience-G experiment-(trial)-ACC embody (include) do-PAST [Themselves-ACC

tasuku to iu koto wa yoku jishu-dokuritsu shite tanin no chikara ni yorazaru no
        help]-T adequately independent-do others-G force-D dependent-not-G

koto nari. Mizukara o   tasukuru no seishin (tamashii) wa oyoso hito taru mono no
be   [Themselves-ACC help-G spirit (soul)]-T [generally human-G

saichi no **yotte** shōzuru **tokoro** no kongen nari. Oshite kore o ieba mizukara
wisdom-G from derive which-G root] is [Presume this-ACC say-if for-oneself

tasukuru jinmin ōkereba   sono hōkoku kanarazu genki jūjitsushi seishin kyōsei naru
help-G people-NOM if-many] their country will surely energy full-do (and) spirit strong-will

koto nari. Tanin yori tasuke o ukete jōju seru   mono wa sono nochi kanarazu
be   [Others-from help-ACC receive succeed-PAST people]-T thereafter surely

otorouru koto ari. **Shikaruni** uchi mizukara   tasukete nasu **tokoro** no koto wa,
decline be [However inside for themselves help do which]-T

kanarazu seichō shite   fusegu **bekarazaru** no ikioi ari.
will surely develop (and) stop not-able-to-G energy have

Kedashi ware moshi tanin no tame ni tasuke o ōku nasan niwa, kanarazu   sono hito
Perhaps [I if others-G for help-ACC much do]-T certainly that person-ACC

o **shite** jiko hagemi tsutomuru no kokoro o genji **seshimuru** koto nari. Kore yue ni
        self-effort-G   spirit-ACC weaken make be This-ABL reason

shiden (kashizuki) no kagen (kibishi sugiru) naru mono wa sono shitei no jiritsu
[teaching (education)-G   too stern (too hard)]-T their disciple-G independence

(hitoridachi) no kokorozashi o   samataguru koto ni shite seihō (seiji) no gunka
(becoming independent)-G resolve-ACC impede   and [politics-G subordinates

(shimo no mono) o atsuyoku (oshitsukeru) suru mono wa jinmin o **shite** fujo o
(general public)-ACC suppress (compel)]-T people-ACC help-ACC

ushinai seiryoku (ikioi) ni toboshi kara **shimuru** koto nari. (emphasis added)
lose energy (vigor) meager make be

Nakamura uses many words and phrases specific to *kanbun kundoku*, as indicated
in boldface in this passage, so the basic tone is *kanbun kundoku* style. Auxiliary
verbs that indicate the past and perfect tense (a marker of *kanbun kundoku* style)
are used only twice (*taru* and *ri*, indicated by boxes). The part marked by dotted
underlining is an explanation added by Nakamura, elaborating on the concept of
self-help (back-translated as "Self-help means to be independent, not dependent
on others' help"). The double underlining indicates expansion and paraphrase.
"Help from without" is rendered as "Those who succeed by dint of other's help,"

and "over-government" is translated as "when politicians oppress the general public." Nakamura added kana on the right side[4] of some kanji compounds to show their pronunciation, and in some cases he put explanations of the meaning in kana on the left side of the compounds. These elaborations and explanations seem to reflect his attitude toward translation—that is, translations should be capable of being read and understood relatively easily. Nishio (1968: 488) claims that Nakamura had in mind readers who needed the pronunciation of Chinese characters to be added in kana and that his translation helped transform the Japanese language from the literary style to a new vernacular style. In his other translations, Nakamura used honorific words such as *tamau*, although the use of honorifics is very rare in *kanbun kundoku* style; so his practice represented a slight deviation from the norm of *kanbun kundoku* style.

Kokusaihō (International law) by Rinshō Mitsukuri (1873)

In 1873, Rinshō Mitsukuri published *Kokusaihō*, a translation of *Introduction to the Study of International Law* written by Theodore D. Dwight Woolsey in 1860.

ST:

We find it necessary for the conception of states, and for their occupying the sphere which the Author of society **has marked out** for them, to predicate of the *sovereignty*, *independence*, and the *equality* of each with the rest. And these its attributes or rights each has a right to preserve; in other words, to maintain its state existence. These three attributes cannot exist apart, and perhaps the single conception of sovereignty, or of self-protection, may include them all.

By sovereignty we intend the uncontrolled exclusive exercise of the powers of the state; that is, both of the power of entering into relations with other states, and of the power of governing its own subjects. This power is supreme within a certain territory, and supreme over its own subjects wherever no other sovereignty has jurisdiction. (emphasis added)

TT:

Kore **motte** kangaureba   kakkoku jōtei no i ni shitagai   kakuji ni sono chi o bunryō
This   with   if-consider   [each-country-G lord-G will-DAT obey each-DAT the sphere-ACC occupy

shite ikkoku o   nasan to **hossuru** ni wa kanarazu   jishu no ken,   fuki no ken,
do   a-country-ACC make-NOM want   in-order]-T necessarily sovereignty-G right, independence-G right

dōtō no ken   naki **atawazu**. **Shikōshite** kakkoku   kono sanken o
equality-G right miss cannot   In-addition [each country these-three-rights-ACC

hoji suru wa **sunawachi** tagaini   sono sonzen o uru no kiso ni shite
hold-do]-T   means   [each-other its-dignity-ACC get-G   basis be and

kono ken   hitotsumo kaku **bekarazaru** mono nari.
these rights at-least-one lack   must-not   be]

Jishu no ken to wa jiyū ni waga kokken o   okonau o   iu.   **Kedashi** kokken o
 Sovereign-right-T   freely its-own power-ACC exercise-NOM mean Certainly power-ACC

okonau wa   takoku no   kōsai o   tsūji jōyaku o musubi **oyobi** jikoku no
 exercise-T [other-country-G relation-INS through treaty-ACC conclude and   own-country-G

jinmin o   tōgyo suru no   kenryoku ni **shite** sono   hōnai ni **oite**
subjects-ACC   govern-G   power   be] (and) its country-within

kore o   saijō no ken to shi   sono jinmin kore o   junpō   sezaru **bekarazaru**
[this-ACC supreme-G right make] [its   people this-ACC abide-by do-not   must-not

mono to su.
     do]

(emphasis added)

Except for the parts indicated by dotted underlining in the source text, which became heavily compressed in the Japanese, Mitsukuri's translation is relatively accurate. The language he uses contains many expressions that originated in literal translations of Chinese classics, and the present perfect form "has marked out" is not translated literally, which was common in *kanbun kundoku* style. Basically, therefore, Mitsukuri's translation conforms to the stylistic norms of *kanbun kundoku* style.

Kyōikushi (History of education) by Shigeki Nishimura (1875)

This is a translation of *History and Progress of Education* (Philobiblius, 1874).

ST:

In the early history of mankind, the instincts **were**, of course, first developed; the body must be protected from atmospheric changes, and the natural clothing of beasts **afforded** the means of accomplishing this; shelter from the sun and rain, and protection from wild beasts **were** the next necessity, and for this purpose, booths **made** from the branches of trees, or huts from their trunks (both of which seem to **have preceded** tents, which, however, **were soon invented**, for the convenience of the shepherd and herdsman), **were constructed.** (emphasis added)

TT:

Jinrui no   hajimete   shōzuru ya onore o yashinau no chi senpatsu su. Ten toki ni
Mankind-NOM for-the-first-time born when self-ACC nurture-G instinct precede Heaven sometimes

kan-on ari.   Kore ni taeru no   hō   nakaru **bekarazu**. Kore ni **oite** jūhi o
cold-warmth be This-DAT endure-G method not-have must-not This-DAT in beast-skin-ACC

mi ni   matoi, **motte** ifuku to nasu. Taiyō no netsu sarani   saegirazaru
body-DAT wear   by-that clothes-ACC do   Sun-G   heat   too not-to-be-protected

bekarazu.   Ametsuyu no shitsu   mata fusegazaru   **bekarazu**.
must-not   Rain-and-dew-G humidity too not-to-be-protected must-not

Yajū no gai no gotoki   mo mata kore o   fusegu **yuen** no sube nakaru
Beasts-G harm-G like-NOM also   this-ACC protect reason-G way not-have

bekarazu. Kore ni **oite** aruiwa   jushi o   ami aruiwa jukan o   kashi
must-not   This-DAT in   either tree-bark-ACC weave or tree-trunk-ACC roof (V)

rosha o tsukuru, (chōbaku o harite   ie to   suru wa   **kedashi** rosha o
hut-ACC   make   ([tent-ACC put-up house-DAT do-NOM]-T certainly hut-ACC

tsukuru no nochi ni ari.   Sono yue wa chōbaku o haru koto   wa
make-NOM   after   there-is That reason-T [tent-ACC   put-up NOM

bokuchiku no gyō o hajimeshi ni   yorite okorishi koto nareba nari.)
   stock-farming-ACC began-NOM-INS   by   developed reason   be

(emphasis added)

This is a relatively accurate translation. The italicized parts of the target text indicate slight paraphrasing or expansion, which shows that Nishimura was trying to make his translation comprehensible for the reader. It does, however, include many Chinese-derived expressions, and the seven past and present perfect tenses in the original passage (indicated in boldface) are not replicated in full in the translation. This is typical of *kanbun kundoku* style.

As can be seen from these three examples, early Meiji nonfiction translations by Enlightenment thinkers and bureaucrats can be characterized as follows. The stylistic norm that they conformed to was largely *kanbun kundoku* style, and there was no major departure from this norm, although some translators tried to make their translations understandable to readers by various means, which gave rise to slight deviations from the norm. The style that the translators chose caused shifts in tenses and other expressions, suggesting that *kanbun kundoku* style was acting as a constraint on the translators. It took two more decades for translators of nonfiction texts to be liberated from the fetters of *kanbun kundoku* style.

Translations of literature

In the translation of literature, a variety of styles competed against each other in the early years of the Meiji period, as was the case with original literary writings. Hayashi (1976: 16) notes that the style of translated literature was not limited to *kanbun kundoku* style, but included the *yomihon* (Edo-period romantic novels) style or *Bakin-chō* style (the *yomihon* style of Bakin Takizawa, a famous writer of the early nineteenth century), and puppet ballad-drama style, which were traditional styles of the Edo period. As indicated above, however, the mainstream style in translations was *kanbun kundoku* style (Hayashi 1976: 16; Morioka 1991b: 431). In contrast to translations of nonfiction works by Enlightenment thinkers, however, a major change occurred in the language of translations of literature in this period. In what follows, I briefly sketch the changes to *kanbun kundoku* style in translations of literature.

Karyū shunwa (Romantic stories of blossoms) by Junichirō Oda (Niwa) (1878)

Karyū shunwa was a famous translation of *Ernest Maltravers* (1827) and *Alice* (1838), both written by Edward Bulwer-Lytton.

> *ST1:*
>
> It **was** one soft May-day that he **found** himself on such an expedition, slowly riding through one of the green lanes <u>of ———shire. His cloak and his</u> <u>saddle-bags comprised all his baggage, and the world was before him "where</u> <u>to choose his place of rest."</u> The lane **wound** at length into the main road, and just as he **came** upon it he **fell** in with a gay party of equestrians. (emphasis added)

> *TT1:*
>
> Tenki   seirō to shite jumoku ussō, kunpū   jōjō to shite saika   ōha   o
> weather-NOM fine   is   trees-NOM lush balmy-wind gently rape-blossoms yellow-waves-ACC
>
> agu.   Toki **atakamo** gogatsu no chūjun ni shite natsu nao   imada atsukarazu.
> raise Season-T just-like May-G   middle is and summer-NOM yet   hot-be-not
>
> Marutsurabāsu tanki ni   gayū o   kokoromin to **hosshi** yakei ni   shōyō
>   Maltravers single-horseman-as expedition-ACC will try   wanted wild-lane-ACC saunter
>
> shi kazan no   fūkei o   kanbō su. Tamatama harukani   ichigun no
> do   summer-mountains-G scenery-ACC view   Accidentally in-the-distance [one-group-G
>
> kitai suna o   kette kitaru o   mitomu. (emphasis added)
> cavalry sand-ACC kick   coming]-ACC saw

> *ST2:*
>
> AND now Alice **felt** that she **was** on the wide world alone, with her child— no longer to be protected, but to protect; and after the first few days of agony, a new spirit, not indeed of hope, but of endurance, **passed** within her. Her

solitary wanderings, with God her only guide, **had tended** greatly to elevate and confirm her character. She **felt** a strong reliance on His mysterious mercy—she **felt**, too, the responsibility of a mother. Thrown for so many months upon her own resources, even for the bread of life, her intellect **was** unconsciously **sharpened**, and a habit of patient fortitude **had strengthened** a nature originally clinging and femininely soft. She **resolved** to pass into some other county, for she **could** neither bear the thoughts that **haunted** the neighbourhood around her, nor think, without a loathing horror, of the possibility of her father's return. Accordingly, one day, she **renewed** her wanderings—and after a week's travel, **arrived** at a small village. Charity is so common in England, it so spontaneously springs up everywhere, like the good seed by the roadside, that she **had** rarely **wanted** the bare necessaries of existence. (emphasis added)

TT2:

Arisu   Marutsurabāsu o tomonaite awazu. Chōzen **to shite omoeraku** ima ya sekai
Alice-NOM Maltravers-ACC visited   met-not Despondently   thought   [[now world

ni tekijū su **beki** mono   nashi to **iedomo** ware hitori no   chikara o   **motte**
in rely-on should person-ACC not-be notwithstanding] I-NOM only-G   ability-INS   with

yoku kono eiji o   yōiku sen. Mata   nanzo hoka no hojo o   matan ya.
well this infant-ACC rear will] In-addition why other-G help-ACC ask

Sunawachi danzen kokoro o kesshite dokuritsu no kokorozashi o tatsu. **Yueni**
Then   resolutely mind-ACC made-up independence-G resolve-ACC set   Therefore

kyūchi no chi o   sari hi ni uta o   hisaide zeni o   koi **motte**   boji no
familiar-G place-ACC left daily song-ACC sell money-ACC ask with-which mother-child-G

kuchi o nori shi nanoka o hete yōyaku hoka no chihō ni   tassu.
  make-a-living   seven-days-later at last other-G region-DAT arrived

Shikaredomo binten **ani** kono karen no shōjo o suten **ya**. Saiwai   eikoku wa
However   why-in-the-earth this pitiful-G girl-ACC abandon Fortunately England-T

jinji no michi okonaware itaru tokoro hito no megumi o uke zaru wa nashi.
  charity-spirit   prevail (and) everywhere [others-G help-ACC   get-not]-T never be
(emphasis added)

Oda's translation has a distinctive feature not found in the preceding examples of translations in *kanbun kundoku* style—that is, the addition of ornamental rhetorical devices specific to Chinese literature (especially poetry), as indicated by the dotted underlining in TT1. The first underlined part means "The weather is fine, the trees are lush, a balmy early summer breeze is gently blowing, and the rape blossoms are like yellow waves." These rhetorical devices seem to be used to make the tone of the work resemble the *kanbun* style familiar to readers of the time. Thus it involves a kind of domesticating translation strategy. The underlined part of ST1 was omitted in the translation, and as Kimura (1972: 389) points out, sometimes a whole chapter was condensed into just a few sentences.

The style of this translation has been characterized as *kanbun chokuyaku* style (literal translation style based on *kanbun*; this is a synonym for *kanbun kundoku* style) (Iwaki 1906: 48; Yanagida 1961: 13; Hayashi 1976: 16). Almost all the past forms in the original passage were rendered as present forms. As can be seen in TT2, heavy use of *kanbun kundoku* style is evident (indicated in boldface), and although *kakari musubi* (a concord construction that is typical of Classical Japanese but is never used in *kanbun kundoku* style) is used twice in TT2 (indicated by boxes), auxiliary verbs are rare, so that the passage exhibits typical features of the *kanbun kundoku* style.

According to Saitō (1998), who compared the usage of the auxiliary verbs *ki*, *tari*, and *ri* in passages of the same length from this translation and *Shinsetsu hachijūnichikan sekai isshū* (an 1878 translation by Chūnosuke Kawashima of Jules Verne's *Le tour du monde en quatre-vingts jours*), the counts for *ki*, *tari*, and *ri* were 31, 17, and 43 in *Karyū shunwa* and 194, 71, and 28 in *Shinsetsu hachijūnichikan sekai isshū*, respectively. This result seems to indicate that *Shinsetsu hachijūnichikan sekai isshū* conforms more closely to the norms of *kanbun kundoku* style than does *Karyū shunwa*. The fact that Saitō did not count the number of present forms means, however, that this assumption is not necessarily tenable.[5] For another group of auxiliary verbs—that is, *keri*, *tsu*, and *nu*, which are rarely used in *kanbun kundoku* style—the numbers were 0, 0, and 2 in *Karyū shunwa* and 97, 6, and 22 in *Shinsetsu hachijūnichikan sekai isshū*. In other words, these texts adhered to the mainstream norms of *kanbun kundoku* style in different degrees, but the extent of departure from the norms seems greater in *Shinsetsu hachijūnichikan sekai isshū* than in *Karyū shunwa* (Saitō 1998: 721), even though they were translated in the same year.

Keishidan by Mokichi Fujita and Yasuo Ozaki (Chisen Asahina) (1885)

It is generally acknowledged that new ground was broken by *Keishidan,* a translation of Bulwer-Lytton's *Kenelm Chillingly*. In the preface, the translator[6] explained his literal translation strategy of giving priority to the form of the original language:

> The novel is the art of language. Therefore, it goes without saying that its beauty lies in the combination of form and content. However, many translators are concerned only with the content and pay no attention to the form.

I have tried to create a new translational style by ensuring that the formal features of the original remain as they are in the translation as much as possible. To that end I did not mind violating Japanese conventions. . . . (1885: 1–2; unless otherwise stated, all translations are my own)

Asahina Chisen, the presumed translator of *Keishidan*, was prepared to "violate home conventions" so that "the translation will be close to the original in terms of adequacy" (Even-Zohar 1990: 50). As Yanagida (1961: 59) puts it, "with the appearance of this translation, translators gained for the first time the wholly conscious expression of a translation strategy," and the earlier "content-centered, unconscious translation strategy was replaced by a conscious translation strategy that put emphasis on both content and form."

ST1:

SIR PETER CHILLINGLY, of Exmundham, Baronet, F.R.S, and F.A.S., **was** the representative of an ancient family, and a landed proprietor of some importance. He **had married** young, not from any ardent inclination for the connubial state, but in compliance with the request of his parents. (emphasis added)

TT1:

Eikoku   Ekisumandamu mura nite Sā Pītā Chiringurī   to ieru wa baronetto no shaku
England-G Exmundham   village at Sir Peter Chillingly   named-T   Baronet-G   title-G

o yūshi, chokusen gakushi kai-in **narabini** kōko gakkai no kaiin nite,   sōō no
   has   F. R. C-member and   F.A.S.-G   member be   adequate

tochi o mo   yūshi, kyūke to kikoe taru Chiringurī ichizoku no chakushū tari. Kono
land-ACC also has   old family   called   Chillingly   family-G   heir   be-PAST This

hito wakaki toki tsuma o   metori taru ga,   motoyori mizukara nozomu tokoro arite
man young when wife-ACC marry-PAST but originally for-oneself   wanted

   kon o   motome taru ni wa arade, mattaku fubo no   i   ni
marriage-ACC seek-PAST   not   entirely parents-G intention-DAT

makase   taru   nari. (emphasis added)
leave   PAST be

The style of this translation and the connection between initial norms and stylistic norms merit close examination. This translated passage shows sparse use of expressions originating in literal translations of Chinese classics (indicated in boldface) and the presence of auxiliary verbs for past and perfect tenses (indicated by boxes), pointing to a decline in the influence of *kanbun kundoku* style. What most distinguished *Keishidan*'s style from preceding translations, however, was the transfer of construals, apparently due to the translator's initial norm of trying to preserve the formal features of the original. As the transfer of construals is one of the major factors that constitute *ōbunmyaku* (European-influenced style), *Keishidan* signals the introduction of *ōbunmyaku* into the weakened *kanbun kundoku* style. Because previous translations had invariably assimilated expressions that were foreign to Japanese, the transfer of construals in *Keishidan* is significant. Consider the following examples:

ST2:

The exception to their connubial happiness was, after all, but of a negative description. Their affection was such that they sighed for a pledge of it; fourteen years **had** he and Lady Chillingly remained unvisited by the little stranger. (emphasis added)

TT2:

Kaku   hyakuji ni   mono kaku koto naki fusai no tada hitotsu no fusoku   ari.
Like this everything-DAT thing lacking   not couple-G only   one-G   insufficiency exist

So wa   shōkyoku no shurui ni zoku suru   fusoku   nare domo, fusai no aijō
That-T [negative-G   kind-DAT belong to] insufficiency] be   but   couple-G affection

ito   fukaki naka ni tsuneni tansoku no tane to   nareri. So o   nanzo to yūni
very deep   while   always   sigh-G   cause-ACC became It-ACC what-ACC say

Chiringurī fujin to   sono otto to wa kekkon no nochi jūyonen no saigetsu o
[Chillingly-G wife and her husband]-T   marriage-G after   14-years-G   time-ACC

heru aida ni **katsute** chishō naru   kahin (shōni o yū) no   mimai ni   ai shi
pass during   once   little-G beautiful-guest (infant)-G visit-DAT meet-PAST

koto nakari shi   koto   **kore** nari. (emphasis added)
case not-be   PAST   ]-NOM this   be

The transfer of source text construals is indicated by dotted underlining. The Japanese expression "shōkyoku no shurui ni zoku suru" is a literal translation of "of a negative description." This expression introduced a new way of encoding (construing) a situation into Japanese, expanding the expressive potential of the Japanese language. Expressions that originated in literal translations of Chinese classics are indicated in boldface, and Classical Japanese-style wording is indicated by double underlining. The past tense *had* is translated as *shi* (past tense, indicated by boxes). The next example shows a literal transfer of a simile.

ST3:

. . . just as, how full soever of sparks a flint may be, they might lurk concealed in the flint till doomsday, if the flint were not hit by the steel.

TT3:

Atakamo musū no   hibana o   ganyū seru hiuchi-ishi mo kanarazu kōtetsu o
As if   [innumerable-G sparks-ACC   contain   flint]-T   also   surely   iron-ACC

ete   kore to   ai   utsu ni   ara zareba   mirai eigō sono   kōki o
gain   (iron)-ACC each other   strike   be-not   forever   its   brightness-ACC

hatsugen suru koto naku shite yamu beki ga gotoku. . . (emphasis added)
     manifest   not   (and)   end   will-G   just-like]

The literal transfer of a simile introduces a novel conceptualization of experience, which could broaden the expressive potential of the target language.

In the following example we see the transfer of a conceptual metaphor (the world is a place we enter and leave).

ST4:

The nurse declared in a frightened whisper that it had uttered no cry on facing the light. It had taken possession of its cradle in all the dignity of silent sorrow. A more saddened and a more thoughtful countenance a human being could not exhibit **if he were leaving the world instead of entering it**. (emphasis added)

TT4:

Uba no   sasayakeru ni wa kono ko nikkō ni mukau   mo taete teikyū   sezu
  [What wet nurse said]-T   [this child sunlight-DAT face   but   least   cry   not]   (and)

yurikago no   uchi monoshizuka ni shite shikamo hisō o   obi   *ima masani*
  [cradle-G   in   quiet   be   and yet   sorrow-ACC have]   [now just

<u>kono yo ni   iden to suru   ni wa ara de masa ni   kono yo o   saran to suru   hito</u>
  world-DAT   going to enter   not   just   world-ACC   going to leave   man

nite mo arawashi e zaru   hodo no   kanashimi o   fukumi   omoi ni   shizumeru
  would-not-express   degree-G   sadness-ACC   have   (and) thought-DAT   be-lost

ganshoku o   teiseri   to ieri. (emphasis added)
complexion-ACC   showed   said]

Conceptual metaphors, when translated literally, could likewise have the effect of enriching the Japanese language. These examples of the literal transfer of the source text construals are a reflection of the attitude toward translation described in the preface of *Keishidan*.

Keishidan marks the turning point in the norms of *kanbun kundoku* style. Here we can see how the choice of initial norms has affected the development of and changes in stylistic norms.

Translations by Shiken Morita

Shiken Morita was a prolific translator of European writers such as Jules Verne, Victor Hugo, and Charles Dickens. In his essay "Hon'yaku no kokoroe" (Hints on translation; 1887/1991: 284), he asserted that even an idiomatic expression such as *engrave in one's mind* should be translated literally and never rendered into the corresponding Japanese idiom (*kimo ni meizu*, i.e. impress on the liver), because a literal translation conveys not only the meaning of the idiom but also how Westerners express the corresponding Japanese concept. Morita also argued against the use of Japanese maxims and proverbs in translation.

With regard to stylistic norms, Morita argued in his 1887 essay "Nihon bunshō no shōrai" (The future of Japanese writing) that the Japanese language should adopt a "communicative but at the same time literal translation style" that closely follows the arrangement of expressions and phrases in European languages (Morita 1887/1991: 237). Thus he explicitly advocated introducing European expressions into Japanese through translation so as to expand the expressive potential of the language. This means that Morita was trying to break away from *kanbun* style and expressions imbued with *kanbun* flavor (Komori 1988: 244). Reflecting his attitudes toward translation and language, Morita's translations show a mixture of Japanese and Chinese-influenced and European-influenced styles, as is evident in *Tantei yūberu* (1898), his translation of Victor Hugo's *L'Espion Hubert*. (This is an indirect translation from the English version, *Hubert, The Spy*, which is included in *Things Seen* (English translation of *Choses Vues*), published in 1887 from Harper and Brothers.)

ST1:

Yesterday, the 20th of October, 1853, contrary to my custom, **I** went into the town in the evening. **I** had written two letters, one to Schoelcher in London, the other to Samuel in Brussels, and I wished to post **them myself**. I was returning by moonlight, about half-past nine, when, as I was passing the place which **we** call Tap et Flac, a kind of small square opposite Gosset the grocer's, **an affrighted group** approached **me**.

They were four refugees, — Mathé, a representative of the people; Rattier, a lawyer; Hayes, called Sans-Couture, a cobbler; and Henry, called little Father Henry, of **whose** profession **I** am ignorant.

"What is the matter with **you**?" **I** said, seeing **them** greatly agitated.

"**We** are going to execute **a man**," said Mathé, as he waved **a roll of paper** which he held in **his** hand.

Then **they** rapidly gave **me** the following details. Having retired since May from the society of **refugees**, and living in the country, all **these** facts were new to me.

In the month of April last **a** political refugee landed in Jersey. The innkeeper Beauvais, who is a generous-hearted fellow, was walking on the quay when the packet came alongside. (emphasis added)

TT1:

Sakujitsu, issen happyaku gojū san nen jūgatsu hatsuka, yo wa tsune ni
Yesterday   1853   October   20th   I-T   usual

kotonarite   yoru ni   iri   funai ni omomukeri. Kono hi yo wa Rondon ni aru
different-from night-DAT enter town-DAT went   This   day I-T London-DAT live

Shōruseru ni   ittsū,   Burasseru ni aru Samyūru ni ittsū   awasete nitsū no
Schoelcher-DAT one letter Brussels-DAT live Samuel-DAT one letter in total two-G

tegami o shitatame *tareba* mizukara kore o   yūbin ni dasan to **hosse**shi nari.
letters-ACC write   PAST and myself them-ACC going to post   wish-PAST be

Kuji han no korooi yo wa gekkō o   fumi tsutsu kaeri kitarite   zakkashō
Nine-thirty-G around I-T moonlight-ACC tread-PROG return come-PAST grocer

Gosusetto no ie no   mae naru gekichi wareware no Tapuefuraku to yoberu
  Gosset-G house-G in front vacant lot   we   Tap et Flac-DAT   call

tokoro o suguru   toki tachimachi hase **kitaru** ichigun no hito ari.
place-ACC pass-NOM when suddenly came-running a group of people there-are

Yo ni   chikazuke *ri*.
Me-DAT approach PAST

Kore yon mei no bōshi   nari *ki*. Kokkai giin Matē, daigennin Ratchīru,
They-T four person-G refugees are-PAST Diet member Mathé   lawyer   Rattier

kutsushō nite Sankonchūru to yobare *taru*   Haesu, **oyobi** oji Henrī to
 cobbler is and Sans-Couture-DAT being-called-PAST Hyes   and   aunt Henry-DAT

yobare *taru* Henrī,   kono hito no waza wa yo   shirazu.
being-called-PAST Henry this man-G   profession-ACC I know-not

Yo wa, hitobito no hanahada gekishi taru iro aru o   mite ie*ri*. "Onmi **ra**
I-T people-NOM greatly   agitated-NOM be-NOM-ACC saw said   You

nanigoto naru ka?" Matē wa sono te ni seru hitotabane no kami o
what's-the-matter Mathé-T his hand-DAT hold one roll-G   paper-ACC

furui tsutsu, "Wareware wa ima ikko no hito o   keiriku sen to   **hosshi**
wave-PROG   We-T   now one-person-ACC execute will-NOM want

yuku tokoro nari" to ie ri.
 go-NOM be NOM say-PAST

Sudenishite hitobito wa, tadachini yo ni   shita no shisai o katare *ri*.
 Then   people-T immediately me-DAT below-G detail-ACC tell-PAST

Kono gogatsu yori irai yo wa bōshi ra no nakama o shirizoki, inaka ni
This   May since I-T refugees-N society-from retired country-DAT

okifushi shi tareba, korera no koto wa issai sōbun   ni te ari *shi* nari.
live   do PAST these-G   facts-NOM all   newly-heard   be-PAST

Saru shigatsu ni ikko no kokujihan no   bōshi ari te, Zerushī ni jōriku
Last   April   one-G   political offender-G refugee be and Jersey-DAT land

se ri. Yadoya o waza to   seru   Būwaisu wa jinshin   aru mono nari *shi* ga,
PAST [Inn-ACC profession-as do-NOM] Beauvais-T generous heart have man   be-PAST but

fune no tsuke*ru* toki,   masani   sanbashi o ayumi ore ri. (emphasis added)
[ship-NOM arrive-NOM when] just-in-time quay-ACC   walk   PAST

What is noteworthy in this translation is that most of the personal pronouns (including the reflexive forms), indefinite articles, plural forms of nouns, repetition of nouns and demonstrative adjectives (all indicated in boldface in the ST) are explicitly translated into Japanese (indicated by boxes). Until then this had been rare in Japanese translations, since pronouns are grammatically optional in Japanese and there is no indefinite article. Morita also replicated various tenses (indicated by dotted underlining), and in the first paragraph the present progressive was rendered as *tsutsu* and *when* was translated as *toki*, both of which were expressions specific to the literal translation of European languages at that time. In the final paragraph, the past progressive form *was walking* was translated using two intransitive verbs and one auxiliary verb, *ayumi + ore + ri*, a construction rarely seen in earlier translations. Morita placed so much importance on the translation of tenses that he expressed dissatisfaction with his own rendition of the present perfect form in the afterword of *Tantei yūberu*. Morita's translation is quite precise, so it was called *shūmitsuyaku* (precise translation). There are no major omissions, and the word order is as close to the original as Japanese grammar allows. His translation retains major characteristics of the *kanbun kundoku* style, but overall the interfusional nature of his translation is apparent. By "*interfusional*" I mean a blending of *kanbun kundoku* style, *wabun* style, and *ōbunmyaku*. Expressions specific to *kanbun kundoku* remain in his translation (indicated by boldface), but the nature of *kanbun kundoku* style has been transformed by the infusion of various elements from *wabun* style and *ōbunmyaku*. Although not numerous, literal transfer of construals is found in other parts of the translation. Thus *kanbun kundoku* style has been transformed into an interfusional style that blends *kanbun kundoku* style, *wabun* style, and *ōbunmyaku*.

Six months after the publication of *Tantei yūberu* there appeared *Aibiki*, Shimei Futabatei's translation of Turgenev's Свидание (The rendezvous), which is famous for its vernacularized style. Kimura (1972: 391) argues that Futabatei produced his translations in vernacular style by carefully reading *Tantei yūberu* and deeply respecting Morita's *shūmitsuyaku* (precise translation). *Kanbun kundoku* style, which had occupied the mainstream position during the first and second decades of the Meiji period, was by this time no longer a constraint on translators, having been transformed into a style that made it possible to translate European languages more freely yet precisely. The interfusion of styles born from translations in the mid-Meiji period provided the basis for the subsequent development of modern Japanese literature.

Conclusion

As we have seen, the mainstream style of writing used in translations in the early Meiji period was *kanbun kundoku* style. In nonfiction translations by Enlightenment scholars and bureaucrats, other styles were rare, probably because *kanbun kundoku* style was a convenient vehicle for assimilating new concepts such as *society* and *freedom* due to its ability to accommodate new kanji compounds that corresponded to such concepts (Ueda 2008: 145). By contrast, the norms of *kanbun kundoku* style in translations of literature underwent gradual but significant changes by the end of the second decade of the Meiji period, incorporating elements of *wabun* (Japanese style) and, above all, *ōbunmyaku* (European-influenced style). Ueda attributes the changes in *kanbun kundoku* style to the fact that it "accommodated new grammar in translating Western languages, such as the introduction of relative clauses and other formulaic expressions" and to "various efforts on the part of individuals to depart from the rules and literary conventions of *kanbun*." From the perspective of Translation Studies (TS), this change in stylistic norms was triggered at least partly by initial translation norms that emphasized the source language, epitomized in the work of the translator of *Keishidan* and in the work of Shiken Morita. The transformation of *kanbun kundoku* style into a mixture of *wabun* style, *kanbun kundoku* style, and *ōbunmyaku* smoothed the way for the upcoming vernacularized style, which helped unify speech and writing in Japan.

Notes

1   The term "style" usually refers to "the set or sum of linguistic features that seem to be characteristic" of a text, which can be identified by comparing "one set of features with another in terms of a deviation from a norm" (Wales 2001: 371–2). In this paper, however, it is used to mean not only the style of individual texts but more particularly the choice of the kind of written language that is used in translations as a collective genre in a particular period.

2 The "Enlightenment thinkers" were people who struggled to modernize Japan by learning from the West in terms of its civilization and material advances. Among the most influential of these thinkers were Yukichi Fukuzawa, Hiroyuki Katō, and Arinori Mori.

3 *Kanbun kundoku* has two meanings: (1) reading Chinese characters with the Japanese reading (i.e. the pronunciation of the Japanese word that has the same meaning as the Chinese word), and (2) translating Chinese as literally as possible into Japanese.

4 Japanese was traditionally written vertically, not in the horizontal format used here, so the kana were appended on the right-hand side.

5 Because *kanbun* has no tense system, it is usually read in the present tense. It is read in the past or present-perfect sense only when so required by the context. Hence the abundant use of *ki, tari,* and *ri* does not necessarily mean that *Shinsetsu hachijūnichikan sekai isshū* adheres more to *kanbun kundoku* norms than does *Karyū shunwa.*

6 Nominally, the translators of *Keishidan* were Mokichi Fujita and Yasuo Ozaki, but it was Asahina Chisen who actually translated the book (Yanagida 1939: 14).

References

Boase-Beier, J. 2006. *Stylistic Approaches to Translation*. Manchester: St. Jerome Publishing.

Catford, J. C. 1965. *A Linguistic Theory of Translation: An Essay in Applied Linguistics*. London: Oxford University Press.

Even-Zohar, I. 1990. "The Position of Translated Literature within the Literary Polysystem." *Poetics Today* 11(1): 45–51.

Hayashi, O. 1976. *Kindai bunshō kenkyū: Bunshō hyōgen no shosō* [A study of modern writing: Varieties of prose expression]. Tokyo: Meiji Shoin.

Ikuta, C. ca. 1907. *Meiji bunshōshi* [A history of Meiji-period writing]. Tokyo: Nihon Bunshō Gakuin.

Iwaki, J. 1906. *Meiji bungakushi* [A literary history of the Meiji period]. Tokyo: Ikueisha.

Kaji, N. 2010. *Kan bunpō kiso* [Fundamentals of *kanbun* grammar]. Tokyo: Kōdansha.

Kayyal, M. 2008. "Salim al Dawudi and the Beginnings of Translation into Arabic of Modern Hebrew Literature." *Target* 20(1): 52–78.

Kimura, K. 1972. "Nihon hon'yakushi gaisetsu" [An outline of the history of translations in Japan]. In *Meiji hon'yaku bungakushū* [Collected works of literary translations in the Meiji period], edited by K. Kimura. Tokyo: Chikuma Shobō, pp. 375–94.

Kisaka, M. 1987. "Gendai ōbunmyaku no hirogari" [The extent of modern European-influenced style). *Kokubungaku: Kaishaku to kyōzai no kenkyū* [Japanese literature: Studies of interpretation and educational material]. 32(14): 124–8.

—. 1988. *Kindai bunshō seiritsu no shosō* [Aspects of the formation of modern writing]. Osaka: Izumi Shoin.

Komori, Y. 1988. *Kōzō toshite no katari* [Narrative as structure]. Tokyo: Shinyōsha.

Langacker, R. W. 2002. *Concept, Image and Symbol. The Cognitive Bases for Grammar*, 2nd edn. Berlin: de Gruyter.

Malmkjær, K. 2003. "What Happened to God and the Angels: HW Dulken's Translations of Hans Christian Andersen's Stories in Victorian Britain OR An Exercise in Translational Stylistics." *Target* 15(1): 37–58.

Matsumura, A. 1977. *Kindai no kokugo: Edo kara kindai e* [The modern Japanese language: From the Edo period to the present]. Tokyo: Ōfūsha.

Meldrum, Y. F. 2009. *Contemporary Translationese in Japanese Popular Literature.* Doctoral dissertation, University of Alberta.

Morioka, K. 1991a. "Sobyō: Genbun itchi-tai no seiritsu suru made" [A sketch of the formation of Japanese vernacular style]. In *Kindaigo no seiritsu: Buntai-hen* [The birth of the modern Japanese language: Style], edited by K. Morioka. Tokyo: Meiji Shoin, pp. 17–43.

—. 1991b. "Ōbunmyaku no keisei" [Development of European-influenced style]. In *Kindaigo no seiritsu: Buntai-hen* [The birth of the modern Japanese language: Style], edited by K. Morioka. Tokyo: Meiji Shoin, pp. 430–40.

—. 1999. *Ōbun kundoku no kenkyū: Ōbunmyaku no keisei* [A study of translating European languages in the same way as translating Chinese into Japanese: Development of European-influenced style]. Tokyo: Meiji Shoin.

Morita, S. 1887/1991. "Hon'yaku no kokoroe" [Hints on translation], reprinted in *Nihon kindai shisō taikei 15: Hon'yaku no shisō* [Compendium of modern thought in Japan, vol. 15: Thoughts on translation], edited by S. Katō and M. Maruyama. Tokyo: Iwanami Shoten, pp. 283–91.

—. 1887/1981. "Nihon bunshō no shōrai" [The future of Japanese writing], reprinted in *Meiji bungaku zenshū 26: Negishi-ha bungaku-shū* [Complete works of Meiji literature, vol. 26: Literary works by the Negishi school]. Tokyo: Chikuma Shobō, pp. 233–9.

Nida, E. A. and C. R. Taber. 1969. *The Theory and Practice of Translation.* Leiden: Brill.

Nishio, M. 1968. "*Saigoku risshihen* no furikana ni tsuite" [On kana glosses to indicate pronunciation in success stories in Western countries]. In *Kindaigo kenkyū: Dai 2 shū* [The study of modern Japanese, vol. 2], edited by Kindaigo Gakkai. Tokyo: Musashino Shoin, pp. 473–88.

Nord, C. 1991. "Scopos, Loyalty, and Translational Conventions." *Target* 3(1): 91–109.

Ōtsuki, K. 1907. *Nihon bunshōshi* [A history of Japanese writing]. Tokyo: Hakubunkan.

Popović, A. 1970. "The Concept of 'Shift of Expression' in Translation Analysis." In *The Nature of Translation*, edited by J. S. Holmes. Bratislava: Publishing House of the Slovak Academy of Sciences, pp. 78–87.

Saitō, F. 1998. "Meijiki ni okeru *Hachijūnichikan sekai isshū* no hon'yaku ni-shu." [Two Meiji-period translations of *Around the World in Eighty Days*]. In *Tokyo Daigaku kokugo kenkyūshitsu sōsetsu hyaku shūnen kinen kokugo kenkyū ronshū* [Collected papers in commemoration of the centennial of the Institute of Japanese Language of Tokyo University]. Tokyo: Kyūko Shoin, pp. 713–27.

Satō, H. 1891. *Nihon gogaku shinron* [New approach to the Japanese language]. Tokyo: Tōkyōdō.

Seko, K. 1968. *Kindai Nihon bunshōshi* [A history of writing styles in modern Japan]. Tokyo: Hakuteisha.

Semizu, Y. 2006. "Invisible Translation: Reading Chinese Texts in Ancient Japan." In *Translating Others*, Volume 2, edited by Theo Hermans. Manchester: St. Jerome Publishing, pp. 283–95.

Shirafuji, N. 1982. "Kundokubun no buntaishi" [A history of styles of *kanbun kundoku*]. In *Buntaishi* [A history of writing styles], edited by Y. Miyaji. Tokyo: Meiji Shoin, pp. 125–48.

Somekh, S. 1981. "The Emergence of Two Sets of Stylistic Norms: In the Early Literary Translation into Modern Arabic Prose." *Poetics Today* 2(4): 193–200.

Takano, S. 1991. "Kanbun kundokutai no gohō." [Usages derived from *kanbun kundoku*]. In *Kindaigo no seiritsu: Buntai-hen* [Formation of the modern Japanese language: style], edited by K. Morioka. Tokyo: Meiji Shoin, pp. 383–403.

Toury, G. 1995. *Descriptive Translation Studies and Beyond*. Amsterdam and Philadelphia: John Benjamins.

Tsukishima, H. 1955. "Kunten-go" [Usages derived from the translation of Chinese into Japanese]. In *Kokugogaku Jiten* [Dictionary of Japanese language], edited by Kokugo Gakkai. Tokyo: Tokyodo, pp. 281–2.

—. 1963. *Heian jidai no kanbun kundokugo ni tsukite no kenkyū* [A study of Heian-period *kanbun kundoku*]. Tokyo: Tokyo Daigaku Shuppankai.

Ueda, A. 2008. "Sound, Scripts, and Styles: *Kanbun kundokutai* and the National Language Reforms of 1880s Japan." *Review of Japanese Culture and Society* 20: 131–56.

Wales, K. 2001. *A Dictionary of Stylistics*, 2nd edn. Harlow, England: Pearson Education.

Yamada, Y. 1935. *Kanbun kundoku ni yorite tsutaeraretaru gohō* [Usages derived from *kanbun kundoku*]. Tokyo: Hōbunkan.

Yamamoto, M. 1964. "Kaikaki no buntai o megutte" [On written styles in Japan's "civilization and enlightenment" period]. In *Gendaigo no seiritsu* [Formation of the modern Japanese language], edited by K. Morioka. Tokyo: Meiji Shoin, pp. 102–30.

Yanagida, I. 1939. *Seiji shōsetsu kenkyū (ge)* [Studies of political novels, vol. 3]. Tokyo: Shunjūsha.

—. 1961. *Meiji shoki hon'yaku bungaku no kenkyū* [A study of literary translations in the early Meiji period]. Tokyo: Shunjūsha.

6

On the Creative Function of Translation in Modern and Postwar Japan: Hemingway, Proust, and Modern Japanese Novels

Ken Inoue

Introduction

The purpose of this paper is to discuss the interaction between translation and creative writing in modern Japan, especially in the period of Shōwa modernism[1] and the early postwar period. By taking up the example of what certain translations of works by Hemingway and Proust contributed to modern Japanese literature, I aim to shed light on the problem of creativity in translation, framing this against the backdrop of a 1940s debate in Japan over the nature of the translation of literature.

Since the cultural turn in Translation Studies (TS), translators have broken free from a subordinate position relative to the original text and author, and there is a growing perception of translators as independently creative writers.[2] In literary translation, above all, the creativity involved in reading and translating is heightened, because the literary translation compounds and multiplies the voices of the original text (Boase-Beier 2006: 148). The main topic I would like to discuss here is the issue of creativity and its function in the process of translation, as well as the role it plays in the development of new literary genres, forms, and styles. To address this issue, I would like to start with a rereading, from the viewpoint of creativity, of the best-known translation controversy in Shōwa Japan.

Translated literature and creativity: Rereading the Rakuchū shomon (Kyōto letters) controversy

In 1944 an exchange of letters about translation took place between Teiichi Ōyama (1904–74), a German literary scholar and translator of writers such as Johann Goethe and Rainer Maria Rilke, and Kōjirō Yoshikawa (1904–80), a scholar of Chinese literature and translator of *Shui-hu zhuan* (*Water Margin*) and poems of the T'ang period. This debate was published in book form in 1946 under the title *Rakuchū shomon* (Kyōto letters).[3] Ōyama asserted that translations of literature should themselves constitute literature. This view was opposed by Yoshikawa, who asserted that translation was a mere expedient and approved of literal translations that did no more nor less than convey the concept of the original text. The diverging arguments in this well-known controversy, as well as Ōyama's naïve literary subjectivity and Yoshikawa's clear, practical approach, have often been pointed out, as Kawamura (1981/2000: 58–78) acutely commented, but insufficient attention has been paid to the essential point of the debate—that is, creativity in translation or how the translation of texts regarded as literary in the source culture should result in texts acceptable as literary in the recipient culture (Toury 1995: 168–9).

Ōyama's main assertions can be summarized in three points:

1. "I would like to think that the translation of literature demonstrates via the medium of translation the kind of literary works that the times naturally call for." (Ōyama in Ōyama and Yoshikawa 1946: 16)[4]
2. "If I were to state the central issue of translation, it is simply this: A translation of poetry must be 'poetry', a translation of a play must be 'a play', and a translation of a novel must likewise be 'a novel.'" (87)
3. "The following is why I state that excellent translations are always born out of an ardent zeal for creating great literature. Namely, the most important feature of the translations by Futabatei and Ōgai was that they determined the new style for writing novels in the Meiji era." (21)

Ōyama's assertion that the translation of literature "demonstrates via the medium of translation the kind of literary works that the times naturally call for" can be interpreted as assigning an appropriate significance and position to the role of translations of literature in peripheral and late-developing cultural spheres. In fact, translations of literature in modern Japan have introduced new genres and led to works of literature that, though too advanced for the society of that time, met the latent needs of the culture and times. It might be easier to understand the major contribution of translations of literature to the introduction and establishment of new genres in Japan by taking an example from the realm of popular literature. It was not until after translations of works by Edgar Allan Poe and Arthur Conan Doyle were introduced at the end of the nineteenth century that genuine detective stories came to be written in modern Japan. Likewise, without the introduction of translations of works by Jules Verne and H. G. Wells, modern Japanese science fiction and adventure stories could never have been established or might have developed in some other form. In the second half of the 1970s it was translations of American horror novels, particularly those by Stephen King, that were primarily instrumental in creating a climate in which Japanese horror novelists could thrive. In this way, translations of literature have often functioned as "the kind of literary works that the times naturally call for."

Next I will examine Ōyama's assertion that a translation of poetry should itself constitute poetry, a translation of a novel should result in a novel, and excellent translation must be born from a strong creative spirit for literature. Yoshikawa refuted this claim by rightly pointing out that the established concepts of a poem and novel involve concrete works and that each work consists of individual words. Poems and novels become established as entities because a work consisting of an accumulation of individual words is integrated into the form of a novel or poem.

> If we overlook individual words, then poetry, plays or novels would never exist. If it were not for individual words, a work of literature would never exist. Therefore we can say that poetry, plays and novels are made up of individual words. Thus it is also possible to reconstruct poetry, plays and novels by taking those individual words carefully and translating them into carefully chosen Japanese. (Yoshikawa in Ōyama and Yoshikawa 1946: 121)

In Ōyama's opinion, however, individual words can be sacrificed to achieve the integration of a whole work.

While Ōyama argued that translations of literature should themselves constitute literature, he was not referring to the use of translations to create literature. If in order to constitute literature it is essential to focus first on individual words and then to translate them, the only way to create translations of literature is to "reconstruct" the work with "carefully chosen" language, as advocated by Yoshikawa. In sum, therefore, the main opposing principles in the *Rakuchū shomon* controversy were as follows:

1. Ōyama: A translation of literature must itself be literature. Success or failure is determined by the existence of a strong creative spirit.

2. Yoshikawa: In practice, the translation of literature is achieved only by
   carefully taking individual words in the original text and replacing and
   reconstructing them carefully in a different language.

The opposing and compatible points of these two propositions had already been
expressed in an essay by Shimei Futabatei (1864–1909) titled "Yo ga hon'yaku
no hyōjun" (My standards for translation; 1906), which arguably constitutes the
origin of modern Japanese translation theory. Referring to his translations of
works by Turgenev, Futabatei first said that "If you think solely of the meaning
when translating a foreign language and attach excessive importance to it, you
will take the risk of harming the original." (Futabatei 1906/1985: 167; trans.
Ryan 1967: 120). Futabatei emphasized the importance of staying true to the
tone and form of the source text, because he respected the original authors and
believed that "one must cherish each and every word" (Futabatei 1906/1985:
168). Futabatei continued as follows:

> Style being inexorably tied to the poetic spirit of the particular author, the
> rhythm will vary with each writer. [. . .] The translator must be sensitive
> to the poetic spirit of each author . . . he must make his mind and body,
> his every action, identical with the original author's and conscientiously
> transfer this poetic spirit to his own version. (Futabatei 1906/1985; trans.
> Ryan 1967: 120)

Futabatei explained that his own translations were not necessarily successful,
because he "lacked the talent" (169; trans. Ryan 1967: 120) to reproduce the
original text. As a result of clinging to the original form, his translations were
rigid and difficult to read. Hence he concluded that it would be better to "simply
show the poetical spirit of the original work," yet he lacked the courage to plunge
into a free translation that focused on the meaning.

Like Yoshikawa four decades later, Futabatei followed the approach of
considering each word carefully and translating them one at a time. Nevertheless,
he felt he lacked the ability to "reconstruct" and "reproduce" them. It is interesting
that Futabatei was aware of the problems with his initial form-oriented approach
and attempted to take a step in the direction of Ōyama's proposed creative
translation methodology. Ultimately, however, Futabatei respected the source
text and maintained his stance on the importance of form. Such a wavering of
ideology that is openly expressed in "Yo ga hon'yaku no hyōjun" contributed to
the broadening of translation theory in Japan and remains significant today.

In the light of Futabatei's thesis, the two propositions in the *Rakuchū shomon*
controversy represent universal conflicts and issues that continue to face every

translator working between languages whose syntax differs greatly. Noteworthy here is the difference between translation based on a "strong creative spirit for literature," as Ōyama advocates, and free translation focused simply on meaning. Ten years before the *Rakuchū shomon* controversy, Ōyama spoke frankly about translation that is based upon a "strong creative spirit for literature":

> Translations of literature are still powerful even if they are slightly difficult to read or the writing is slightly convoluted. . . . The central task of translation—to express the fragrance of a foreign language, which is easily destroyed and dispersed—should first and foremost be performed by a writer. (Ōyama 1934b: 710)

In short, when Ōyama refers to a "strong creative spirit for literature" what he has in mind is translations by a writer such as Futabatei or Ōgai Mori (1862–1922), who were both mentioned in *Rakuchū shomon*. We can assume that the essence of a "strong creative spirit for literature" refers to "literary insight," which is brought to bear when one chooses a text for translation (Ōyama, in Ōyama and Yoshikawa 1946: 18) and which has the potential to eventually lead to the creation of a new writing style.

The background to Ōyama's principle and his idealistic theory of a writerly translation lies in Goethe's translation theory. In particular, in Goethe's third phase of translation[5] the translation is no longer a substitute for the original text, but of equal status. According to Ōyama (1934a: 1148), if a translation is strictly faithful to the source text, "the third, previously unattainable, stage of translation is reached" as a result of "sacrificing [target language] national characteristics to some extent." Translations by Ōgai and Futabatei are sometimes criticized for being overly elaborate and straying from the original, but Ōyama (1947/1970: 315–16) argued strongly that "Ōgai and Futabatei's translations are based upon Goethe's 'third translation method . . .' and their works introduced literature that must be written in Japanese in the form of translation."

Regardless of whether Ōyama properly understood Goethe, it becomes clear that in fact there is no great contradiction between his translation method born from a "creative spirit for literature" and Yoshikawa's manner of reconstructing a poem, a play, and a novel. The contrast between their approaches should not be depicted in terms of a sterile binary opposition (such as the dichotomy between free and literal translation that has long been discussed in the history of translation theory), but in terms of differing emphases on principles (1) and (2).

What is at issue here is creativity in translation. In essence, translation is carried out on the basis of principle (2) with the support of principle (1). The process of demonstrating creativity does not, however, always follow the same path. Rather, it also happens that in implementing principle (2), translations that are faithful to the source text and suppress principle (1) might create new expressions and new writing styles, so that they act as a creative stimulus for other contemporary literary expression. To give another example, Ōyama's "ardent zeal for creating great literature" aids in the choice of work to translate, thus releasing a writer's creativity and potentially resulting in excellent translations. This creativity is produced by the writer-translator merging his or her mind with that of the original author, incorporating the writer's spirit into his or her own expressions. In the following section, we shall consider this point more concretely by taking up the examples of Hemingway for "creative stimulus" and Proust for "merging" and "incorporating."

The impact of Hemingway-style prose

In June 1929 *Shi to shiron* (Poetry and poetics), a leading Shōwa modernism periodical edited by the poet and critic Yukio Haruyama (1902–94), issued a special feature (volume 4) that surveyed the world's modern poets. In the American section, Haruyama introduced two leading twentieth-century American novelists, Sherwood Anderson and Ernest Hemingway, in addition to many American modern poets, such as Carl Sandburg, Hart Crane, and T. S. Eliot. Haruyama wrote a short introductory essay on Hemingway, and this was probably the first introduction of Hemingway in Japan. In June 1930 a feature on America in volume 8 of *Shi to shiron* included nine modern American short stories, eight of which were translated from the experimental literary periodical *Transition* (1927–38), published in Paris and distributed mainly through Shakespeare and Company. Tellingly, there was a portrait of Hemingway on the page before the table of contents, and of the nine short stories it was Hemingway's "Hills Like White Elephants" (*Men without Women*, 1927) that was accorded particular attention. The translator of "Hills Like White Elephants," Sei Itō, was a critic and writer who had translated James Joyce's *Ulysses* and D. H. Lawrence's *Lady Chatterley's Lover* in the 1920s. In January 1931 volume 10 of *Shi to shiron* included another Hemingway short story, "Indian Camp" (*In Our Time*, 1925), this time translated by Manabu Orita.

Ritsu Oda's translation of Hemingway's *A Farewell to Arms* (1929) was published in September 1930 under the title *Buki yo saraba*. In January the following year translations of Hemingway's short stories "The Killers" (*In*

Our Time, 1925) and "Wine of Wyoming" (*Winner Take Nothing*, 1933)[6] were published by Shinchōsha in *Sentan tanpenshū* (Modern short stories), a volume in the *Amerika sentan bungaku sōsho* (Modern American literature) series. Thus translations of Hemingway's works were first introduced into Japan in 1930. These translations preceded the reactions to Hemingway's writing in literary circles, as Matsuo Takagaki (1890–1940) and other pioneers of research on American literature only began to refer to Hemingway from about 1933.

Oda, the translator of *A Farewell to Arms*, was less a translator than an adapter. He took original material and, straying from the source texts, proceeded to retell the stories. It was only Hemingway who motivated Oda to attempt a translation faithful to the original, rather than using his usual adaptive translation method. Oda found distinction and charm in the realism and lack of sentimentality of Hemingway's prose. In the preface of *Sentan tanpenshū* (1931), Jirō Hayasaka (one of the translators) wrote that Hemingway's charm derived from his transcending of sentimentalism and from his clear, expressive style. In other words, Hemingway's style was accepted in Japan as a clear and new writing style that portrayed the mechanism of modern psychology at a time when there were keen expectations of new psychological novels and intellectualism in literature, following on from the establishment of naturalism in the late nineteenth century and antinaturalism in the 1920s.

The concise, perceptive realism and clear, energetic rhythm of Hemingway's prose dispensed with superfluous decoration, but translating this prose into Japanese presented certain challenges. *A Farewell to Arms* was translated as *Buki yo saraba* just a year after its original publication in 1929. At first glance, Oda's translation appears to be merely a literal rendition, but in his foreword Oda said he remembered feeling an intense interest in the outstanding realism and lack of sentimentality in the original. In this light, we can see that Oda's translation employs a new style of Japanese characterized by short sentences and repetition of the perfective *ta* verb ending, with fidelity to the literary form being underpinned by the translator's empathy with the author's intentions and dry realism. Although rendering Hemingway's prose "literally" in the form of a string of short sentences ending with the *ta* perfective form was arguably a kind of mistranslation, this played a productive role in giving rise to a new literary style in Japanese. From the late 1940s to the early 1950s, this was to become established as the "hard-boiled" literary style that influenced many talented postwar Japanese novelists, including Kunio Ogawa, Shintarō Ishihara, and Takeshi Kaikō, and this new writing style also influenced subsequent translations of Hemingway from 1950 onward.

It was Hemingway's short stories, however, that best demonstrated his characteristic style, so I would like to present Sei Itō's translation of "Hills Like White Elephants" as an example. This short story mainly consists of a conversation between a young couple. The plot and characters are built up through the recurring subject of an abortion. While Hemingway's most important stylistic characteristics are how he uses everyday expressions with an up-tempo and conversational omissions that have major implications, here I would like to focus on the descriptive aspect in the penultimate paragraph:

> He picked up the two heavy bags and carried them around the station to the other tracks. He looked up the tracks but could not see the train. Coming back, he walked through the barroom, where people waiting for the train were drinking. He drank an Anis at the bar and looked at the people. (Hemingway 1997: 54–5)
>
> Kare wa futatsu no omoi kaban o tazusaete mukō no rēru made hakon*da*. Kare wa senro o miwatashita ga kisha wa mienakat*ta*. Kaerimichi ni kare wa kisha o matte hitobito ga bīru o nondeiru bārūmu o tōt*ta*. Kare wa Anisu o hitotsu nonde hitobito o miwatashi*ta*. (emphasis added)

The subject of all four sentences in Hemingway's original is *he*. There is also a succession of direct, very simple verbs—*pick, look, see, walk, drink*—without any accompanying adverbs or adverbial phrases. The only adjective is *heavy*. There are no subordinating conjunctions that constitute an adverbial phrase, and there is only one relative clause, introduced by *where*. Literal translation of this passage resulted in numerous short sentences that start with the personal pronoun *kare* (*he*) and end with the perfective form *ta* (or its variant *da*). This produces a dry, crisp impression, sometimes even more so than in Hemingway's original.

It was not until the 1950s that Japan fully accepted Hemingway. In 1954 a leading postwar critic, Masahito Ara (1913–79), took up the subject of the relationship between Hemingway and Japanese literature, arguing that Hemingway's literary actions, his "vitalism" and his "hard-boiled" literary style were beyond what Japanese authors could handle. Therefore, argued Ara (1954: 126), it was difficult to imagine that Hemingway would have an effect on Japanese literature in the near future. In the latter half of the 1950s, however, several major Japanese publishing houses published Hemingway's paperbacks, with Mikasa Shobō issuing a "complete works" anthology in ten volumes. Ara's prediction proved at least partly inaccurate, mainly in the fields of detective and adventure novels in the latter half of the 1950s, when the *Kare wa . . . ta* model of narrative linkage proliferated, along with short, fast-tempo conversations.

In a 1933 essay titled "Atarashii bunshō e no kōsatsu" (A study of new prose style), Sei Itō stated that unlike in Western prose, where the verb comes directly after the subject, "a picturesque expression in Japanese" is characteristically produced by placing a long succession of adverbs, adjectives, and nouns after the subject, with the verb coming at the end. "In brief, if one is trying to draw a picture, one limits oneself at first to the frame. One then aims towards the centre, gradually revealing various parts. Finally one takes the verb, with one movement revealing the direction" (Itō 1933/1973: 224). According to Itō, the unique characteristics and subtle sensitivity of Japanese expression produce the contrast of adjective, adverb, and noun in the frame formed by subject and verb, thereby creating a "passive moving form." Thus Hemingway's dynamic writing style, which clearly shows the direction of movement with its pairing of subject and verb, is unequivocally foreign to the characteristics of Japanese writing. It is precisely because of such foreignness, however, that a literal translation sometimes functions with great effect and cultivates new forms of expression.

Translation of Marcel Proust and the rhythm of prose

The introduction of Hemingway to Japan largely overlaps with the period in which the introduction of Marcel Proust began in earnest. Literal translations of Hemingway works almost incidentally brought about a new writing style by using the fundamentally foreign structure of his language, and as a result Hemingway's prose influenced Japanese literature in a creative direction. Proust's influence, despite the essentially similar foreign structure of his language, was deeply connected to Ōyama's "ardent zeal for creating great literature" for the following reasons. First, the literary world, especially young writers such as Tatsuo Hori (1904–53) and Motojirō Kajii (1901–32), showed a keen reaction to and enormous interest in the translation of Proust's works in the early 1930s, because it suggested a way to depict a stream of consciousness by means of a series of long sentences. Secondly, some of these writers, Hori in particular, attempted to approach the essence and secret of Proust's style and creativity by reading his works in the original or translating them.

Proust's short novels and his literary fragments and sketches had already been translated in the mid-1920s. Then in January 1930 Shūichi Hotta translated and edited *Purūsuto zuihitsu* (Proust essays), which contained Proust's short novels and subsequent critical reviews. Perhaps the most crucial factor in the introduction of Proust to Japan, however, was the translation of "Combray," the first chapter of *Du côté de chez Swan* (volume 1 of *Á la recherche du temps perdu*, 1913–27). This was translated by Ryūzō Yodono (1904–67), a friend of Kajii. The translation was serialized in four issues of a periodical from October 1929 to January 1930[7] and published in book form by Musashino Shoin in July 1931. Kajii reacted swiftly to Yodono's translation. In a letter to Yodono in July 1931 he expressed his frank observations of Proust's writing style and the quality of the translation (Kajii 2000: 421–2). Kajii paid much attention to Proust's "distinctive way of thinking," "the uniqueness of his writing style" and his manner of describing the wide world through a narrow inner world. On this basis Kajii indicated the unclear points of Yodono's translation, based on the expectation that translations should be "understandable in one reading."

Unlike the introduction of works by Hemingway, works by Proust were translated and introduced to the Japanese public at the same time as they were being studied by writers and the literary world. In the early 1930s certain periodicals played a key role in the study of Proust.[8] Japanese Proustians were equally interested in Proust's concept of "involuntary memory" and his writing style, as discussed in Kajii's letter.

In the early 1930s Tatsuo Hori, one of the leading novelists in the period of Shōwa modernism, published five essays on Marcel Proust, and in two of these he tried his hand at translating some paragraphs by Proust. A close examination reveals that through this exercise Hori learned how to render prose depicting a stream of consciousness into long sentences in Japanese. Some of Proust's motifs and this approach to translating Proust left their mark on Hori's important original works, *Utsukushii mura* (1933; trans. Barry, *Beautiful Village*, 1967) and *Kaze tachinu* (1936–8; trans. Ineko Sato, *The Wind Has Risen*, 1947). Since then a Proust-like style has played an important role in shaking up the naturalistic mode of writing fiction that had long been the mainstream in literary circles in Japan.

Among the studies of Proust, the noteworthy study relevant to contemporary Japanese literature is "Purūsuto no yaku ni tsuite" (On the translation of Proust, 1934) by Kyūichirō Inoue (1909–99). Inoue joined in Yodono's project of translating works by Proust (Nakano 2002: 501–3), and after World War II he completed his translation of *Á la recherche du temps perdu*. In the essay "Purūsuto no yaku ni tsuite," Inoue acclaimed K. Scott Moncrieff's English translations of Proust and said that "Proust's emotional writing strangely accords with Japanese. . . . A close look at Jun'ichirō Tanizaki's *Tade kuu mushi* [1928;

trans. Edward Seidensticker, *Some Prefer Nettles*, 1955] . . . and Tatsuo Hori's *Utsukushii mura* [1933; *Beautiful village*] proved that Proust's writing has the potential to be translated into subtle and beautiful Japanese" (1934: 44). In other words, these Japanese novels might suggest a proper style for translating Proust works into modern Japanese.

Hori continued to absorb modern Western literature throughout his entire life. He was a unique novelist in modern Japanese literary history because he never tried to hide Western writers' influences on his essays or novels. Hori continually emulated Western writers such as Jean Cocteau, Raymond Radiguet, Prosper Mérimée, Goethe, Fyodor Dostoevsky, Rainer Maria Rilke, and Claude Mauriac.

It was in August 1928 that Hori mentioned Proust for the first time in a letter to his close friend, Kiyoshi Jinzai (1903–57), a writer, critic, and translator who had apparently shown Hori a work by Proust. In his five short articles about Proust, which were published in the early 1930s, Hori showed a keen interest in Proust's Bergsonism,[9] his "involuntary memory" and his writing style. In one of these articles, "Zoku Purūsuto zakki" (More notes on Proust, 1933), Hori compared his own literary style with Proust's as follows:

> My preference for simple writing is troubled by Proust's careless, confusing writing style . . . up until now I have preferred genuine confusion to imperfect simplicity. (1977, vol. 3: 388)

In "Purūsuto no buntai ni tsuite" (On Proust's style, 1934), Hori mentioned Proust's attempt to distinguish the mental from the sentimental and the instantaneous, and he highlighted Proust's unique "rhythm of writing" and "subtle taste of writing" (1977, vol. 3: 409). In his short articles Hori often translated Proust and quoted his paragraphs. In this particular essay, he translated Proust's description of asparagus in a dining hall based on the premise of "free translation." Proust's original text is as follows:

> Il me semblait que ces nuances célestes trahissaient les délicieuses créatures qui s' étaient amusées à métamorphoser en légumes et qui, à travers le déguisement de leur chair comestible et ferme, laissaient apercevoir en ces couleurs naissantes d'aurore, en ces ébauches d'arc-en-ciel, en cette extinction de soirs bleus, cette essence précieuse que je reconnaissais encore quand, toute la nuit qui suivait un dîner où j'en avais mangé, elles jouaient dans leurs farces poétiques et grossières comme une féerie de Shakespeare, à changer mon pot de chambre en un vase de parfum. (Proust 1987: 119)

In Scott Moncrieff's English rendition, which was highly acclaimed by Kyūichirō Inoue, the translation meanders along, connected by many relative pronouns, as follows:

> I felt that these celestial hues indicated the presence of exquisite creatures who had been pleased to assume vegetable form, who, through the disguise which covered their firm and edible flesh, allowed me to discern in this radiance of earliest dawn, these hinted rainbows, these blue evening shades, that precious quality which I should recognise again when, all night long after a dinner at which I had partaken of them, they played (lyrical and coarse in their jesting as the fairies in Shakespeare's *Dream*) at transforming my humble chamber into a bower of aromatic perfume. (Proust/Moncrieff 1929: 164)

Proust's sentence is thus reproduced as a single sentence, but in Japanese this is no easy task. As pointed out by Sei Itō in his argument above, it is the existence of the relative pronoun in European languages and its absence in Japanese that constitute one of the greatest differences between these languages (Itō 1973: 226–7). In a related vein, in *Bunshō tokuhon* (A guide to writing good prose, 1934/1983: 124) Tanizaki pointed out that "In the Japanese language, it is not effective merely to add words; on the contrary, this obscures the meaning."

Although Hori referred to his translation of Proust's description as a "free translation," he used various linguistic and literary devices (effective use of appositives, inserted comments, commas, and, most notably, postpositional words) to render this sentence as one sentence in Japanese:

> Sō iu kono yo naranu nyuansu no seika, watashi ni wa sono asuparagasu ga, nandaka aru bimyōna ikimono ga omoshiro-hanbun ni sonna yasai ni henshin shite iru yōna ki ga shi, soshite sono hensō (tabeyō to omoeba taberareru, katai niku no) goshini marude ano akebono no umareyō to shite iru yōna iroai, ano niji no shitagaki no yōna iroai, aomi o obita yūgure no kiento shite iru yōna iroai to natte, sono fūgawari na essensu ga—sore o ban-meshi ni tabeta ban wa, yonaka zutto, Sheikusupia no fearī mitai na shiteki de bakabakashii fāsu demo enzerarete iru ka no yō ni, watashi no nyōbin o kōsuibin ni kaete shimau tokoro no, sore hodo fūgawari na essensu ga, sono uchi ni mitomerareru yōni watashi niwa omowareta. (1977, vol. 3405)

As Inoue stated, Hori's attempt can be seen as an essential step to make Proust's writing into "beautiful, subtle Japanese." Splitting a European-language sentence such as this one by Proust, which uses various relative pronouns, into shorter Japanese sentences would truncate the thoughts, feelings, and rhythm that flow continuously in the original. In fact, from around the time of writing *Tade kuu mushi* (*Some Prefer Nettles*), Tanizaki put all his stylistic focus into writing long, smooth, and elaborate sentences in Japanese. A year before presenting this translation about the asparagus, Hori wrote the following long, complicated sentence in *Utsukushii mura*, similar to what Tanizaki had earlier attempted:

> Dandan sono bessō ga chikazuite kuru ni tsure, watashi wa masumasu shinzō o shimetsukerareru yōna ikigurushisa o oboeta ga, sate, iyoiyo sono bessō no mukō ni, sukkari ake-hanashita madowaku no naka kara, watashi no mioboe no aru furui entakushi no ichibu ga mie, sono ue niwa, hitobito ga shokuji kara tachi-satte kara mada mamonai to itta yōni, marumerareta napukin dano, kudamono no kawa no nokotte iru sara dano, kōhī-jawan dano ga, mada katazukerarezu ni chirakatta mama, mabushii kurai yōtō no hikari o abite hikatte iru no o, watashi wa jibun demo igai na kurai na reiseisa o motte mitomeru koto ga dekita. (1977, vol. 1: 391–2)

> The closer we got to the villa, the more my heart tightened. Presently we were passing right in front of the white picket fence that enclosed their villa. Looking across the fence-enclosed lawn, bright with the light that came from the window left wide open, I could see part of the round table I remembered so well. After eating supper they had left without clearing away the stiffly curled napkins, plates full of peelings, and coffee cups: I looked at these things glittering in the bright light with a calmness I never thought myself capable of.[10] (Barry 1967: 33–4)

Inoue (1934: 44) regards Hori's writing style in *Utsukushii mura* as a model for translations of Proust. If the relationship between cause and effect in Inoue's essay is reversed, it reveals that Hori wrote *Utsukushii mura* under the influence of Proust's style. In brief, after he learned "genuine confusion" from Proust's writing he attempted to change his "simple writing style" in *Utsukushii mura*.

Michihiko Suzuki, the second Japanese to complete a full translation of *Á la recherche du temps perdu*, stated his aims in translating Proust as follows:

> What I would like to bring out in the text is the author's breath, or the "rhythm" of his writing. This consists of Proust's long sentences and unique way of thinking, with relative pronouns, commas, colons, semicolons etc. included in one breath, which then continues talking, expanding or inserting different expressions. (2001: 213)

Likewise, it was because Hori was able to synchronize with Proust's "rhythm of writing" that he could absorb Proust's texts into his own creative works. To assimilate the author's "way of thinking" and "rhythm of writing" is the same as

Futabatei's concept of absorbing and reproducing the author's "poetical spirit." We can also take the view that Hori, with his largely successful intention of merging with the author's spirit, implemented Ōyama's idea of a "creative spirit for literature."

Rhetorical or structural? The creative aspect of translation

In modern Japan the key agents in translation have gradually and successively shifted from literary figures to journalists, to scholars, to professional translators. In the 1950s a dual structure was established whereby pure literature was translated by scholars, and popular literature by professional translators. There is little disputing the fact that after this period what Lawrence Venuti calls "transparent" translation, in which the translator seeks "invisibility" (Venuti 1995/2008), became increasingly regarded as the model approach to translation in Japan. To put it the other way around, up until the 1940s most Japanese translations primarily functioned as the effect of foreign literary styles, exhibiting the literary influence of the original. With the Japanese translations of Hemingway and Proust that are the main focus of this paper, it is also the case that "translation is scandalous because it can create different values and practices, whatever the domestic setting" (Venuti 1998: 82). Shinobu Origuchi (1887–1953), a poet and eminent authority on Japanese literature and folklore, once stated that "the connection between our lives and foreign languages overall is extremely limited. However, it is precisely because of this . . . that we can have great hopes of unprecedented expressions." (Origuchi 1950/1997: 145). When Origuchi says "foreign languages" here, he means "translated texts." Origuchi hoped that through the translation of languages with a completely different structure from Japanese, "unprecedented expressions" could be created by breaking free from the habitual (conventional) elements of Japanese.

Meisei Gotō (1932–99) was an author and translator who was influenced by the grotesque humor techniques of Gogol and Kafka. When comparing his own Gogol translation with the highly regarded 1930s' translations of Hajime Hirai (1896–1946), Gotō wrote that:

> As you know, Hirai's translations read like a kind of humorous writing . . . . However, I realized the problem lies not in the "style," but in the "rhetoric." In other words, I thought that Hirai's translations are not stylistic, but rhetorical. I therefore thought of the opposite when I attempted to create my translation. (1981/1990: 288)

In fact, what Gotō calls "style" is the "structure" or "narrative" in the sense defined by Russian Formalists, whereby sentences are related and connected together, and what Gotō calls "rhetoric" refers to a more superficial and more individual system of verbal expressions (Gotō 1981/1990: 223, 261). His terminology is unique and somewhat confusing, but his distinction between these two approaches to translation is important. Simply put, according to Gotō there are two types of translation: "rhetorical" translation and "stylistic" or "structural" translation. If we follow Gotō's terminology, we can conclude that Hemingway's influence was more "rhetorical" and Proust's influence was more "stylistic."

Conclusion

This essay has outlined how works by Hemingway and Proust were translated in Japan in the early Shōwa era and how these translations and their creative functions introduced new styles and expressions to Japanese literature. Translations of Hemingway showed their creative function mainly in the "rhetorical" aspect. As Tanizaki indicated, "Japanese has grammatical rules on tense, but nobody follows them precisely" (1934/1983: 132). The use of verbs in Japanese is dependent on aspect (perfective and continuative), not tense (Kudō 1995), so always translating the past tense in Hemingway's texts into the perfective *ta* or *da* forms is a kind of mistranslation. Nevertheless, Oda's series of short Hemingway sentences translated with *ta* endings was, on a rhetorical level, what Origuchi called an "unprecedented" expression. After the 1950s this became established as a masculine, active writing style in popular Japanese literature.

Hori's translations of Proust, whose writing consists of long sentences in a series of clauses connected by relative pronouns, were likewise unconventional on a "rhetorical" level. They also showed their creative function on a "structural" level and, as a technique for describing the continuation of the inner mind or consciousness, fascinated various Shōwa modernist writers, such as Hori himself and Motojirō Kajii. The "structure" of Proust's writing style compelled translators to assimilate and recreate his "way of thinking" and "rhythm of writing." Looking back on his experience of translating Baudelaire, Takehiko Fukunaga (1918–79), a writer who studied under Hori, commented as follows:

> When I finish translating a work, I write it out on paper by pencil. This is probably compensational behaviour for not being able to create my own poetry. (1967/1988: 228)

In a sense, the ultimate goal of the creative function of translated texts on a "structural" level is to act as "compensational behaviour" in relation to the author's creativity. Proust and translations of his works influenced many prominent Japanese writers in the postwar era, such as Fukunaga and Shin'ichirō Nakamura (1918–97), who also studied under Hori, and the writer Shōhei Ōoka (1909–88).

Steiner (1975/1992: 246) has argued that "In a very specific way, the translator 're-experiences' the evolution of language itself, the ambivalence of the relations between language and world, between 'languages' and 'worlds.' In every translation the creative, possibly fictive nature of these relations is tested." In the translation and reception of Proust and Hemingway in the transitional period of Japanese literature between Shōwa modernism and the postwar era, we can see a good example of what Steiner calls "the creative, possibly fictive nature" of such relationships.

Notes

1   This period was approximately from the late 1920s to the early 1930s when, in rivalry with the school of proletarian literature, modernist writers published many little magazines.

2   See Susan Bassnet and Peter Bush (eds), *The Translator as Writer* (London &and New York: Continuum, 2006) and Manuela Perteghella and Eugenia Loffredo (eds), *Translation and Creativity: Perspectives on Creative Writing and Translation Studies* (London &and New York: Continuum, 2006).

3   Rakuchū means "in the city of Kyoto." Both Ōyama and Yoshikawa taught at Kyōto University at that time.

4   Unless otherwise stated, all English translations from essays and criticism in Japanese are mine.

5   In Goethe's first phase translators learn to translate sense-for-sense, but in the second phase they discover that this is a kind of violence to the source text and return to literalism. Goethe comments on the three phases of translation as follows: "The first acquaints us with the foreign country on our own terms; a plain prose translation is best for this purpose. [. . .] A second epoch follows, in which the translator endeavors to transport himself into the foreign situation but actually only appropriates the foreign idea and represents it as his own. [. . .] the third epoch of translation . . . is the final and highest of the three. In such periods, the goal of translation is to achieve perfect identity with the original, so that the one does not exist instead of the other but in the other's place." (Goethe1819/2004: 64–65).

6   The translator of "Wine of Wyoming" was Tomoji Abe (1903–1973), a novelist and critic who introduced twentieth-century English critical theory to Japan in the 1930s. Abe had already published some short articles about Hemingway's stories in the periodical *L'Esprit Nouveau* in July 1930.

7   The periodical was *Bungaku* (Literature), and Tatsuo Hori and the well-known writers Yasunari Kawabata (1899–1972) and Riichi Yokomitsu (1898–1947) worked there as editors and staff members.

8   *Shinbungaku kenkyū* (New literature studies) and its supplementary volume *Purūsuto kenkyū* (Proust studies, 1932) were both edited by Sei Itō, while another periodical also called *Purūsuto kenkyū* (Proust studies, 1934) was edited by the scholar of French literature Fumio Kume (dates unknown).

9   Bergsonism is the philosophy of Henri Bergson, who focused upon "the continuous nature of experience" and argued that "the flow of life becomes the prime datum falsified by mechanistic and scientist philosophies" and that this "flow is an active, melting process or 'pure' time, quite different from abstract time of natural science." (Blackburn 2005. 40).

10   Barry has translated Hori's single sentence into four English sentences.

References

Ara, M. 1954. "Heminguwē no sekai to nihon bungaku" [The world of Hemingway and Japanese literature]. In *Heminguwē kenkyū* [Hemingway studies], edited by M. Shiga. Tokyo: Eihōsha, pp. 123–7.

Barry, G. S. 1967. *Beautiful Village. Selected Works of Tatsuo Hori*. Tokyo: Sophia University Faculty of Foreign Languages English Department.

Blackburn, S. (ed.) 2005. *The Oxford Dictionary of Philosophy*, 2nd edn. Oxford and New York: Oxford University Press.

Boase-Beier, J. 2006. *Stylistic Approaches to Translation*. Manchester: St. Jerome Publishing.

Fukunaga, T. 1967/1988. "Bōdorēru, waga dōrui" [Baudelaire, my kindred]. In *Fukunaga Takehiko zenshū* [The complete works of Takehiko Fukunaga], vol. 18. Tokyo: Shinchōsha, pp. 226–30.

Futabatei, S. 1906/1985. "Yo ga hon'yaku no hyōjun" [My standards for translating literature]. In *Futabatei Shimei zenshū* [The complete works of Shimei Futabatei], vol. 4. Tokyo: Chikuma Shobō, pp. 166–70.

Goethe, J. 1819. "West-Östlicher Divan." In *The Translation Studies Reader*, 2nd edn, 2004, edited by L. Venuti and translated by S. Sloan. New York and London: Routledge, pp. 64–6.

Gotō, M. 1981/1990. *Warai no hōhō: Aruiwa Nikorai Gōgori* [The method of laughter or Nikolai Gogol]. Tokyo: Fukutake Shoten.

Hemingway, E. 1997. *Men without Women.* New York: Charles Scribner's Sons.

Hori, T. 1977. *Hori Tatsuo zenshū* [The complete works of Tatsuo Hori], vols 1 and 3. Tokyo: Chikuma Shobō.

Inoue, K. 1934. "Purūsuto no yaku ni tsuite" [On the translation of Proust], *Purūsuto kenkyū* [Proust studies] III: 40–4.

Itō, S. 1973. *Itō Sei zenshū* [The complete works of Sei Itō], vol. 13. Tokyo: Shinchōsha.

Kajii, M. 2000. *Kajii Motojirō zenshū* [The complete works of Motojirō Kajii], vol. 3. Tokyo: Chikuma Shobō.

Kawamura, J. 1981/2000. "Hon'yaku no nihongo" [Japanese of translated literature] in J. Kawamura and O. Ikeuchi. *Hon'yaku no nihongo* [Japanese of translated literature]. Tokyo: Chūōkōronsha, pp. 11–192.

Kudō, M. 1995. *Asupekuto・tensu taikei to tekusuto* [Aspect-tense system and texts]. Tokyo: Hitsuji Shobō.

Nakano, C. 2002. "Senzen ni hon'yaku sareta Purūsuto no sakuhin" [Translation of Proust before the war]. In Philippe Michel-Thiriet. *Jiten Purūsuto hakubutsukan (Quid de Marvel Proust)*. Edited by M. Hokari and translated by H. Yuzawa, C. Nakano, and H. Yokoyama. Tokyo: Chikuma Shobō, pp. 501–9.

Oda, R. 1930. *Buki yo saraba.* Tokyo: Tenjinsha.

Origuchi, S. 1950/1997. "Shigo toshite no nihongo" [Japanese as poetical language], *Origuchi Shinobu zenshū* [The complete works of Shinobu Origuchi], vol. 32. Tokyo: Chūōkōronsha, pp. 137–56.

Ōyama T. 1934a. "Gēte no hon'yakuron" [Goethe's translation theory]. *Eigo kenkyū* [English studies] 26(10): 1148.

—. 1934b. "Sakka no hon'yaku" [Translations by writers]. *Eigo kenkyū* (English studies) 27(8): 710.

—. 1947/1970. "Hon'yaku bungaku ron" [Essay on translated literature]. In *Bungaku nōto* (Notes on literature). Tokyo: Chikuma Shobō, pp. 310–17.

Ōyama, T. and K. Yoshikawa. 1946. *Rakuchū shomon* [Kyōto letters]. Ōsaka: Akitaya.

Proust, M. 1929. *Swann's Way.* Vol. I. Translated by C. K. Scott Moncrieff. London: Chatto and Windus. Phoenix Library.

—. 1987. *Á la recherche du temps perdu 1.* Paris: Gallimard.

Ryan, M. G. (trans.). 1967. *Japan's First Modern Novel:* Ukigumo *of Futabatei Shimei.* New York and London: Columbia University Press.

Steiner, G. 1975. *After Babel: Aspects of Language and Translation.* Oxford and New York: Oxford University Press (2nd edn, 1992; 3rd edn, 1998).

Suzuki, M. 2001. "Hon'yaku no kanōsei: *Ushinawareta toki o motomete* no zen'yaku o oete" [Translatability: On completing the translation of *Á la recherche du temps perdu*], *Subaru* 23: 5–6.

Tanizaki, J. 1934/1983. *Bunshō tokuhon* [A guide to writing good prose]. In *Tanizaki Jun'ichirō zenshū* [The complete works of Jun'ichirō Tanizaki], vol. 21. Tokyo: Chūōkōronsha, pp. 87–246.

Toury, G. 1995. *Descriptive Translation Studies and Beyond*. Amsterdam and
    Philadelphia: John Benjamins.
Venuti, L. 1995. *The Translator's Invisibility: A History of Translation*, 2nd edn. London
    and New York: Routledge, 2008.
—. 1998. *The Scandals of Translation: Towards an Ethics of Difference*. London and New
    York: Routledge.

7

Translating Place-Names in a Colonial Context: Two Dictionaries of Ainu Toponymy

Nana Sato-Rossberg

Introduction

The process of compiling a place-name dictionary from scratch resembles the process of writing an ethnography. Neither task involves a written original. Instead, the original texts are produced by the translators/ethnographers themselves. To compile their dictionaries of place-names used by the indigenous Ainu people of northern Japan, the two translators studied here—Hōsei Nagata (1838–1911) and Mashiho Chiri (1909–61)—went out into the field, talked to the locals and observed before finally authoring the dictionary entries.[1] I will refer to this work as "translation" rather than "lexicography" because, as will be seen below, the information conveyed in the final product is in both cases not just about lexical correspondences; the emphasis is clearly on explanation of the underlying culture and cultural knowledge. The similarity between the tasks of ethnographers and translators has been noted by many scholars (Tedlock 1983; Asad 1986; Clifford and Marcus 1986, Clifford 1988; Rubel and Rosman 2003; Chambers 2006; Sturge 2007). So far, however, this argument has been made mostly in relation to typical ethnographical work, and the matter of place-name dictionaries has attracted little attention. Furthermore, most of these ethnographies were written for an anglophone audience. Extending the perspective to other cultures (in this case, Japan) is therefore important so as to achieve a broader and more representative view.

How are place-names, which are often deeply related to the underlying culture, to be explained in another language that reflects a different worldview—that is, how are they to be translated? The concept of culture itself is already problematic, as it changes depending on the time, place, or people. Rather than working on the basis of a particular definition of culture, I will therefore try to see culture here in the sense in which it was understood in the two place-name dictionaries under consideration. To understand Ainu culture, it has to be seen from Ainu eyes. Similar points have often been made by other cultural anthropologists who regard themselves as cultural translators, translating the culture of the Other. Keith Basso (1996) has emphasized that the life knowledge and culture of indigenous peoples are attached to places. To understand and translate place-names, translators need to know the culture behind them. The two questions of how these particular translators understood the Ainu culture reflected in place-names and how they translated them will be the guiding themes here.

The essay focuses on the *Chimei Ainu-go shō-jiten* (Small dictionary of Ainu place-names; 1956a) by Chiri and an earlier dictionary, *Hokkaidō Ezo-go chimei kai* (Interpretation of Ezo-language place-names; 1891), by Nagata. The time lag between these two dictionaries should be taken into consideration, as well as the different roles played by Chiri and Nagata as translator-ethnographers. Yet it was not these factors, but differences in their understanding of Ainu place-names and culture, that produced the tension between Nagata and Chiri.

Chiri was a native anthropologist in the classical sense (Jones 1970), while Nagata was a *wajin* employed by the governor of Hokkaido, a large island in the north of Japan (*wajin* were Japanese who originated from the mainland of Japan).[2] Until Chiri published his dictionary, Nagata's was the most comprehensive Ainu place-name dictionary available. It was reprinted four times, and many famous Japanese scholars praised it uncritically. Chiri, however, criticized this dictionary harshly on the grounds that Nagata did not understand the Ainu worldview (1956a: 73–120). Hence it is important to illuminate the Ainu worldview that made sense to Chiri. I will demonstrate that his dictionary questioned and challenged a notion of understanding the Other that was common among Chiri's readers. This led him to develop his own understanding of dictionary translation/compilation—an understanding that was, in retrospect, a visionary approach.

The first section of this essay outlines the history of Japanese colonization of the Ainu, with which many readers might be unfamiliar, as well as the relevance of Ainu place-names in this context. The second section sketches the biographies of Nagata and Chiri, as these are important for understanding their differing approaches. Neither Nagata nor Chiri has received much attention so far, even in Japan. The third and fourth sections take a closer look at their dictionaries, referring to Basso's ideas, and the fifth section compares the two dictionaries. An analysis of various aspects of the dictionaries clarifies the differences in their understanding of Ainu place-names and culture. Chiri's rendition of place-names resembles the approach that Kwame Anthony Appiah (1993) has called "thick translation." A closer examination of Chiri's method of explaining place-names will offer new perspectives on how to see the Other.

Historical background and Ainu place-names

Under pressure from foreign countries around the mid-nineteenth century, Japan initiated a rapid modernization process. In order to determine clear national borders as part of this process, Japan incorporated the Ryukyu islands to the south and the northern island of Ezo into its territory and renamed them Okinawa and Hokkaido. The indigenous Ainu people were living in what became known as Hokkaido. From 1869, when the Meiji government established the Hokkaido Colonization Board[3] on this island, the Ainu were forced to comply with Japanese family register requirements, and traditional Ainu religious celebrations and customs (e.g. earrings and beards) were prohibited. Restrictions were placed on the fishing of salmon and the hunting of deer, both of which were important food sources for the Ainu. Because many Japanese migrated to Hokkaido, the conditions in which the Ainu lived underwent rapid change, and they were often forced to move from the lands they had traditionally occupied. The Ainu were soon outnumbered by *wajin*—in 1873 official records counted 16,272 Ainu in Hokkaido, constituting just 14.63 percent of the island's total population (Siddle 1996: 59). In 1886 the Hokkaido government was established, and in 1899 it became responsible for enforcing the Hokkaido Former Aborigines Protection Act. This law was mainly aimed at encouraging Ainu people to engage in farming and to send their children to school. At school, Ainu children had to speak Japanese, and this ban on speaking Ainu at school led to a rapid loss of the Ainu language. According to Siddle (1996: 70–1):

> The Protection Act represented the systematisation of a policy of assimilation. Assimilation (*dōka*) meant, in this instance, the transformation of the Ainu into model Imperial subjects through the eradication of their former language, customs and values. While displaying superficial similarities to early Meiji cultural policies that prohibited "backward" folk customs and suppressed local dialects at school in order to bring "civilisation" and enlightenment to "ignorant" Japanese peasants, Ainu policy was quite different in that it was a systematic policy designed for a subordinate and inferior native population under a colonial regime.

Before the Japanese occupation, Ainu culture had been maintained by oral tradition, and place-names were not written down or documented. A sound geographical orientation was important for Ainu in order to know where to fish, hunt, and collect plants. Detailed knowledge about places such as capes, steep mountain paths, or strong river currents could be life-saving. Places were named to satisfy the needs of the people who lived there, and so they went well beyond mere or arbitrary labels.

To learn these place-names, the two translators studied here had to visit the actual locations and ask Ainu people about the names they were using, or they had to rely on similar efforts by others. As mentioned above, in this sense the translator's work was close to that of an ethnographer. Ainu place-names often refer to topographical features of the landscape, and thus it was natural not only to ask about the names used but also to examine the topography directly.

To grasp the views and wisdoms of indigenous people, it is vital to understand the cultural significance they attach to geographical locations. Places are an environment for culture and offer it a foundation (Basso 1996). The names by which indigenous people refer to places provide clues to understanding the relationships among people, culture, and environment. However, literal translations of indigenous place-names often fail to convey the nuances the names have in the native language.

Hōsei Nagata and Mashiho Chiri

Hōsei Nagata (1844–1911) was born near present-day Tokyo. In his day, the Japanese were striving to learn about the West, and toward this end they translated many nonfiction Western works, including books such as *On Liberty* by John Stuart Mill (1859; first translation published in 1872 as *Jiyū no ri*), Henry Thomas Buckle's *History of Civilization in England* (1862; first translation published in 1875 as *Eikoku kaikashi*), and Peter Parley's *Universal History* (1862; first translation published in 1876 as *Bankokushi*). These books contained many foreign words referring to concepts new to Japan, and translators struggled to coin equivalents in Japanese.

Nagata, too, was working as an English-Japanese translator. His works are not yet well researched, but apparently he was accustomed to translating despite an incomplete knowledge of the source culture. His first translation, a textbook on natural history, was published in 1873, and his translations were often done to produce school textbooks. In his day the textbook system was not strictly regulated, so textbooks were freely produced and published.[4] Nagata's Bible translation (three volumes published from 1873), interestingly titled *Seiyō oshiegusa* (A text for learning about the West), has been singled out for praise by the Bible scholar Kiyoshi Kinoshita for its quality. It was published shortly after the ban on Christianity in Japan was lifted and, according to Kinoshita (1973: 21, 23), it was the first Bible translation of this era[5] by a Japanese. There is also "Map of the earth" (*Ansha chikyū zukai*, 1875), which does not cite the source text but names Hōsei Nagata as the translator. The approach adopted in this book resembles that in his later Ainu place-name dictionary:

新カレドニア島　ニューゼルランド」[6] の西北ニアリ (1875: 77)

[Shin Karedonia tō Nyūzerurando no seihoku ni ari]

(New Caledonia is to the northwest of New Zealand.)[7]

From this translation work Nagata might have obtained hints on how to compile a place-name dictionary.

The details of how and why Nagata went to Hokkaido are not clear,[8] but in 1881 he became a member of the Hokkaido Colonization Board, and in 1882 he took up the task of establishing Kyū Dojin Gakkō (Schools for Former Aborigines), using a special fund from the emperor. He also began to learn the Ainu language. In 1888 Nagata was commissioned to prepare a place-name dictionary by the director of the Hokkaido Office, which was the main agency for implementing colonization policy in Hokkaido. The Office had been pursuing a development plan since 1874, and in line with this the Hokkaido Colonization Board was surveying the land of Hokkaido in preparation for constructing roads. Nagata's dictionary was apparently meant to support this work and to promote the economic exploration of unknown land. In the introduction to his dictionary, Nagata writes: "Plants, vegetation, birds, beasts, fishery products, ores, or even insects—where these exist, there will surely also be corresponding place-names. Therefore, once you hear the place-names, you easily know the geography and have the key to finding special products" (1891: 1).

From a very different background to Nagata's, the linguist and ethnologist Mashiho Chiri (1909–61) was born in Hokkaido as an Ainu. A translation from Ainu to Japanese that he produced as a teenager came to the attention of the famous Japanese linguist Kyōsuke Kindaichi (1882–1971), who studied Ainu sagas. Supported by Kindaichi, Chiri enrolled at the Imperial University of Tokyo, studying Western literature and then linguistics. He became one of the leading Ainu researchers of his time and part of a "first elite" that emerged from this indigenous people. As a "native anthropologist," he left many works on his views of the Ainu people and Ainu culture, as well as many translations of Ainu narratives.[9] In line with the strict assimilation policy that was codified by law and in place from 1899 to 1997,[10] Chiri's parents taught him Japanese as his first language (in terms of time and fluency). Yet he called the Ainu language his mother tongue:

> I have rarely heard my parents speak in the Ainu language. Therefore, unlike my elder sister Yukie, who was raised by our grandmother in Chikabumi village in Asahikawa, we brothers[11] did not know our mother tongue until after boyhood. (1937/1981: 169)

As this passage shows, Chiri learned the Ainu language after he grew up. He subsequently made dictionaries for use in translations from his first language (Japanese) into his mother tongue (Ainu) or from his mother tongue into his first language. His personal background gives his works a particular tension that goes beyond mere lexicography. Chiri is said to have felt a strong mission as a "native anthropologist," and he tried to carry out research from an "insider's perspective."[12] His comment below, however, reveals additional motivations:

> People who do not understand the Ainu language write research papers about it, riding the waves of the mass media. Then, because I expose their wrong research and occasionally write honest things, they criticize me for being "narrow-minded" or "arrogant"; that's how things stand. *In reality, even in the academic world, an honest person will look like a fool. To protect my dignified isolation and continue my simple work steadily is my tiny source of patriotic spirit.* (1960/2000: 13, emphasis added)[13]

This is an excerpt from an article on "patriotic spirit" published in 1960 by *Asahi shinbun*, a leading Japanese newspaper. It is difficult to determine from this piece whether in Chiri's mind the word "patriotic" refers to Japan or the land of the Ainu that existed long ago. Nevertheless, it appears from the underlined sentences that the source of his patriotism was a principled morality, rather than attachment to a particular country. No matter how we might judge them today, Chiri was true to his beliefs, even in the face of strong criticism from colleagues about his unconventional views. Because of this strong resolve, Chiri did not compromise on his research. This might have been another reason for producing his series of unique dictionaries.

Among Chiri's works are several Ainu-Japanese dictionaries that focus on different topics, such as *Bunrui Ainu-go jiten Shokubutsu-hen* (Classified Ainu dictionary—Botany; 1953), *Bunrui Ainu-go jiten Ningen-hen* (Classified Ainu dictionary—Humans; 1954), *Chimei Ainu-go shōjiten* (Small dictionary of Ainu place-names; 1956), and *Ainu-go kemono mei shū* (Dictionary of Ainu beast names; 1959). At the time Chiri compiled his dictionaries, linguistic geography[14] was the mainstream method among Japanese linguists. Chiri mentioned this method in *Bunrui Ainu-go jiten Shokubutsu-hen* (Classified Ainu dictionary—Botany) and borrowed from this method there, but did not adopt it in any of his other dictionaries. Instead he followed his own method, which accumulated information on each dictionary entry more or less independently.

Hōsei Nagata's dictionary

According to Nagata, it took him eight years to complete his dictionary. Hokkaido is as large as Austria, and the only possible ways for Nagata to travel at that time were by foot or horse, so collecting place-names was hard work. In the introduction to his dictionary Nagata writes that to learn about place-names he interviewed old Ainu men and women: "to understand Ainu place-names, it is necessary to ask elderly Ainu people who live at that place. Ainu place-names live only in those people's minds; when they die, the place-names will die too" (Nagata 1891: 2). It is evident that he was fully aware that the Ainu language was threatened with extinction.

There are several indications that Nagata thought that Ainu place-names had a literal meaning in the Ainu language and that understanding this language leads to the meaning of the place-names. In his explanatory notes, Nagata recorded when he visited different locations and how he found out the meanings of place-names. He explains that in the Hidaka district he did not find an "elderly person" to interview and so had to rely on old maps. From transcriptions of place-names on the map, he then inferred their translations. In the Kushiro district he combined an interview with an old Ainu lady, Ete Nozawa, with information from a map. Nagata explains that in the Toshima district he found that the local Ainu dialect had distorted the place-names, so he sought to find the "original Ainu sounds," again by comparison with a map (1891: 12). Obviously, Nagata had difficulties finding proper and accurate pronunciations. He also writes: "The Ainu language exhibits vowel shifts (*tsūon*) and dialects, so place-names also contain these vowel shifts and dialects" (1891: 6). It remains unclear how he handled these variations. For Nagata, the correct pronunciation was important, because it would determine his translation (1891: 12). As is apparent from these notes, he felt that finding the "original pronunciations" was much more challenging than subsequently translating these words into Japanese.

Nagata first wrote each Ainu place-name in the Roman alphabet, then in the phonetic katakana script, followed by the Japanese translation:

Pet paro ペッ　パロ 河口 [pet paro *kakō*; the mouth of a river].

In most cases, Nagata translated the words simply from Ainu into Japanese. Sometimes, however, he added explanations, as in the following examples:

Kuraromai クラロマイ　機弓場　アマポヲ置キ熊ヲ捕ル處.

Kuraromai Kuraromai　Kikyūjyo　[a place to set up a bow] Amapo o oki kuma o toraeru tokoro [a place to put *amapo* [a trap] and catch a bear].

Kurumat oma nai クルマッ　ヲマ　ナイ 日本人ノ澤昔工夫ノ妻此ニ死シタリ故ニ名クト

Kurumat oma nai kuruma　woma　nai nihonjin no sawa [the Japanese swamp] mukashi kōfu no tsuma kokoni shishitari yueni nakuto [So named because once upon a time the wife of a Japanese miner died here.]

Basically, however, Nagata's approach and the formatting of the lines were very close to a word-for-word translation. Nagata understood that Ainu place-names have meanings, and he occasionally explained the cultural background attached to place-names, perhaps adding such information when he received it from Ainu informants. However, he did not attempt, as Basso later advocated, to understand the views and wisdoms of the indigenous people.

Mashiho Chiri's dictionary

In 1960 Chiri published the booklet *Muroran-shi no Ainu-go chimei: Chimei no yurai, densetsu to chizu* (Ainu place-names in Muroran city: Origin, legends, and maps). This was a joint work with Hidezō Yamada (1899–1992), a friend of Chiri and a nonacademic researcher of Ainu place-names. The booklet explains Ainu place-names as follows:

Names were gradually given to places by the Ainu inhabitants, who needed this knowledge for their lives, and the names have survived until now in various places. Some of the place-names are extremely old, while others are relatively new, although even the "new" ones we are investigating seem to be over 100 years old. Yet such new words are very rare, and many of the names must have existed for more than hundreds or thousands of years. An ancient will, geographic configuration and grammar are apparent from those old place-names; they are not comprehensible in terms of our ordinary understanding or knowledge. (1960: 44)

Regardless of the accuracy of this claim, this passage reveals the feeling for the history associated with place-names that underpinned Chiri's understanding of Ainu place-names.

In a paper titled "Abashiri-gunnai Ainu-go chimei kai" (Understanding Ainu place-names in Abashiri district; 1958/2003), Chiri wrote that "the old place-names were named by Ainu who had completely different perspectives on life from today's Ainu. It would obviously be wrong to try to understand those old place-names from a contemporary Ainu perspective, since they reflect the special Ainu life and thought of an old era" (1958/2003: 269). Hence even contemporary Ainu (probably meaning also Chiri himself) need to see through the eyes of old Ainu to understand Ainu place-names and their meanings. Chiri also tried to understand Ainu history through place-names:

> **Chise-ne-sir, -i** The meaning is house-shaped mountain. But the house here is not a contemporary Ainu house. Rather, this indicates that Ainu houses in old times were pit dwellings. The Ainu call this form **toy-chise** (dirt house), and the main body of the house is buried in the ground; it cannot be seen from the outside. Only the roof can be seen from the ground. Thus, if we say "house-shaped mountain," the actual mountain does not look like a house with walls, as we might imagine from the word "house." There are no walls; it just looks as if the roof has been brought down to the ground—in other words, a triangular-shaped mountain. Place-names like these probably arose when the Ainu people lived in pit dwellings. (1956a: 354)

When Chiri explained this word in his dictionary, he did not mention Nagata at all. Explaining the same word elsewhere, however, he criticized Nagata's rendition, writing that "Nagata translated *chise-ne-sir* as 'house mountain.' When translating it properly today, it should be rendered along the lines of 'a mountain that looks like a roof.' If it is translated as 'house mountain,' the [Ainu] 'history' will die" (1956b: 269–70). Thus, documenting the meanings of place-names was also for Chiri a way to inscribe Ainu history.

In his introduction to *Chimei Ainu-go shō-jiten* (Small dictionary of Ainu place-names) Chiri wrote:

> To understand place-names correctly, first of all we must apprehend the meaning of the words and of the physical shape. [. . . .] This dictionary will be useful not only for place-name researchers, but also for Ainu language researchers. [. . . .] If this dictionary makes some small contribution to promoting correct Ainu language research, it will be of great satisfaction to me. (1956a: 337)

As exemplified above, Chiri often used the words "correct" or "accurate" in relation to Ainu-related research, apparently implying that previous research was not always accurate.

Unlike Nagata, Chiri arranged place-names in alphabetic order. Like Nagata, he first wrote them in the Roman alphabet. He then added the pronunciation in a mixture of katakana and hiragana to indicate where to stress the words—for example, **nay-po** なイポ (a stream). **Na**な is written in hiragana and **i-po**イポin katakana, and the use of hiragana indicates that the stress should be placed on *na*. This mixing of hiragana and katakana looks very unusual to the Japanese eye, but Chiri used this method to ensure proper pronunciation. It is far more striking for readers than stress marks, which are also known in Japanese. Chiri's dictionary also gives more detailed explanations than Nagata's dictionary. For example:

> **At, -i/-u** Bark of an elm: an elm tree is called **at-ni**. This means "a tree to take **at** [elm bark]." This tree appeared to be of special interest to the Ainu because they used the fibers of the elm to make **Attushi** [a type of dress]. This word often appears in place-names. (1956a: 347)

> **iso-mokor-us-I 【K】** [K meant that the word was collected in Karafuto, i.e. Sakhalin.] Trace of a sleeping bear. = **kamuy-hechiri-box**. If you find such places in the mountains, you must not go there (bears often sleep there). (1956a: 364)

As these examples show, Chiri strove to explain the contexts of place-names. This attitude resembles what Clifford Geertz advocated with his call for "thick description." According to Geertz (1973: 14), culture provides a context, and understanding a society's practices and discourses requires describing them within this context. Chiri does not explicitly make this link to "culture" in his dictionary, but the contents of the dictionary reveal how much he cared about culture and how important he thought it was to understand the Ainu point of view.

Chiri took great care to convey how Ainu people understood place-names, and he tried to explain the details of their words and thought. The following example stresses how the Ainu and Japanese refer to salmon:

> **ichan, -i** spawn hole of trout or salmon; commonly called a moat. – Salmon have sparkling silver scales when in the sea. Japanese fishermen call them **shirokke** (white hair = white skin), Ainu call them **hereus-chep** (sparkling shining fish) or **heru-ram** (shining scales). When these salmon change to spawning colour, in other words, a beech-tree colour skin, Japanese fishermen call them **bunakke** (beech-tree colour) and Ainu call them **pet-e-chi-chep** (burned fish in the river). After the salmon swim to the upper reaches of the river and begin to dig the moat, their name changes again. Male salmon are called **ikuspe-tuye-p** (salmon that cut the pillars) and female salmon are called **mose-p** (salmon that cut the thatch) or **moskar-pe** (ditto). Ainu people see salmon couples work together to prepare a palace for the birth. Therefore, if *someone* just translates this as "spawn hole" or something like that, this person ignores the Ainu's feelings. (1956a: 363; emphasis added)

The "someone" here possibly refers to Nagata's translation below:

> **Ichan** イチャン salmon's egg place, a place where the salmon dig the sand and put their eggs. (1876: 66)

In fact, Chiri often responded to Nagata's dictionary in his *Chimei Ainu-go shō-jiten*. The following section gives an even clearer example of how he challenged Nagata's dictionary.

Comparison of the translations

There is an Ainu expression **pon pet**, which Nagata translated as "small river" (1892: 302, 347). Like Nagata, Chiri translates this as "small river," but he adds more detail:

> . . . but if one translates **pon** as small and **poro** as big without further investigation, one does not actually understand Ainu place-names. **Poro** and **pon** are both derived from the word **po** (child). [. . .] The original

meaning is still vivid in the place-names. For words such as island, pond or bay, if two of those exist at the same place, the Ainu thought of and named them as **poro** (big) for parent and **pon** (small) for child.... (1956a: 98–100)

Poro as parent, *pon* as a child—this is an example of the personification of nature. Chiri believed that this personification is important in order to grasp the meaning of Ainu place-names. To understand this point better, let us consider a different word, *horka*. Chiri explains this as follows:

The meaning is "retrace." In the context of place-names, it refers to a branch of a river that turns in the direction of the sea in the headwaters. In ancient times, the Ainu believed that rivers are creatures and they climb from the sea up to the mountains. When a river changed direction from climbing up the mountain to down towards the sea, the Ainu expressed this by the word **horka**.... (1956a: 30–1)

Nagata translated this as "back-flowing." Chiri commented on this rendition in his book *Ainu-go nyūmon* (An introduction to the Ainu language):

There are place-names called **horka-pet** or **horka-nay**. Up to now, these were translated as "backward-flowing river." In particular, Nagata ceremoniously inserted a note saying: "When the tide comes in, the water flows back into the river, therefore it is named backward-flowing." (1956b: 43)

To the Ainu, however, rivers are creatures. This personification was a very important point for Chiri in understanding Ainu place-names. In his view, Nagata understood Ainu place-names only from the *wajin* perspective, without understanding the underlying culture.

The final pages of Chiri's dictionary display another aspect of translating the land as a living creature. Two maps of Hokkaido and Karafuto (present-day Sakhalin) are juxtaposed with the sketch of a naked woman, with the body parts labeled with Ainu words. Chiri's explanations often establish etymological or anecdotal relationships between the names of geographic locations and body parts, reflecting his view that the Ainu understood topography, plants, and their living environment as creatures just like human beings.[15] For Chiri, as we have seen, Ainu place-names often contain references to the human body.[16]

Other aspects of the daily life of the Ainu are also linked to place-names.

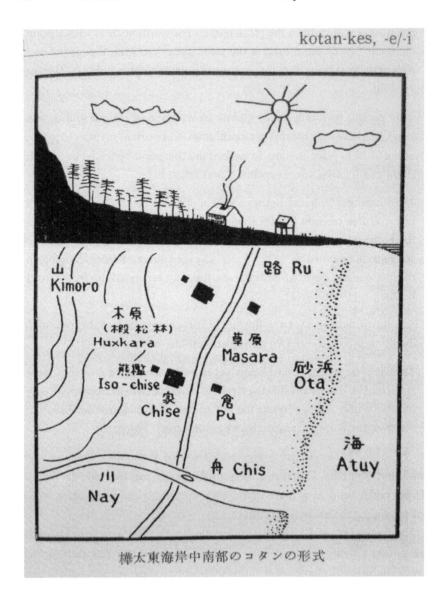

樺太東海岸中南部のコタンの形式

This picture, which Chiri included in his dictionary, illustrates the word *kotan*, explained by Chiri as follows:

> **kotan**: village. However, it is something different from what we[17] imagine as a village. If there is only one house, it is a **kotan**. If there is only temporary housing, it is still a **kotan**. If there is a house, whether temporary or permanent, it is called **kotan**. (1956a: 50)

How was *kotan* understood in the world of the Ainu? As shown in Figure 7.1, in a *kotan* there is usually a house (*chise*), a bear's cage (*iso-chise*), a storehouse (*pu*), and so on. If Chiri had translated *kotan* simply as "village," readers would very probably imagine a Japanese village. By inserting the illustration, he enabled readers to conceptualize the Ainu image of a village. Using images, Chiri appeals to and entertains readers both visually and intellectually. He draws on several methods to make his translations "thick." Another example can be found in the entry for the word *rep*:

> **rep**: 1. "the sea distant from the shore." 2. "the part of the river which is closer to the centre, as seen from the river bank." 3. "the part of the fireplace which is closer to the centre, as seen from the edge of the fireplace." The Ainu were fishermen, so they also projected their life at sea inside their house. Thus they denote the fireplace's edge as the shore and the place inside the fire as offshore. In an old song, a captain who sits at the edge of the fireplace while having worrisome thoughts is innocently drawing something in the ashes of the fireplace. Or this word is used to describe the gesture of somebody who is trying to say something but cannot, which is expressed like this . . . .
> (1956a: 106–7)

Chiri then inserts an excerpt from an Ainu chanted myth. As mentioned above, the Ainu did not have a written culture prior to Japanese colonization. Instead, they had a rich tradition of storytelling. Chiri cited several Ainu chanted myths and epics in this dictionary. He believed it would be impossible to appreciate Ainu place-names without understanding their relationship to other aspects of Ainu culture, including oral narratives. Readers would misunderstand the existence of the Ainu, their lives, and their history, all of which are integrally associated with place-names. Thus a literal translation is inadequate for conveying a full understanding of Ainu place-names.

Conclusion

Earlier I referred to Basso (1996: xiii–xviii), who convincingly stressed the importance of geographic locations for understanding the "views and wisdoms of indigenous people." Knowledge of their myths and epics, which contain their wisdom, also helps to understand the meanings they attach to geographical locations. The Ainu lived in an organic relationship with nature. Place names are just fragments of the bigger Ainu picture of the world. Yet the translator can attempt to link these fragments into a context by resorting to various techniques.

Chiri offered holistic explanations in an effort to highlight particularities in the recognition of meanings and to overcome "untranslatability." As we have seen, he inserted not only detailed explanations, but also illustrations and sometimes even full Ainu myths into his dictionary.

As noted above, Appiah has suggested making translations "thick" by adding glosses and explanations. He writes:

> To offer our proverbs to American students is to invite them, by showing how sayings can be used within an oral culture to communicate in ways that are complex and subtle, to a deeper respect for the people of pre-industrial society. (1993/2000: 400)

I see a common ground between Appiah and Chiri. Words such as "pre-industrial" or "primitives" are used as a contrast to "industrial" or "civilized." The Ainu were placed on a "primitive" level by *wajin*, and Chiri had to accept this. Just as Chiri strove to make his readers understand the Ainu worldview, Appiah's insistence on the Akans' cultural background constituted a critique of a narrow Western perspective. The Ainu people were called *rettō minzoku* (inferior people) by the Japanese because, for instance, they did not have a script and did not farm in the way *wajin* did. Indeed, their lifestyles were quite different from those of *wajin*. Chiri tried to highlight these differences between the two cultures in his dictionary. To challenge the *wajin* point of view, he needed to resort to techniques now known as "thick translation." This is the key to understanding Chiri's work on dictionaries.

For Nagata, the organic relationships between place-names and people or culture were very probably not important to understanding Ainu culture. He might not even have been aware of these relationships. For him, knowing the "meanings" of Ainu place-names was sufficient, as this was what he was ordered to investigate by the Hokkaido Office. For Chiri, however, making a dictionary of place-names was a way of meeting the challenge of giving recognition to different views and a way of bringing readers' attention to those who had been living in their place in a different time.

The question remains as to how to translate the culture attached to place-names. Word-for-word translation cannot meet the task because, as Basso argued, it is vital to understand the culture-dependent meanings attached to geographical locations and toponyms. Thick translation is surely one answer, but there is no fixed or specific way for making translations thick (see Cheung 2007). In a scenario such as the one we have discussed, the choice between the various competing options will always be a challenge for translators. Upon this choice depends the very representation, image, and perception of the Ainu culture.

Notes

1   One early general dictionary of Ainu language published in Japan was *An Ainu-English-Japanese Dictionary and Grammar* (1889/1905, Kyōbunkan) by the British missionary John Batchelor (1854–1944), who helped establish a school for Ainu children in Hokkaido. Batchelor devoted his life to missionary work among the Ainu. For details, see the biography by Futami (1963).

2   By contrast, the term *nihonjin* (Japanese) encompasses Japanese citizens of all ethnicities.

3   This was the government agency that administered Hokkaido and the islands belonging to Hokkaido from 1869 to 1882.

4   The first regulations for the school system in Japan were issued in 1872. In the early years translated works such as *Gakumon no susume* (An encouragement of learning) by Yukichi Fukuzawa were used as textbooks. See Ishii (1993: 291).

5   There had been some partial Bible translations during the "Christian century" (1549–1638), when European missionaries had a presence in Japan.

6   Parentheses as in original.

7   All translations are mine.

8   Hosaka (1983: 15) writes that "in order to have a rest, he probably went for a spa treatment, which was popular at that time."

9   See Sato-Rossberg (2008, 2011) regarding Chiri's other translations.

10   In 1997 the Hokkaido Former Aborigines Protection Act of 1889 was replaced by the Law for the Promotion of Ainu Culture and Dissemination and Cultivation of Knowledge of Ainu Tradition.

11   Chiri had an elder brother.

12   See Fujimoto (1994) and Minato (1982).

13   The Ainu storyteller Kura Sunazawa wrote that one day Chiri shouted at a journalist "You fool us. You always write lies," and then he snatched the journalist's notebook and pencil and threw them in his face (1983: 331).

14   Western linguistic geography was imported to Japan around the beginning of the twentieth century. By focusing on words for general objects, linguistic geographers investigate how these objects are named in different areas and then, using mapping tools, they attempt to reconstruct the history of words and languages.

15   This view of the earth as organic, a creature like humans, is not unique to Chiri. As Anne Buttimer (1993: 155) points out, "Traces of an organicist world-view can be found in the Vedic myths of Purusha, in Chinese poetry and legend, in pre-Socratic doctrines and the Hippocratic school of medicine."

16   Yamada (1969: 13) points out unaccountable leaps in Chiri's explanations, but remains vague in detailing this criticism.

17   Chiri often writes "we" rather than "I" in his articles. It is often not clear whom he meant to include in this plural. The reader can only guess.

References

Appiah, K. A. 1993/2000. "Thick Translation." In *Translation Studies Reader*, edited by
    L. Venuti. London and New York: Routledge, pp. 389–401.

Asad, T. 1986. "The Concept of Cultural Translation in British Social Anthropology."
    In *Writing Culture: The Poetics and Politics of Ethnography*, edited by J. Clifford and
    G. E. Marcus. Berkeley: University of California Press, pp. 141–64.

Basso, K. H. 1996. *Wisdom Sits in Places*. Albuquerque: University of New Mexico Press.

Batchelor, J. 1889/1905. *Ainu-eiwa jiten* [An Ainu-English-Japanese dictionary and
    grammar]. Tokyo: Kyōbunkan.

Buckle, H. T. 1862. *History of Civilization in England*. New York: D. Appleton and
    Company.

Buttimer, A. 1993. *Geography and the Human Spirit*. London: John Hopkins University
    Press.

Chambers, C. 2006. "Anthropology as Cultural Translation: Amitav Ghosh's *In An
    Antique Land*." *Postcolonial Text* 2(3): 1–19.

Cheung, M. P. Y. 2007. "On Thick Translation as a Mode of Cultural Representation."
    In *Across Boundaries: International Perspectives on Translation Studies*, edited by
    D. Kenny and K. Ryou. Newcastle upon Tyne: Cambridge Scholars Publishing,
    pp. 22–37.

Chiri, M. 1937/1981. *Ainu mintan-shū* [Ainu folk tale stories]. Tokyo: Iwanami.

—. 1956a. *Chimei Ainu-go shō-jiten* [Small dictionary of Ainu place-names]. Hokkaidō:
    Hokkaidō Shuppan Kikaku Sentā.

—. 1956b. *Ainu-go nyūmon* [An introduction to the Ainu language]. Hokkaidō:
    Hokkaidō Shuppan Kikaku Sentā.

—. 1958/2003. "Abashiri-gunnai Ainu-go chimei kai" [Understanding Ainu place-names
    in Abashiri district]. In *Chiri Mashiho chosaku shū 3* [Mashiho Chiri anthology 3],
    edited by M. Oka. Tokyo: Heibon, pp. 269–313.

—. 1960/2000. "Aikoku-shin: Watashi wa kō omou" [What is patriotic spirit? My views],
    in *Wajin wa fune o kuu* [*Wajin* eat boats], edited by M. Chiri. Hokkaidō: Hokkaidō
    Shuppan Kikaku Sentā, p. 13.

Chiri, M. and H. Yamada. 1960. *Muroran-shi no Ainu-go chimei: Chimei no yurai,
    densetsu to chizu* [Ainu place-names in Muroran city: Origin, legends and maps].
    Hokkaidō: Private Printing.

Clifford, J. 1988. *The Predicament of Culture*. Cambridge: Harvard University Press.

Clifford, J. and G. E. Marcus. 1986. *Writing Culture: The Poetics and Politics of
    Ethnography*. Berkeley: University of California Press.

Fujimoto, H. 1994. *Chiri Mashiho no shōgai* [The life of Mashiho Chiri]. Tokyo: Sōfūkan.

Futami, G. 1963. *Ainu no chichi John Batchelor* [John Batchelor—Father of the Ainu].
    Sapporo: Nireshobō.

Geertz, C. 1973. *The Interpretation of Culture*. New York: Basic Books.

Hosaka, T. 1983. "Fujimura Kensei ni manekareta Nagata Hōsei to sono chosho *Seiyō oshiegusa*" (Hōsei Nagata, who was invited by prefectural governor Kensei Fujimura, and Nagata's book *A Text for Learning about the West*). *Bulletin of Yamanashi Gakuin University. Humanities and Sciences* 6: 1–28.

Ishii, K. 1993. *Nihon no rekishi, vol. 12—Kaikoku to ishin* [Japanese history, vol. 12—Foundation of the country and the Meiji restoration]. Tokyo: Shōgakkan Library.

Jones, D. K. 1970. "Towards a native anthropology." *Human Organization* 29(4): 251–9.

Kinoshita, K. 1973. "Nagata Hōsei nenpu" [Hōsei Nagata chronological list]. *Momoyama Gakuin Daigaku Kirisuto ronshū* [Momoyama Gakuin University anthology of Christian essays] 9: 21–31.

Mill, J. S. 1859. *On Liberty*. London: Longman, Roberts, and Green.

Minato, M. 1982. *Ainu minzoku to Chiri Mashiho-san no omoide* [Ainu people and memories of Mashiho Chiri]. Tokyo: Tsukiji.

Nagata, H. 1873. *Seiyō oshiegusa* [A text for learning about the West]. Osaka: Bun'eidō.

—. 1875. *Ansha chikyū zukai* [Map of the earth]. Osaka: Kokusei.

—. 1876. *Shōgaku jintai kyūri mondō* [An elementary schoolchild's questions and answers about the human body]. Osaka: Private Publication.

—. 1891/1972. *Hokkaidō Ezo-go chimei kai* [Interpretation of Ezo-language place-names]. Tokyo: Kokusho Kankōkai.

Parley, P. 1862. *Universal History*. London: Ivison, Phinney & Co.

Rubel, P. and A. Rosman. 2003. *Translating Cultures: Perspectives on Translation and Anthropology*. Oxford: Berg.

Sato-Rossberg, N. 2008. "Chiri Mashiho's Performative Translations of Ainu Oral Narratives." *Japanese Studies* 28(2): 136–48.

—. 2011. "Bunka o hon'yaku suru" [Translating culture—Creative translations of Ainu chanted myths by Chiri Mashiho]. Sapporo: Sapporodō.

Siddle, R. 1996. *Race, Resistance and the Ainu of Japan*. London and New York: Routledge.

Sturge, K. 2007. *Representing Others. Translation, Ethnography and the Museum*. Manchester: St. Jerome Publishing.

Sunazawa, K. 1983. *Kusukuppu Orsipe: Watashi no ichidai no hanashi* [The story of myself]. Hokkaido: Hokkaidō shinbunsha.

Tedlock, D. 1983. *The Spoken Word and the Work of Interpretation*. Philadelphia, PA: University of Pennsylvania Press.

Yamada, H. 1969. *Hokkaidō no Ainu-go chimei jūni wa* [Twelve stories of place-names in Hokkaidō]. Hokkaidō: Private Printing.

8

Japanese in Shifting Contexts: Translating Canadian Nikkei Writers into Japanese

Beverley Curran

What is different about Japanese in the Americas?

In "What's Different about Translation in the Americas?" Edwin Gentzler discusses the evolving languages, linguistic and cultural interference, and lapses in transnational memory that are particular to places where "native indigenous tribes and languages, combined with immigration and globalization patterns, characterize the linguistic make-up" (2002: 9). Although Gentzler's essay is mainly concerned with the character of translation found in obscure or ignored cultural communities (see also Gentzler 2008), it makes an important point about linguistic assimilation. Where language has been suppressed or has broken down or disappeared, there is not just loss, but damage:

> The effect of the past on the present though often erased or covered up . . ., often returns to haunt the present. For ethnic minorities in the Americas, this past and the language in which the stories were told, is becoming increasingly important to communities to enable them to understand the present. (Gentzler 2002: 17)

The present chapter suggests that an awareness of the effects of linguistic and historic pasts is crucial to understanding not only the present, but also the future. Such an awareness can also open up a reconsideration of the notions of both diaspora and translation as grounded in relationships with a lost homeland or previous text and allow us to see them instead as indicators of futurity and impending change.

At the heart of the two novels discussed in this paper, Joy Kogawa's *Obasan* (1981) and Kerri Sakamoto's *The Electrical Field* (1998), lies the uprooting, internment, and dispersal of Japanese Canadians (Nikkei—i.e. Japanese migrants and their descendants) who were living on the west coast of Canada. These events followed in the wake of the bombing of Pearl Harbor and accelerated linguistic assimilation, leaving many Japanese Canadians estranged from their Japanese language and cultural identity and ambivalent about their relationship to Canada. In these two novels, the anglophone Canadian Nikkei writers incorporate fragments of Japanese that have survived assimilation, doing so as a way of remembering and a mode of repair. When Japanese is used in English novels in this strategic manner, how does it survive in translation into Japanese, and how does it continue to show a special linguistic and cultural relationship to both Japanese and English, as well as a specific Canadian history?

This paper considers the translation of Japanese into Japanese in texts that are marked by diglossic relationships with both English and Japanese by looking at some examples from the Japanese translations of Kogawa's *Obasan* (translated by Sari Nagaoka in 1998 as *Ushinawareta sokoku*) and Sakamoto's *The Electrical Field* (translated by Maya Koizumi in 2002 as *Mado kara no nagame*) in order to understand how the translators responded to the particular demands of these works that speak so fluently of linguistic damage and assimilation accelerated by uprooting and internment. In the English texts the Japanese words are positioned, often playfully, as new Canadian words rather than as the detritus of a language lost in assimilation, but in the translation of these terms there is little attempt by the Japanese translators to maintain the "thickness"[1] initiated by the authors in order to challenge Canadian identity, let alone stretch the limits of the Japanese language in order to challenge the limits of Japanese identity. In a close but necessarily selective reading of *Obasan* and *The Electrical Field* in Japanese translation, I focus on orthographic devices and the striking potential of the four writing systems in Japanese (Chinese characters, the hiragana and katakana syllabaries, and the Roman alphabet) in terms of their graphic and political implications. I examine how interlingual and intralingual translation rub against each other to create a provocative friction that sparks a sense of diasporic writing as a crucial resource for understanding translation in general,[2] as well as how the Japanese translation of such writing might also provide both creative and critically self-reflexive commentary.

Obasan and *Ushinawareta sokoku*

Obasan was published in 1981, a year before the Charter of Rights and Freedoms recognizing the collective rights of linguistic and indigenous minorities was added to the Canadian Constitution. This novel was the first fictional treatment by a Japanese Canadian writer of the internment of Japanese Canadians. It tells the story of a family uprooted from their home in Vancouver on the west coast of Canada following the bombing of Pearl Harbor on December 7, 1941; their forced removal to an internment camp in the interior of British Columbia; their further relocation to Alberta at the end of World War II (Japanese Canadians were not allowed to return to the Pacific coast until 1949); and how this experience continues to resonate in their lives decades later. *Obasan* presents characters operating under linguistic and social constraints amid the "intolerable confusion of finding the citizen and the alien in the same body" (Sinfield 1992: 35). The story of the internment, both the event and its afterlife, is told using different voices in English and Japanese, so as to redirect the history of internment and redraw the map of what constitutes "Canadian" identity. The novel is a narrative of cultural translation—that is, the translation of a Canadian citizen into an enemy alien, the translation of someone viewed as Japanese into someone recognized as Canadian. In the following discussion I would like to look at some of the ways the novel "stretches" language in its use of both Japanese and English and at the lack of stretch in the Japanese translation, which limits the linguistic possibilities that Kogawa has set in motion.

The title of Kogawa's novel, *Obasan*, uses Japanese to assert a Canadian subject. This word, which means "aunt" or "(older) woman," is an unfamiliar one to most anglophone readers. Its use is typical of how Japanese appears in much Nikkei writing, where all that remains after linguistic assimilation are single words or formulaic expressions. However, as a word that has survived assimilation, "Obasan" carries great weight in this text. Using it as both the title of the book and to refer to a character, Kogawa weaves gender and language into a narrative of national exclusion, while also foregrounding relationships. The families in her novel are described as intimate "to the point of stickiness, like mochi" (24).[3] The Japanese "sticking" to the English of this novel includes linguistic relationships that emphasize affect, "those resonances that circulate about, between, and sometimes stick to bodies and worlds, and in the very passages or variations between these intensities and resonances themselves" (Seigworth and Gregg 2010: 1). "Obasan" as character and title creates another stickiness between the narrative and the material text, linking the significance of the old woman who is the stone of silence within the novel, a "silence that will not speak" with the text, which names her, and its "silence that cannot speak" (n.p.). In addition, there is Emily, another obasan. Neither the reticent obasan (Aya) nor the loquacious Aunt Emily has been assimilated: Obasan has not ventured across linguistic and cultural barriers; Aunt Emily has made the crossing, but is unwilling to let her Japanese language or identity disappear, even though she takes her Canadian citizenship seriously. As an earnest activist, she is intent on using language to unite and heal a dispersed community: "We're gluing our tongues back on," she explains, and is unapologetic about any clumsy speech acts:"It takes a while for the nerves to grow back" (43).

In one sense, the Japanese translation by Sari Nagaoka recognizes the strategic use of Japanese in the novel. In her "Afterword" Nagaoka points out that she has rendered in katakana all Japanese used in Kogawa's text so that the reader can see where it has been used: "Romanized Japanese used in the original text is explicitly rendered in katakana in the translation" (Nagaoka 1998: 465; my translation). Nagaoka's translation does not, however, convey the "sticky" ramifications of Kogawa's use of Japanese, which affect not only the English of the novel but also how the Japanese in the novel is translated. Further, the Japanese word obasan is not retained as the title of the translation. Instead, either by editorial decision or that of the translator, the title becomes *Ushinawareta sokoku*, or "lost homeland." This title change frames the story of diaspora and exile only in terms of "deprivation and dispossession," which limits the sense of diaspora to being "essentially a matter of the past, stressing the work of collective memory as "foundational" in an uprooted people's relationship to a 'homeland'" (Edwards 2006: 91), a comparison between "here" and a longed-for "there." In terms of translation, however, diaspora and diasporic writing draw attention to linguistic and cultural imbalances within societies.

For Nagaoka, the English title of Kogawa's novel obviously refers to the first-generation migrant Aya obasan, but not exclusively. As the translator explains in her Afterword (p. 465), the term obasan is an inclusive one that embraces with love and respect all *mō wakakunai onnatachi*, or women who are no longer young, and it imbues the title with an unmistakable air of nostalgia for a particular construction of Japanese femininity. The choice of *Ushinawareta sokoku* for the title of the translation arguably ups the nostalgia, but focuses on place rather than a woman, replacing obasan with a "mother country" or "fatherland." Does the Japanese reader (including the translator) read the lost country as Canada or as Japan? Nagaoka does not use the titular term *sokoku* (homeland) when she translates a passage in which Emily has written "I am Canadian" (47) as "Watashi wa kanadajin de aru" (79), but every reference to "my native land" (48) is translated as *watashi no bokoku* (p. 79). *Sokoku* and *bokoku* both carry the meaning of "homeland," but when this term is complicated by migrancy, *sokoku* places a greater emphasis on an "ancestral" homeland, while *bokoku*, literally "mother country," is closer in meaning to the country of one's birth or "native land." This suggests that the translation positions Japan, and not Canada, as the lost land, whereas the author was intent on asserting the rights of Japanese Canadians as Canadian citizens and insisting on redress for the Canadian government's crimes of seizure and internment. "Seeking the full rights of citizenship, including the right to see redress [was] a large part of what 'Japanese Canadian' meant, throughout the 20th century" (Miki 2005: 12)—that is, recognition as Canadian citizens, not Japanese. What would have been the effect if the title had been untranslated, leaving Obasan as a word in the Roman alphabet? In Canada, this word was unfamiliar vocabulary that was nevertheless Canadian; in Japan, incorporating obasan into one of the available writing systems would provoke a different relationship to the word and what and whom it signifies.

What has been lost by the renaming of the novel is the idea that there are Japanese words and people that are crucial to telling a Canadian story and that this specific vocabulary will have to be acquired by anglophone readers for the narrative to unfold. Naomi Nakane, the niece of the two obasan, operates within the story as a language teacher, correcting pronunciation in and outside the classroom, introducing new words that are crucial to a radical rereading of a historical period that overshadows the names of citizens like Nakane or Kato with those of Pearl Harbor and the Yellow Peril. The latter term, a racist expression of the fear of East Asian encroachment on the West, distinguished the Asian in America as a foreigner, regardless of birthplace, citizenship, linguistic proficiency, or length of residency. The internment, as an immediate consequence of Pearl Harbor, demonstrated how quickly the Japanese Canadian could be translated into a foreigner and an enemy. When Naomi uses the term Nisei, for example, it provokes a language lesson during a dinner date, as she reaches for a napkin to spell the word and explain its meaning:

> "N-i-s-e-i," I spelled, printing the word on a napkin. "Pronounced 'knee-say.'
> It means 'second generation.'" Sometimes I think I've been teaching school
> too long. I explained that my grandparents, born in Japan, were Issei, or
> first generation, while the children of the Nisei were called Sansei, or third
> generation. (9)

Although Kogawa offers explicit and implicit explanations of the Japanese terms she uses, she does not italicize them to identify them as foreign terms. As a Canadian writer using Japanese and English, she writes her problematic relationship with each language into both languages. Kogawa resists italics and puts both languages side by side; Japanese seeps into the English text "umi no yo, like the sea" (2) and leaves its residue on the English, even when it ebbs. By incorporating "Nisei" into the narrative as a Canadian word, Kogawa not only inserts Japanese into the English text, but also stretches the meaning of the Japanese diaspora to include not only those three generations identified by their degree of separation from Japan, but others whose linguistic or cultural identity is Japanese. When we look at the Japanese translation, however, we see that Nagaoka's decision to use katakana to distinguish the Nikkei author's Japanese simultaneously reinstates both the barriers dismantled by the linguistic seepage in *Obasan* and the frustrating identity issues faced by Japanese Canadians viewed as Japanese in Canada and considered foreigners in Japan as soon as they speak.

Obasan also brings attention to the Canadian government's use of such euphemisms as "evacuation" to couch the uprooting and internment of Canadian citizens. It was a term eventually employed by many Japanese Canadians to describe their own history "from the moment of uprooting following Pearl Harbor on December 7, 1941, to the final lifting of restrictions on April 1, 1949" (Miki 2005: 50). "Evacuation" makes a socially engineered crime sound like a natural disaster; by being called an "evacuation," the internment becomes a protective safety precaution and the "camp" a mountain getaway. In the novel, Aunt Emily explains the term this way:

> "It was an evacuation all right," Aunt Emily said. "Just plopped here in the wilderness. Flushed out of Vancouver. Like dung drops. Maggot bait."
>
> None of us, she said, escaped the naming. We were defined and identified by the way we were seen. A newspaper in BC headlined: "They are a stench in the nostrils of the people of Canada." (139–40)

The "evacuation" confounds the boundary in Canadian history between inclusive and exclusive citizenship, in which the "inner" (Japanese) Canadian citizen is expelled and becomes an outer "enemy alien," despite holding official citizenship as a Canadian. The particular contours of this event are marked by the physical ex-pulsion and re-pulsion that "founds and consolidates culturally hegemonic identities along sex/race/sexuality axes of differentiation" (Butler 1990: 133). The "excretory function" becomes "the model by which other forms of identity-differentiation are accomplished. In effect, this is the mode by which Others become shit" (Butler 1990: 134). The term "evacuation," then, is not just a euphemism but also a fabrication that is then translated into the very fabric of actual lives and "inscribed on the surface of bodies" (Butler 1990: 136).

How is a word with the thickness and stretch of "evacuation" translated on the surface of the page? Nagaoka offers two renditions: *tachinoki*, followed immediately by *haisetsu* in parentheses. The parenthetical term, with its reference to bodily elimination, is precisely the reading that Aunt Emily is riffing on in this passage, but *tachinoki* means "forced removal," which indeed the uprooting was. What this translation fails to show is that "evacuation" was used to intentionally frame the uprooting and internment as ostensibly benign. A term such as *hinan* (escape or evacuation to a safe place) comes closer to the Canadian government's use of "evacuation," because it turns the removal of Japanese Canadians from the coast into a measure to ensure their own safety, rather than an expulsion of those perceived as a threat to national security. In this case, instead of an explanation, the writing systems available in Japanese could have been put to use to visually and semantically thicken the translation of "evacuation" so as to suggest multiple meanings or allusions or to indicate ironic intention.

Judy Wakabayashi (2006: 3) has drawn attention to the tension and "uneasy embrace" in which *rubi* glosses[4] exist with the words they modify and has pointed out the resistance and outright aversion to the textual disruption and complications that their appearance seems to provoke in some Japanese critics. Because of this, the use of *rubi* in the Japanese translations of these Canadian texts could perform as well as elaborate the uneasy relationship of the Nikkei in Canada and could register Japanese being used in shifting contexts. The different writing systems and reading indicators available to the Japanese translator (kanji, katakana, hiragana, the Roman alphabet, and *rubi* glosses), as well as their mix, allow words to be presented in ways that let meanings shimmer suggestively. Bespoke combinations of kanji can also be created, because the intended phonetic and semantic readings can be supplied by the *rubi* glosses. In short, instead of being limited to a single word choice or an annotation to make a choice clear, the translator working into Japanese can often have her cake and eat it. This can be especially useful as a way to savor the linguistic crumbs of Japanese used in a text like *Obasan*. Consider, for example, the playful way that English and Japanese are used by Naomi and even by her brother Stephen, who "is always uncomfortable when anything is 'too Japanese'" (261), including language. Forced to take a detour down a gravel road, a lone truck passes and sends a rock into the windshield of the car in which Aunt Emily, Naomi, and Stephen are travelling:

"Sakana fish," Stephen mutters as he steps on the brakes.

Aunt Emily looks startled. "What did you say?"

> Some of the ripe pidgin English phrases we pick up are three-part inventions—part English, part Japanese, part Sasquatch. "Sonuva bitch" becomes "sakana fish," sakana meaning "fish" in Japanese. On occasion the phrase is "golden sakana fish." (262)

Like "Nisei," a particular expression is being explained here. Imaginative invention is a necessary part of making a language to feel at home in. Yet instead of using the writing systems available in Japanese not only to make this bilingual wordplay understood but also to perform it in Japanese translation, Nagaoka again resorts to explaining the joke in a parenthetical comment: the pronunciation of "golden sakana fish," that is, goldfish, is close to "goddamn sonuvabitch" (405). Although the translator tries to give meaning to this wordplay in Japanese and English, she does not attempt any play of her own to represent the hybrid mix of Japanese and English by means of the multiple writing systems available to her in Japanese. Nor does she give equal weight to "Sasquatch," the third component of the hybrid tongue being spoken. The translation, *kaijūgo* ("monsterspeak"), suggests deviation or monstrous distortion, perhaps, of the other two languages. But "Sasquatch" is a derivation of a Salish First Nations term for a local monster, also known as Bigfoot. Kogawa's wordplay is thus also an overlapping linguistic location of all inhabitants of the West Coast, and it suggests that a mix of European, Asian, indigenous tongues, and the imagination is necessary to articulate the multiple histories of that place and its peoples. It also subtly draws our attention to the First Nations people of the Pacific coast, whose history has not differentiated between the colonizer and the immigrant, seeing both Canadians of European ancestry and of Asian ancestry as invaders. As Gentzler has observed more generally about translation in the Americas, the past and the languages in which stories of communities are told are important to understanding the present, but more specifically, their translation provides a way to understand the movements of languages within the movements of multiple intersecting groups "narrated and valuated in different ways and to different ends" (Edwards 2006: 92). Japan, too, finds itself among such vexed linguistic and cultural milieu. Disglossia and social exclusion have been played out in its relationship with its own diaspora, and tension exists between an expansion-justifying wartime ideology of an ethnically diverse Japanese people and the postwar construction of homogeneity that translated former Japanese, such as resident Koreans, into resident aliens.

The Electrical Field and *Mado kara no nagame*

In the terms of translation, the Redress Movement among Japanese Canadians in the 1980s had a domesticating agenda that emphasized a seamless Canadian citizenry, placing an emphasis on the violation of citizenship rights in the "loss of community and the trauma of uprooting" (Miki 2005: 248) that scarred the personal and cultural histories of Japanese Canadians. This emphasis on being Canadian citizens encouraged linguistic as well as cultural assimilation among Canadian Nikkei. In particular, many Nisei who had experienced internment were determined to integrate themselves through language and education and to distance themselves from their "Japanese" identity. In their efforts to be recognized as "Canadian," the Japanese language was lost but the visibility of a "Japanese" body remained. Kerri Sakamoto's 1998 novel *The Electrical Field* focuses on the problematic relationship that many Canadian Nikkei have had with their embodied identity and its perceived lack of legitimacy. As poet and activist Roy Miki explains:

> The elusive phenomenon known as "assimilation" never ceased to provoke an uneasy tension between my personal awareness and the marking of my body. While social forces encouraged assimilation through language, thought, and performance, the movement of my body continued to be tracked as the other—the "Jap" in the midst. "Canadian," in this context, assumed meanings that extended well beyond the mere attribute of citizenship and came to occupy the boundary line between presence and absence—between being somebody and being nobody. (Miki 2005: 14)

Kerri Sakamoto's novel is about the reverberations of two crimes of betrayal that unsettle the Japanese Canadian community: one crime is the Canadian government's unjust internment of Japanese Canadians, while the other is the sensational murder of Chisako Yano, the Japanese wife of a Nikkei activist, and her Canadian boss and lover. *The Electrical Field* was published post-Redress but is set in the seventies, when the term "redress" was a largely unfamiliar one, stirring in the "social cauldron of . . . a period marked by the emergence of identity politics, in which the ideology of assimilation was [being] subsumed by a new buzz word, 'multiculturalism'" (Miki 1998: 202). (In the 1970s, Sakamoto's Japanese translator, Maya Koizumi, was in Steveston, a fishing village at the mouth of the Fraser River, gathering oral histories of the endemic racism in the fishing industry against Japanese Canadians.) Sakamoto's novel is not so much concerned with the fact of internment as it is with affect: the emotional toll and psychic damage. It focuses on the problematic relationship that many Canadian Nikkei have had with their embodied identity and its perceived lack of legitimacy. From the very start of *The Electrical Field* this is expressed in linguistic terms, as Miss Saito, the novel's first-person narrator, corrects the terms used by the young girl Sachi to refer to their neighbors when the 13-year-old comes to tell her that the Yano family is missing. This is the first indication of how carefully Miss Saito polices her own English and why she seldom speaks Japanese—that is, she is ashamed of how she sounds.

The historical fact of internment of Japanese Canadians is at the heart of *The Electrical Field*, as it is in *Obasan*, but its darkness is engaged in a different way. Instead of approaching the injustices as moral issues and focusing on the straightforward abrogation of citizens' rights, Sakamoto takes a queer position that can be called "camp," an attitude marked by deliberate linguistic excess that fashions language into a pose, which emphasizes how language can be appropriated and manipulated. As described by Susan Sontag in Note 34 of "Notes on Camp":

> Camp turns its back on the good-bad axis of ordinary aesthetic judgment. Camp doesn't reverse things. It doesn't argue that the good is bad, or the bad is good. What it does is offer for art (and life) a different—a supplementary— set of standards. (Sontag 1964)

Both the Canadian government and the Redress Movement operated along the moral and aesthetic axes of good and bad. The aesthetic was at work in the racialized nature and emphasis on visibility and appearance that were at the heart of the exclusionary measures of the federal Canadian and provincial British Columbian governments. The Redress Movement emphasized the ability of Japanese Canadians to "fit in" and their aspirations to be recognized as "Canadian" and to be acknowledged as productive nation-builders. *Obasan* uses multiple voices and the collective language of redress to insist on the recognition of "Japanese Canadians" as "Canadians" and to resist an "official" government discourse rendering them as suspect "Japanese."

In *The Electrical Field*, by contrast, Miss Saito's aesthetic standard is Japan, constructed out of her imagination and a selective vocabulary. She embodies and enacts an arrested pulsion, an aching desire to be translated beyond the rejection or embrace of citizenship. Oriented toward a Japan she has never seen, she uses her small cache of Japanese words, learnt mainly in the schoolyard of the Japanese school prior to internment or behind the *ofuro* in the internment camp, to both stage absence and to "pretend . . . an identity into existence"

(Apter 1999: 134). Whereas Kogawa uses Japanese to assert a Canadian identity, Sakamoto employs it to imagine a Japanese linguistic identity that really exists only as a performance. Like "camp talk," the faulty, suggestive, and ironic play of Miss Saito's Japanese, as well as her obsession with proper English use, offers "textures of negotiation" (Harvey 2003: 128) that require the reader to be attentive to possible and alternative meanings. The collective displacement and experience of the camps is reworked in Miss Saito's performance of a persona. In personal terms, we might call her a camp construction in the sense of theatrical overplay; in historical terms, we might call her a camp deconstruction, psychically shattered like other Nisei caught up in internment. Given this, a camp approach to the Japanese translation could draw attention to the way Japanese or its perceived lack is excessively attended to in the novel. In *Intercultural Movements:* American *Gay in French Translation* (2003), Keith Harvey draws attention to the way that italics in English representations of camp talk contribute to what could be called "a stylistics of the emphatic":

> This stylistics makes use of a whole cluster of devices—for example, the grammatical feature of moodless exclamation and the semantic characteristic of hyperbole—each of which needs to be taken account of alongside the typographical feature as instrumental in encoding the position of "the drama queen." Important also is a recognition that italics are a *written* device .... Indeed, while italics may represent the kind of speaker investment (excitement, emotiveness) that might well result orally in heightened stress patterns, they may also underline the presence of citationality—as most obviously, in their co-occurrence with foreign terms. (Harvey 2003: 139)

Like Kogawa in *Obasan*, Sakamoto never puts Japanese words in italics, but her intention is not to naturalize the words as Canadian ones, but rather to heighten their performance and expose the artificial construction of identities. She not only foregrounds the fictional basis of racism that constructs a body that is then truly abused, but also draws attention to the negative self-images of many Canadian Nikkei as fake, inferior Japanese, as well as second-class Canadian citizens. Sakamoto's translator, Maya Koizumi, like the translator of *Obasan*, renders all Japanese terms used in Sakamoto's novel in katakana. However, because Sakamoto intends the use of Japanese by Miss Saito to expose the artificial rather than authentic basis of identity, the katakana in this case operate like italics to give the Japanese words a camp emphasis and mark them as cited or borrowed words, distinguishing the use of these "Japanese" words in a different context.

The Electrical Field is less intent on getting the word out to Canadians than on getting the words out in Japanese. The first use of Japanese by the narrator Miss Saito is "nihonjin" (Japanese): "we nihonjin, we Japanese" (1), a reference echoed in English that here includes Japanese born in Canada and unable to speak Japanese. Miss Saito uses the word to make a sweeping statement about Japanese and their bodies: "we nihonjin, we Japanese, hardly perspire at all" (1). Koizumi chooses to downplay this first inference of a homogenous Japanese body by translating the phrase as *watashitachi nihonjin* instead of *wareware nihonjin*. Although both expressions mean "we nihonjin," the latter refers to an in-group and has been put to ubiquitous use to set up the us–them binaries between Japan and the world, Japan and Asia, Japanese and gaijin, Japanese and Nikkei—and, by extension, *nihongo* (the Japanese language) and *seiyōgo* (Western languages), or even *kokugo* (Japanese as a national language; Japanese for Japanese) and *nihongo* (Japanese as foreign language study). Here Miss Saito is including herself in a group that she actually feels distinct from, which is all the more reason to iterate a mantra of inclusion, but the translator chooses a bland option.

Again there is a title change in the Japanese translation of *The Electrical Field*. Sakamoto's title summons an image of the fields of electrical towers in suburban Ontario, where the story is set and where the writer grew up. Sakamoto has explained, however, that when she was living in New York as a graduate student, those fields seen from the air on flights home provoked further associations:

> I couldn't help but see a parallel in the aerial photographs of the camps I pored over in the National Archives in Ottawa: the row upon row of identical plots and houses in the flat, open valley floor. The mountains [where the camps were] seemed to suggest their counterpart in the electrical towers . . . . Oppressive and authoritarian, the currents they transmitted were invisible, relentless and powerful. (Fujimoto 2002: 106)

The Japanese title, *Mado kara no nagame* (The view from the window), focuses on the gaze and the visible, the inside and the outside, as well as the repressed nature of the narrator. The idea of being implicated in a crime is a powerful one in this novel, but the sense of the energy coursing through relentless and invisible circulating currents has been erased in the Japanese title.

In Koizumi's translation, Miss Saito's Japanese is always rendered in katakana, as are the Japanese names—for example, Saito san, Yano san. In conversations between Miss Saito and the Japan-born Chisako, however, Chisako's Japanese is sometimes rendered in kanji, intensifying the difference Miss Saito feels between herself as an inferior Nikkei copy and Chisako, an "authentic" Japanese, as well as her sense that Chisako considers herself superior. Whenever the translator renders Chisako's Japanese in katakana in the conversation, it gives it a patronizing feeling, as if she is speaking down to Miss Saito; we can almost hear her slowing down, as if she were talking to a child. Koizumi does not, however, exploit the different scripts available to the Japanese translator when dealing with Chisako's relationship to English. Miss Saito recognizes Chisako's overly careful pronunciation and imagines her practicing, "making sure her tongue touched the edge of her teeth and roof of her mouth in just the right way, pronouncing a word over and over. *Lovely, lovely.*" (Sakamoto 1998: 116). That excessive care is not "heard" in the katakana ラブリー (*raburī*; lovely) that the translator chooses. These English words italicized in Sakamoto's text could have been rendered in the Roman alphabet in order to evoke not just the complicated relationship Miss Saito has to Japanese and English, but also the complex linguistic and cultural relationship that many Japanese people in Japan have with English and language learning. That is, the construction of an identity is performed in this language learning: the practice and monitoring of pronunciation by both Chisako and Miss Saito attempt to erase "unevenness," thereby paralleling the construction of national identity in both Canada and Japan.

Rethinking intralingual translation

Leo Chan has observed that "most theoretical models [of translation] are founded on a concern for how meaning is transmitted from one linguistic system to another. But if the systems are not themselves separate, but implicated in each other, the notion of translation as a process of transferring meaning immediately becomes destabilized" (Chan 2002: 68). This destabilization blurs Roman Jakobson's familiar distinctions between interlingual, intralingual, and semiotic translation (1959/2000). Canadian Nikkei writers writing mainly in English, such as Kogawa and Sakamoto, knead Japanese into their writing, as well as silence and an ambivalent relationship to English. Japanese becomes a borrowed, residual, or imagined language used sparingly and strategically to form, situate, and specify a conflict between text and context and between voices heard and heeded and those that are not understood and thus dismissed or suppressed.

The Japanese translations of these works were undertaken by engaged Japanese women aware of the historical context and committed to their project.

Their afterwords show their recognition of the importance of the use of Japanese in the novels, and this recognition is carefully marked in both translations; the visual ripples created by the katakana draw attention to texts comprised of words from various linguistic sources. Nevertheless, neither translator takes advantage of the multiple Japanese writing systems, or their afterwords, to unsettle and complicate the multiple meanings in these novels. *Obasan* and *The Electrical Field* are superficially similar in terms of their shared subject matter and use of Japanese and English, but the intent of the narrative and the use of these languages in each novel are radically different. While Kogawa seeks redress and national inclusion, Sakamoto's Miss Saito is linguistically crossdressing, trying on possible identities to mask her discomfort with her own. Their translators recognized and marked the use of Japanese in these diasporic novels, but overlooked the range of possibilities available in Japanese to raise reader awareness of the language's global circulation and intralingual diversity and even to provoke a reassessment of the historical reasons for and implications of the multiple writing systems in Japanese. When stories of the diaspora return in translation, they need special handling to uncover a repressed past and aid understanding of the present and the future in Japan, as in the Americas, or anywhere else in this world in flux.

Notes

This research was supported by a Grant-in-Aid for Scientific Research (C) Research No 21520291.

1   The "thickness" I am referring to here is Kwame Anthony Appiah's description of a thick translation that "seeks with its annotations and its accompanying glosses to locate the text in a rich cultural and literary context" (Appiah 1993: 817).
2   Although not concerned with Japanese or the politics of diglossia in translation, Meir Sternberg's 1981 article "Polylingualism as Reality and Translation as Mimesis" offers a cogent discussion of the tension between language and translation as communicative and mimetic modes and approaches to the translation of heterolingual literary texts.
3   *Mochi* is a glutinous pounded rice cake.
4   *Rubi* are glosses in small type ("ruby" was a printing type size equivalent to 5.5 points) that appear above or alongside words or phrases in Japanese texts to provide phonetic or intended readings.

References

Appiah, K. A. 1993. "Thick Translation." *Callaloo* 16(4): 808–19.

Apter, E. 1999. *Continental Drift: From National Characters to Virtual Subject*. Chicago and London: University of Chicago Press.

Butler, J. 1990. *Gender Trouble: Feminism and the Subversion of Identity*. London: Routledge.

Chan, L. T. 2002. "Translating Bilinguality: Theorizing Translation in the Post-Babelian Era." *The Translator* 8(1): 49–72.

Edwards, B. H. 2006. "The Futures of Diaspora." *Prime* 24: 91–109.

Fujimoto, Y. 2002. "Positioning of the Private Eye/I in Kerri Sakamoto's *The Electrical Field*." *Kanada bungaku kenkyū* [Canadian literary studies], 10: 105–34.

Gentzler, E. 2002. "What's Different about Translation in the Americas?" *CTIS Occasional Papers* 2: 7–17.

—. 2008. *Translation and Identity in the Americas: New Directions in Translation Theory*. London and New York: Routledge.

Harvey, K. 2003. *Intercultural Movements: American Gay in French Translation*. Manchester: St. Jerome Publishing.

Jakobson, R. 1959/2000. "On Linguistic Aspects of Translation." In *The Translation Studies Reader*, edited by L. Venuti. London and New York: Routledge, pp. 113–18.

Kogawa, J. 1981/1992. *Obasan*. New York: Doubleday.

Koizumi, M. (trans.). 2002. *Mado kara no nagame*. Tokyo: DHC.

Miki, R. 1998. "Unclassified Subjects: Question Marking 'Japanese Canadian' Identity." In *Broken Entries: Race, Subjectivity, Writing: Essays*, edited by R. Miki. Toronto: Mercury Press, pp. 181–2.

—. 2005. *Redress: Inside the Japanese Canadian Call for Justice*. Vancouver: Raincoast Books.

Nagaoka, S. (trans.). 1998. *Ushinawareta sokoku*. Tokyo: Chūōkōronsha.

Sakamoto, K. 1998. *The Electrical Field*. Toronto: Vintage Canada.

Seigworth, G. J. and M. Gregg. 2010. "An Inventory of Shimmers." In *The Affect Theory Reader*, edited by M. Gregg and G. J. Seigworth. Durham, NC and London: Duke University Press, pp. 1–25.

Sinfield, A. 1992. *Faultlines: Cultural Materialism and the Politics of Dissident Reading*. Oxford: Clarendon Press.

Sontag, S. 1964. "Notes on 'Camp.'" http://interglacial.com/~sburke/pub/prose/Susan_Sontag_-_Notes_on_Camp.html, accessed November 1, 2010.

Sternberg, M. 1981. "Polylingualism as Reality and Translation as Mimesis." *Poetics Today* 2(4): 221–39.

Wakabayashi, J. 2006. "Translating in a Forked Tongue: Interlinear Glosses as a Creative Device in Japanese Translations." *Translation and Interpreting Studies* 1(2): 3–41.

9

Pretranslation in Modern Japanese Literature and what it tells us about "World Literature"

Irmela Hijiya-Kirschnereit

Making Japanese literature "fit" for world literature

The notion of "world literature" has been discussed again and again in the context of Translation Studies (TS), but rarely has Japanese literature played a role in these considerations. The present contribution attempts to address some of the reasons for this omission and clarifies how translation relates to "world literature" in the Japanese case, focusing particularly on the notion of pretranslation. This is understood here as a more or less consciously executed act of "editing" a work to make it more palatable to a presupposed international standard.

Translation—or more exactly, linguistic translation—becomes necessary only when we assume that the potential readership of a work transcends the borders of the language in which the text was written. As long as we naïvely equated language, ethnicity, culture, and nationality, as has often been the case when speaking of "Japanese literature" in particular, the issue of translation might have been regarded as of little consequence. From the point of view of this seemingly closed system, the idea of actively reaching beyond its confines seems hard to conceive of, much less materialize. Japanese writers throughout most of Japanese history, including the twentieth century, might not have harbored aspirations to be read beyond the borders of their home country, even though the majority of them were avid readers of foreign literature, Chinese or European. This one-way traffic in the communication of Japanese writers and intellectuals with the world outside Japan in the nineteenth and twentieth centuries, but also in earlier stages of their history, has formed a rich and productive field of research in the past two or three decades, but it has also helped consolidate Japan's image at home and abroad as a nation that is open to input from the world but simultaneously closed to the outside, with all the associated positive and problematic connotations. Now at last the time seems ripe to learn more about Japan's role not as a receiver, but as a giver in an internationalized world, and to shed new light on the perceived information imbalance.

On opening doors to the world from the inside

To Japanologists like myself, a new age seemed to announce itself when the Japan Foundation launched its new quarterly periodical *Japanese Book News* in 1993, based on an understanding of the need to "provide a window for Japanese books that contribute to the reservoir of human knowledge and the advancement of mutual understanding between Japan and the rest of the world," as the introductory paragraph in the inaugural issue put it (left of the Table of Contents, n.p.). This issue addressed the "Information Imbalance," with a "tremendous amount coming in and only a bare trickle going out of Japan," and it cited "the great differences between Japanese and other languages" as "one of the biggest barriers" and "cultural taste" as "another stumbling block" (n.p.) for the international dissemination of Japanese literature. This new publication, together with some other initiatives that were started in the 1990s, such as Japanese translation support programs and translation prizes, finally displayed a proactive stand toward the longstanding vague discomfit with the imbalance in the flow of information. The Japanese side had at last realized that there was need for action on the part of those who feel that they are under- or misrepresented, instead of simply lamenting the indeed deplorable state of affairs. To my mind, *Japanese Book News* was an important step in the direction of seeing publications in the Japanese language as part of a global intellectual community and marketplace.

On the other hand, I also realized that the awareness of the global dimension of literature is unevenly developed among Japanese writers. Many of them do not seem to care very much about being translated, at least into languages other than English. They might have all kinds of reasons for this attitude. As the editor of a 32-volume series of Japanese literature with a renowned German publisher from 1990 to 2000,[1] I more than once experienced a situation in which the Japanese author refused to grant translation rights. Even in the case of translation into English, famous and popular Japanese writers such as Ryōtarō Shiba (1923–96) appear to have stubbornly declined to be translated.[2] Perhaps it is because of their general scepticism toward translation, or perhaps they are simply satisfied with their domestic market, or perhaps things are more complex.

It is interesting in this respect to study the statements of Japanese writers in the column titled "In Their Own Words" at the back of *Japanese Book News* from 1996 onward. This column was obviously created to provide a forum for Japanese writers to discuss issues of "Translating and Being Translated," which is also the title of the first instalment of this column, authored by the famous novelist Haruki Murakami. This column has since featured articles by many Japanese writers. While it would certainly be worthwhile studying these brief essays in a more systematic manner, my general impression after reading dozens of them is that of a curiously parochial and self-sufficient worldview. Exceptions of course prove the rule. Where do Japanese writers position themselves? Is it that they do not care about being part of "world literature?" Perhaps they are not even aware that they already are.

Japanese literature in a transnational dimension

Even with modern and contemporary Japanese writers there is a certain scepticism toward or even lack of interest in being translated into foreign languages, as I have observed in the context of discussing this issue with writers and intellectuals. I would interpret this as a possible effect of one of the core myths of modern Japan—that is, the untranslatability of Japanese forms, in spite of the perplexing fact that Japanese modernization is itself based on translating into Japanese, as many authors have stressed. It is the direction that makes the difference, as if "things Japanese," including language, cannot be transmitted from inside to the outside world. It is a kind of "waterproof" construction whereby all outside information can easily reach Japanese ground while knowledge or notions regarded as specific insider property are to be retained. It is this thinking that forms the background to the well-known Japanese claim to uniqueness that is central to the genre of Nihonjinron (so-called discourses on Japanese uniqueness), which has flourished since the 1970s and is still popular today.

Meiji writer Ōgai Mori (1862–1922) serves as a fine counter-example to this tendency. Perhaps it is no coincidence that in a novella written in 1911 Ōgai (as he is usually known), himself a prolific translator and transmitter of Western knowledge since his years of study in Germany from 1884 to 1888, self-consciously conjures up the notion of "world literature" (*sekai no bungaku* in his wording)—an expression coined in Germany in the 1770s and widespread since its 1827 use by Goethe.[3] Ōgai's text, titled "Hyaku monogatari" (A hundred tales, 1967), depicts a narrator who attends a party where an old-fashioned game of telling ghost stories is to be played—the "hundred tales" of the title. The relevant passage appears right at the beginning of the text, after two brief opening paragraphs:

> I know well enough that in fiction no explanations are provided, but here I flatter myself, as perhaps would anyone, in thinking that if a tale such as this were to be translated into any of the European languages, then, when it joined the literature of the world, readers in other countries would doubtless have difficulty in fathoming its meaning; they would be convinced that the writer had created something altogether preposterous. Therefore, I have decided to begin my tale with an explanation. (trans. Rimer 1994: 183)[4]

Here Ōgai coquettishly refers to his story being translated into European languages, which would make it part of "the literature of the world" in his view. This gesture serves at least two purposes. The self-conscious reference effectively paints a global horizon for Ōgai's story, with its deliberately traditional setting. At the same time it serves as a narrative device to provide information deemed necessary for his Japanese readers, who are just as dependent on the ensuing explanation as would be "readers in other countries." In this fascinating story Ōgai not only makes his Japanese readership aware of the transnational dimensions of literature by making them imagine the story being translated into other languages, but also offers a kind of very early example *avant la lettre* of the phenomenon now termed pretranslation.

This expression in the sense used here was brought up in a discussion of Arabic literatures translated into European languages, when Jenine Abboushi Dallal (1998) maintained that contemporary Arabic authors tend to "pre-translate" their works for an implied European audience, because they feel they have to explicate for "Western" readers what is common cultural knowledge among Arabs. Instead of entering into the controversial discussion around this notion in the case of Arabic literatures, let me note that "pre-translation" in this sense is also at work in Japanese literature. I am referring to the practice on the part of some Japanese authors of making their texts more easily accessible to an international audience by avoiding cultural specifics and/or by elaborating on cultural specifics that are self-evident to readers of Japanese. Ōgai's tongue-in-cheek remark about having to explain the ghost story game because his text might be translated into a European language is an early example of awareness of the perceived necessity of adjusting one's text to the needs of a globalized readership. Yet Ōgai is perhaps unique in using this awareness playfully as a narrative device.[5]

Japanese authors pretranslating their works

How do other Japanese authors pretranslate their texts? Turning to contemporary writers, one immediately thinks of Haruki Murakami's works, with their relatively unspecific contemporary settings in nameless cities that could be any metropolis from Tokyo or Osaka to Shanghai or Los Angeles. Take, for example, his novel *Afutādāku* (2004), which is written in partly unidiomatic Japanese with an overabundance of sentence subjects (which are often implicit in Japanese writing) and with expressions, figures of speech, and gestures that seem more English than Japanese. One might attribute these stylistic characteristics to Murakami's work as a translator of anglophone literature or to a conscious decision to give his literature a foreign and quasi-cosmopolitan ring in Japanese. On the other hand, the translatability of Murakami's works into other languages is due in part to his pretranslation or explanation of things or attitudes that are self-evident to Japanese. I wonder how Japanese readers react to the detailed and circumstantial description in *Afutādāku* of how to access and use a "love hotel" (Murakami 2004: 50), something about which no Japanese adult needs any explanation. This is how the passage reads in Jay Rubin's translation *After Dark* (2007: 34):

> The two walk in through the front door of the Alphaville. Guests at this hotel choose their room from large photos on display in the foyer, press the corresponding numbered button, receive their key, and take the elevator straight to the room. No need to meet or talk to anyone. Room charges come in two types: "rest" and "overnight." Gloomy blue illumination.

Yet perhaps such instances have a kind of alienation effect on Japanese readers—provided they notice these adaptations to an international readership's assumed expectations in the first place.[6] On the whole, the architectural and technological settings in Murakami's works are so devoid of culturally specific features that one might expect from this novel nothing but such catering to a globalized kind of lifestyle-feeling. If we read this novel as just another version of the young consumerist-oriented urban novel, that's that.

Forms of pretranslation, be they linguistic features or, more commonly, related to the content, clearly hint at a dual framework, with two different audiences being addressed at the same time—that is, Japanese readers and what Ōgai would have called "readers in foreign countries." Their cultural knowledge is, of course, much more difficult to assess. It seems safe to assume, however, that the frame of reference of authors who "pre-translate" their works can be pinned down to readers of European languages (if we presume a conservative stand identical with Ōgai's perspective) or, more realistically perhaps, readers of English on a globalized scale, with an American readership as the primary audience. This assumption goes hand in hand with the observation that quite a few Japanese writers seem to have a biased preference for translations into English rather than other languages, as was pointed out earlier in the context of experiences with the series of translations into German titled *Japanische Bibliothek*, where more than once we were denied translation rights on the basis of the author's wish to have a translation into English first. Nobody, of course, can ignore the hegemony of English in international communication, but literary markets are quite another matter, although this topic calls for more discussion than is possible here.[7]

Advantages and problems of pretranslation

Of course, pretranslation is not confined to literature written in Arabic or Japanese. In an interview in 2005, Japanese-born British writer Kazuo Ishiguro admits to doing his utmost to avoid local color in his writing (see Schader 2005). He suspects that he is the first in his generation to work from the very outset with the question of translatability in mind, in a linguistic as well as a cultural sense. Thus Ishiguro confesses to abstaining from English wordplay or puns. He also avoids describing characters by brand names or the names of the restaurants they frequent, for "this kind of information may make sense to a reader living in London, but not to someone in Norway or Kansas City" (my translation). Ishiguro goes so far as to scrutinize his subject matter according to its global compatibility, suggesting that there are topics that might be important in an English context but not necessarily in other parts of the world.

So what then could be problematic about pretranslation in a Japanese novel if even anglophone authors with a wide international circulation frankly admit to adjusting their works to the assumed expectations of a globalized readership? In the case of Ishiguro at least, it seems that his strategy of writing for an international market, embraced from his very beginnings as a professional author, has worked out well, and the fact that he writes in English will certainly have facilitated his success. Yet can his example serve as a model for other writers, particularly those in other languages and cultures? And in any case how do we measure Ishiguro's success? Are we counting sales figures, the number of translations into other languages, literary prizes or what? And how much of this success can be attributed to his pretranslation as distinct from other aspects of his work?

In the case of contemporary Japanese literature, pretranslation is just one strategy out of many that serve to make a work compatible with a wider transcultural literary scene. While pretranslation is carried out by authors themselves, other strategies of making Japanese literature fit for a world market are applied at a later stage by translators or by editors or readers of the target language. The forms of editing are manifold indeed, and it would take another paper to deal with them or even to list them all.[8] I will limit my observations here to a few remarks concerning cooperation between authors and translators in this respect.

Once sensitized to the phenomenon, readers of contemporary Japanese works will have no difficulty in identifying instances of pretranslation with other authors. Yukio Mishima could perhaps be regarded as an early instance. Some critics (e.g. Ryan 1974) read the intention of catering to an international audience into his tetralogy *Hōjō no umi* (The Sea of Fertility), with its theme of reincarnation and heavy explanation of Buddhist philosophy, particularly in the third volume titled *Akatsuki no tera* (The Temple of Dawn, 1969). If this observation hits the mark, it also points to one of the problematic aspects of pretranslation—namely, a tendency toward self-orientalizing or self-exoticizing that has also been observed and criticized (e.g. Abboushi Dallal 1998, Ettobi 2003) in the case of contemporary Arabic authors.

Whereas many authors are not qualified to check what has happened to their work in the target language and others might not even be interested as long as the book looks nice and royalties are flowing in, some authors are fairly explicit about how they want to be translated. In one of Mishima's German versions, we find a note stating that the work was translated from the English rendition at the author's demand. Was it that Mishima distrusted German translators more than English ones? And was his distrust so strong that he instead opted for a relay translation? We will never know.[9]

We could also draw here on the example of Haruki Murakami's double standard whereby he opts for a globalized version on the basis of English translations of his works, which might differ substantially from the original Japanese version, as was the case with *Nejimakidori Kuronikkuru* (3 vols, 1994–5; *The Wind-up Bird Chronicle*, 1997) and other novels. Murakami is obviously convinced that the editing—the shortening and straightening out[10] of a number of episodes and scenes in order to adapt the work to American readers' tastes and standards—produces an "international" version of his works that Murakami wants to see as the basis for translations into other languages. While it is perfectly legitimate for an author to decide if, when and how his works are translated, it might come as a surprise that this Japanese author proactively supports the hegemony of American literary tastes.[11]

The backdrop to my observations concerning strategies of making Japanese works of literature compatible to international standards (however those standards are defined) is the question of so-called world literature, and it is this topic that I want to reconsider in the remaining part of this paper.

Implications of "world literature" or the "world republic of letters"

As noted above, the concept of "world literature" was forged in the European period of Romanticism, when the foundation for the development of different national literatures all over Europe was laid. While Goethe's reflections on what he termed the "free trade of concepts and feelings"[12] (or world market of intellectual goods) are regarded by many scholars as an anticipation of the contemporary entanglement of literatures and cultures, the concept has nevertheless been controversial, being regarded as based on a Eurocentric vision or, as others have maintained (among them sociolinguist Katsuhiko Tanaka), as accentuating the very notion or "ideology" of national literatures that it intends to transcend (Tanaka 1993: 156–8, 176). Others therefore speak of an international literary space with "its own mode of operation: its own economy, which produces hierarchies and various forms of violence; and, above all, its own history," a point made by Pascale Casanova in her reflections on the "World Republic of Letters" (2004: 12).

I started out with the observation that some Japanese writers might not even be interested in having their works cross linguistic and cultural borders. And yet Japanese writers have been part of a global literary space for many generations now. Their choice of topic and style is also shaped by a globalized consciousness, whether or not they are aware of it. After all, modern Japanese literature, through its reception of and mostly one-sided dialogue with the international literary and cultural scene since the late nineteenth century, as well as through Japan's agency in the contemporary world, reflects and configures modern experiences, which more often than not transcend national borders. The notion of "world literature" is, of course, not identical with the global literary space, and it remains contested. Perhaps David Damrosch's pragmatic understanding is helpful here. He takes world literature to encompass "all literary works that circulate beyond their culture of origin, either in translation or in their original language," adding that a work "only has an *effective* life as world literature whenever, and wherever, it is actively present within a literary system beyond that of its original culture" (Damrosch 2003: 4). The continuing definitional debate as to whether world literature should be seen as an established body of *classics*, as an evolving canon of *masterpieces*, or as multiple *windows on the world* is reframed by Damrosch's suggestion that these conceptions are not mutually exclusive and that they should therefore be allowed their ongoing value (Damrosch 2003: 15). So let us base our understanding of "world literature" on the presumption that a work is alive in a number of cultures and languages other than its origin, that it is read, discussed, and perhaps adapted, and that it inspires other works in the target cultures.

This phenomenon can already be observed with many Japanese literary works. According to the most recent bibliography of translations of modern Japanese literature into German (Stalph et al. 2009: vii), there were about 1,800 German translations of 1,553 Japanese works between 1868 and March 2009, produced by 544 translators. This is just one example, from one language, and the fact is that whether or not we are aware of it, Japanese literature is indeed, at least potentially, part of the literary life of other nations.[13] This aspect deserves much more critical attention on the part of scholars and critics, as well as readers and the authors themselves. What makes a Japanese work "fit" for "world literature"? Does the author have to keep an international readership in mind while writing? Does she have to pretranslate? Does he perhaps orientalize his work or, alternatively, try to strip it of local color?

When Korean star author Kim Young Ha was asked in an interview about the reaction of European readers to his novels, he responded that these readers seemed to have felt that an Asian or ethnic Korean touch was missing in his works (Neue Zürcher Zeitung 2009). He acknowledged that this might have been a natural consequence of the fact that his novels are situated in a historical moment when Western consumer culture was booming in South Korea. To the extent, then, that present-day South Korea is part of a globalized world, the local color expected by international readers seems to fade, at least on the surface. Nevertheless, when asked about the possible globalization of Korean literature—a literature which, according to his explanation, retains certain characteristics such as a pronounced preference for short narrations and a lack of light genres such as pulp fiction—Kim stated that although this might happen eventually, it cannot and should not be a goal. It is this kind of critical reflection and self-reflection that I would like to see in respect to Japanese literature as well, with Japanese writers and readers, translators of Japanese literature, and scholars of Japanese literature in and outside Japan producing a lively discourse about what it means to translate and be translated, what the role of English is or should be in this context, and what to make of strategies of adapting to an international market. It will take professional critique of translations in the target countries with feedback to Japan to make the idea of Japanese literature as "world literature" come to greater life. My appeal—what an old-fashioned thing to do!—is therefore addressed to all players in this complex game.

Tasks for the target language

As one example of what a target culture can do to foster the reception of foreign literature, let me introduce a bibliography of reviews of Japanese literature in German translation between 1968 and 2003 (Ando et al. 2006). In close to 900 pages (with four indexes) this bibliography systematically lists the full texts of all such reviews that were published in German-language newspapers with national circulation in former West and East Germany, as well as Switzerland and Austria. It serves as a tool for research into how Japanese literature has been received in this market and what part it plays in the wider continental book market. Another indispensable tool takes the most basic form of reliable dictionaries. For the past decade or so we have been working to enhance the quality of translations from Japanese by compiling a Comprehensive Japanese-German Dictionary (*Wadoku daijiten*). This is the largest bilingual dictionary for Japanese that has ever existed, with over 130,000 main entries (*midashi-go*) and more than a million words (*tango*), including subentries. The first of three volumes (A–I; 2,540 pages) was recently published with countless sample sentences from literature and with sources given (Stalph et al. 2009). These examples illustrate what contributions from the Japanese studies side in the target culture might look like. Although these contributions are mostly hidden from public view, because they are too basic to attract attention, they too contribute, in their modest and unspectacular way, to making Japanese literature part of "world literature."

What is needed is a platform for more serious discussion of what happens with and because of Japanese literature in an international context. The English expression "world-readable" has implications that we have not yet fully understood, and while the bias toward European literature is waning steadily in the "world republic of letters," we need to study its mechanisms and institutions of legitimation. Recognizing Japanese literature as an important and original player on the world stage requires all parties—the authors first, but also translators, researchers, critics and, of course, experienced and curious readers—to acknowledge Japanese works, not necessarily for their "Japaneseness," but for their individual aesthetic qualities as a work of art.

Japanese literature, world literature and Translation Studies (TS)

In the context of TS, the problems discussed in this paper point in two directions. On the one hand, this concerns the globalization of the canon—if we are willing to accept a notion of "canon" in the twenty-first century at all. Generally speaking, we have been observing the abdication of the Western canon for some time now, but the trade imbalances of the twentieth century and earlier still seem largely intact. Much of this has to do with the hegemony of English in international communication, but in this paper I have tried to show that the reasons are more complex and can also be found in intransigent attitudes on the part of some Japanese authors. Pretranslation, which I have singled out as a strategy on the part of certain Japanese writers, serves as a focal point for discussing some of the difficult options and unclarified dependencies in the international traffic of literature. It goes without saying that this strategy is not "unique" or particularly common with Japanese writers but can be observed with writers of other languages as well, as demonstrated in this paper.

Emily Apter is one of the major players in recent TS who have taken up the dispute over world poetry and the anxiety of global influence (see Owen 1990) to meditate on the options of a so-called Third World Literature (in this case from Algeria) in the world literary market—that is, the choice between what she calls "the dangers of becoming translatable" (Apter 2006: 108) and remaining ignored. Much of what she discusses in the context of the dispute about the popularity of the Chinese writer Bei Dao's translated poetry, which has been accused of "cozy ethnicity" and of catering to an "implicit nostalgia for China's traditional heritage" and a "deeply ingrained Orientalism" on the receiving side (Apter 2006: 101), echoes the discussion of the Japanese examples presented above. There is no easy solution in sight for the problem of what Apter calls "being blacked-out or whited-over in the international public sphere of letters" (Apter 2006: 108).

Yet it is obvious that the Japanese case is underrepresented in this discussion. For instance, Lawrence Venuti, another major protagonist in TS, refers to current practices in his now-standard work *The Translation Studies Reader*, but he would certainly have modified his statements had he considered examples of translations from Japanese.[14] At the same time, however, Venuti alerts us to the second direction of inquiry that results from our analysis of strategies for standardizing Japanese literature—that is, the fact that there cannot be one globalized and "straightened-out" version of a Japanese text. As Venuti writes,

> The foreign text is rewritten in domestic dialects and discourses, registers and styles, and this results in the production of textual effects that signify only in the history of the receiving language and culture. (Venuti 2004: 485)

Japanese literature on a global level can therefore be realized only as an aggregate of different versions in as many languages as possible, each with a life of its own. Studying their semantic and stylistic differences and culture-specific "textual effects" could form another avenue to understanding the poetic potential of what has conventionally been termed the "original." Studies like these have not only enriched the field of TS,[15] they also show how this field contributes to a transcending of the narrow confines of the study of national literatures. In an age when it is obvious that Japanese literature is part of the "international public sphere of letters," the discipline of *kokubungaku* (the study of Japanese literature) will benefit from this border-crossing through the fresh perspective that TS offers for approaching Japanese texts. As Jonathan E. Abel has stated in regard to translations of Classical Japanese texts into modern Japanese, "Translations do share something with the translated, but this sharing is not the communicating of one text's message to another, the erasing of one by another, the domineering of one over another, or the embellishment of one text at the expense of the other. This sharing is the being-in-common, the standing-in-relation between two texts." (Abel 2005: 155). Through sophisticated application of a TS-informed approach to Japanese works and their variants in other languages, we can expect exciting new vistas for "Japanese literature" to prosper.

Notes

1 The series *Japanische Bibliothek* (Japanese Library) was published with Insel Publishers, then Frankfurt/M. and Leipzig. It features some pre-modern but mostly modern and contemporary authors.

2 See Fogel (2006). More recently, however, translations of works by this particular author have appeared in English.

3 See Schamoni (2008). Incidentally, it was this scholar of Japanese literature who excavated August Ludwig Schlözer as a precursor to Goethe, who is generally credited with the "invention" of the term "'world literature."

4   I want to thank Wolfgang Schamoni, Ōgai's German translator, for alerting me to this text.

5   Another writer with an eye for the effects of being translated is Jun'ichirō Tanizaki (1886–1965), who in his 1927 essay Jōzetsuroku ("Tongue on the Loose") acknowledged that his aim was to write a "Western" style, rather than a beautiful style, and that he was embarrassed to admit that while writing it he had constantly kept in mind whether it would be easily translatable into English. I want to thank Judy Wakabayashi for this hint. Tanizaki's opposition of "beautiful" versus "Western" style, by the way, refers us to another fascinating issue in this context, namely the idea that the style of translations from European languages into Japanese constitutes a so-called Third Literature (*dai-san no bungaku*) situated between original Japanese texts and literature in foreign languages. On the idea of Third Literature, as propagated by the translation scholar Ken Itō, see Hijiya-Kirschnereit (2001): 27–28.

6   Much Japanese writing aimed even at domestic audiences also has "foreign" touches as a result of over a century of contact with foreign texts.

7   I have dealt with this issue in a number of articles. See, for example, Hijiya-Kirschnereit (1994).

8   I have dealt with these aspects in a number of papers. See, for example, Hijiya-Kirschnereit (1993) and ((ed.) 2001).

9   On Mishima's directions concerning the translation of his works, see also Donald Keene's remarks in the panel discussion documented in Hijiya-Kirschnereit (2010).

10   By this what I mean is an ironing out of obvious contradictions on the level of the plot or other aspects awkward to Western readers who, since the days of the literature of realism, are more sensitive to violations of the laws of probability.

11   I have discussed this problem under the rubric of the Hollywoodization of Japanese literature (Hijiya-Kirschnereit (ed.) 2001). Jay Rubin, translator of Murakami's *Nejimakidori Kuronikkuru* and other works, has responded to this discussion on editing in the appendix to his book *Haruki Murakami and the Music of Words* (2002) without, however, dealing with the problem of "Hollywoodization."

12   "Freihandel der Begriffe und Gefühle," in Goethe's talks with Eckermann (1827). See Schrimpf's essay on Goethe's notion of world literature, explaining Goethe's idea of an exchange of intellectual goods on the marketplace of all nations (Schrimpf 1968: 45–8). Goethe's explanation about the "world market of intellectual goods" and the "free trade of notions and feelings" can be found in Goethe (1993): 157–8.

13   The reception of Yukio Mishima as material and literary motif in various literatures is a concrete example of what it means for Japanese literature to be part of the literatures of the world. See my essay "Sekai no bungaku to Mishima" (Yukio Mishima in the literatures of the world) in Hijiya-Kirschnereit (ed.) (2010).

14 One thinks of his observation that "Dates, historical and geographical markers, the characters' names—even when the names are rather complicated and foreign-sounding—these are generally not altered or only in rare cases (e.g. Russian names)." (Venuti 2004: 484). Translations from Japanese literary works seem to ignore these rules much more frequently than Venuti might imagine.

15 An example is the study *Anders Gesagt/Autrement Dit/In Other Words* (Utz 2007), which compares various English and French versions of German-language works by Hoffmann, Fontane, Kafka, and Musil.

References

Abboushi Dallal, J. 1998. "The Perils of Occidentalism: How Arab Novelists are Driven to Write for Western Readers." *Times Literary Supplement*, April 24, 8–9.

Abel, J. E. 2005. "Translation as Community: The Opacity of Modernizations of *Genji monogatari*." In *Nation, Language, and the Ethics of Translation*, edited by S. Bermann and M. Wood. Princeton and Oxford: Princeton University Press, pp. 146–58.

Ando, J., I. Hijiya-Kirschnereit, and M. Hoop. 2006. *Japanische Literatur im Spiegel deutscher Rezensionen* [Japanese literature reflected in German reviews]. Munich: Iudicium Publishers.

Apter, E. 2006. *The Translation Zone: A New Comparative Literature*. Princeton: Princeton University Press.

Casanova, P. 2004. *The World Republic of Letters*. Translated by M. B. DeBevoise. Cambridge and London: Harvard University Press.

Damrosch, D. 2003. *What Is World Literature?* Princeton: Princeton University Press.

Ettobi, M. 2003. "La traduction comme représentation d'une étrangère: le cas dela [sic] littérature arabe traduite en anglais et en français" [Translation as representation of a stranger: the case of Arabic literature in English and French translation]. http://oress.concordia.ca/numero4/essai/ettobi.shtml, accessed December 28, 2009.

Fogel, J. 2006. "On Translating Shiba Ryōtarō into English." In *Historical Consciousness, Historiography, and Modern Japanese Values*, edited by James C. Baxter. Kyoto: International Research Center for Japanese Studies, pp. 153–65.

Goethe, J. W. 1993. *Die letzten Jahre: Briefe, Tagebücher und Gespräche von 1823 bis zu Goethes Tod. II* [The final years: Letters, diaries, and conversations from 1823 until Goethe's death], edited by H. Fleig. Frankfurt/M.: Deutscher Klassiker Verlag.

Hijiya-Kirschnereit, I. 1993. "Von der Übersetzbarkeit japanischer Literatur" [On the translatability of Japanese literature]. In *Traumbrücke ins ausgekochte Wunderland: Ein japanisches Lesebuch* [Dream Bridge into Hardboiled Wonderland: A Japanese Reader], edited by Irmela Hijiya-Kirschnereit. Frankfurt/M.: Insel Publishers, pp. 71–83.

—. 1994. "Nihon bungaku shōkai habamu eigo yūsenshugi" [How the hegemony of English impedes the introduction of Japanese Literature]. *Asahi shinbun* (evening edition), November 15, p. 11.

—. 2001. "Murakami Haruki o meguru bōken: Bungaku shijū sōdan'no fuchōon" [A Wild Murakami Haruki Chase: "Dissonances" in the Literary Quartet], *Sekai*, January 2001: pp. 193–9.

Hijiya-Kirschnereit, I. (ed.). 2001. *Eine gewisse Farbe der Fremdheit: Aspekte des Übersetzens Japanisch-Deutsch-Japanisch* [A certain colour of foreignness: Aspects of translation Japanese-German-Japanese]. Munich: Iudicium Publishers.

—. (ed.). 2010. *MISHIMA!—Sono fukugō bunkateki gensen to kokusaiteki inpakuto.* [Mishima!—Worldwide impact and multicultural roots]. Kyoto: Shōwadō.

Mishima, Y. *Hōjo no umi.* Vol. one: *Haru no yuki* (Spring Snow). Tokyo: Shinchōsha 1969; Vol. two: *Honba* (Runaway Horses). Tokyo: Shinchōsha 1969; Vol. three: *Akatsuki no tera* (The Temple of Dawn). Tokyo: Shinchōsha 1970; Vol. four: *Tennin gosui* (The Decay of the Angel). Tokyo: Shinchōsha 1971. Translated as *The Sea of Fertility* [Harmondsworth, Middlesex, England: Penguin Books, 1985].

Mori, Ō. 1967. "Hyaku monogatari" [A hundred tales]. In *Mori Ōgai shū 1, Nihon bungaku zenshū 4.* Tokyo: Shūeisha, pp. 291–303.

—. 1994. "*Hyaku monogatari*: Ghost Stories." In *Mori Ōgai, Youth and Other Stories*, edited by J. T. Rimer. Honolulu: University of Hawaii Press, pp. 182–96.

Murakami, H. 1996. "Translating and Being Translated.'" In *Japanese Book News* 16, 22.

—. 2004. *Afutādāku.* Tokyo: Kōdansha. Translated by Jay Rubin as *After Dark* (New York, NY: Alfred A. Knopf, 2007).

Neue Zürcher Zeitung. 2009. "Literatur als Wunschmaschine" [Literature as a wishing machine] (Interview with Kim Young Ha, by Ho Nam Seelmann), May 30, 2009. http://kimyoungha.com/english/shoebox/Entries/2009/5/30_Interview_at_Neue_Zurcher_Zeitung(German).html, accessed December 30, 2009.

Owen, S. 1990. "What Is World Poetry: The Anxiety of Global Influence." *The New Republic* (November 19, 1990): 28–32.

Rubin, J. 2002. *Haruki Murakami and the Music of Words.* London: Harvill Press.

Ryan, M. 1974. "The Mishima Tetralogy" (Review). *Journal of Japanese Studies* 1(1): 165–73.

Schader, A. 2005. "Die leisen Lügen der Erinnerung: Eine Begegnung mit dem Schriftsteller Kazuo Ishiguro" [The soft lies of memory: Meeting writer Kazuo Ishiguro], *Neue Zürcher Zeitung*, August 27, 2005. www.nzz.ch/2005/08/27/li/articleCYIZT.html, accessed December 30, 2009.

Schamoni, W. 2008. "'Weltliteratur'–zuerst 1773 bei August Ludwig Schlözer" [World literature—first in 1773 with August Ludwig Schlözer]. *Arcadia—International Journal for Literary Studies* 43(2): 288–98.

Schrimpf, H. J. 1968. *Goethes Begriff der Weltliteratur* [Goethe's notion of world literature]. Stuttgart: J.B. Metzler.

Stalph, J., I. Hijiya-Kirschnereit, W. Schlecht, and K. Ueda. 2009. *Großes japanisch-deutsches Wörterbuch* [Comprehensive Japanese-German Dictionary] Vol. 1 (A–I). Munich: Iudicium Publishers.

Stalph, J., C. Petermann, and M. Wittig. 2009. *Moderne japanische Literatur in deutscher Übersetzung. Eine Bibliographie der Jahre 1868–2008* [Modern Japanese literature in German translation: A bibliography of the years 1868–2008]. Munich: Iudicium Publishers.

Tanaka, K. 1993. *Kotoba no ekorojii: Gengo, Minzoku, "Kokusaika"* [Ecology of words: Language, ethnicity, "internationalisation"]. Tokyo: Nōsan gyoson bunka kyōkai.

Tanizaki, J. 1927. "Jōzetsuroku" [Tongue on the loose]. In *Tanizaki Jun'ichirō zenshū* [*The collected works of Jun'ichirō*], vol. 20, 4th printing, 1990. Tokyo: Chūō kōron, pp. 71–166.

Utz, P. 2007. *Anders Gesagt/Autrement Dit/In Other Words*. Munich: Hanser.

Venuti, L. 2004. "Translation, Community, Utopia." In *The Translation Studies Reader*, 2nd edn, edited by L. Venuti. New York and London: Routledge, pp. 482–502.

10

Transcreating Japanese Video Games: Exploring a Future Direction for Translation Studies in Japan

Minako O'Hagan

Overview

Behind the growth of today's game industry as a major global digital entertainment sector lies the significant role played by Japanese game companies such as Nintendo, Sega, and Sony Computer Entertainment (hereafter abbreviated as Sony) since the early days of the industry's development. Industry insiders generally agree that without Japanese contributions the game sector would not have gone beyond "a passing fad" (Aoyama and Izushi 2003: 424). Commenting on the power shift in the video game industry from the United States to Japan, Consalvo (2006: 132) cautiously remarks that the flow of cultural dominance for consoles and many major games is currently in the direction from East to West, "with Japan leading production, the USA and Europe following." Taking into consideration the longstanding association of video games with Japan, this chapter explores the relatively new translation research domain known as game localization, with the aim of exploring a potential direction for Translation Studies (TS) that is currently under development in Japan.

Video games originated in the late 1950s in the United States, which dominated the market until the so-called Atari crash saw the fall of the United States game industry in the early 1980s (Kent 2001). At the same time Japanese arcade games such as *Space Invaders* (Taito, 1978) and *Pac-Man* (Namco, 1980) enjoyed early international successes. In the game console era—starting with the 1983 release of Nintendo Famicom in Japan, known as Nintendo Entertainment System (NES) elsewhere, subsequently followed by Sega Saturn and Sony PlayStation, both in 1994—Japan's dominance in the international arena became apparent, both as a major hardware manufacturer (platform holder) and as a game developer/publisher. In the new millennium, in 2001, Microsoft entered the scene as a platform holder while Sega abandoned that role, instead focusing solely on producing games as a third-party publisher.

The game industry is dynamic, with technological innovation constantly changing the landscape. For example, enhanced Internet environments in the last few years have contributed to the worldwide popularity of massively multiplayer online games (MMOGs), while Microsoft's Kinect for Xbox360 and Sony's Move for PlayStation3 are more recent attempts by these platform holders to introduce a new gameplay experience through new types of player interface technologies, following the earlier success of Nintendo Wii. Furthermore, games are now spreading to a wider population with casual games to be played on mobile phones, while social games are another growing sector tied in with social networking platforms such as Facebook. While acknowledging these new trends, the present study focuses on the localization of console games, which occupy the largest share within the game sector and are thus commercially the most significant sector for game localization. The console sector is currently dominated by Nintendo, Sony, and Microsoft as the key platform holders who are also involved in game development and publishing, making their positions even more powerful. The console sector is structured in such a way that it relies on sales of game software, while the hardware itself is sold at a loss (Kerr 2006: 57). This further highlights the vital importance of software publishing and, in turn, localization of games to generate income from international markets, which are divided into different territories.

Commenting on the characteristics of the Japanese video game industry, Aoyama and Izushi (2003: 425–6) argue that Japan's strength in consumer electronics and its tradition of the visual art forms of manga and anime facilitated Japan's prominence in the game industry, successfully marrying its technological strength in electronics with existing cultural forms. The introduction of distinctive game characters, as opposed to the more abstract objects prevalent in early arcade games, and the development of a meaningful storyline are often regarded as Japanese contributions and linked to manga and anime (Kohler 2005: 5–7). Video games are cultural products that can be seen as a successful fusion of culture and technology, leading to what some call "techno-orientalism," where high-tech has become particularly "associated with Japaneseness" (Morley and Robins 1995: 168; qtd in Consalvo 2006: 124). Having been largely absent in the game studies literature, localization issues that are particularly significant for the international viability of Japanese games are more recently attracting the attention of some scholars who have become more aware of the diverse cultural and linguistic backgrounds of players, pointing to the importance of localization issues (Consalvo 2011: 343; Taylor 2011: 379).

Given this background, the focus on video game localization seems entirely justified in order to explore a potentially productive direction of TS in Japan, drawing in particular on some specific Japanese practices in localizing games. Against the backdrop of increasing criticism of the discipline as having privileged European-centric views (e.g. Tymoczko 2007; Baker and Saldanha 2009; Wakabayashi and Kothari 2009), this chapter turns attention to some little-known game localization practices undertaken by a major Japanese game company. Applying the concept of "transcreation" in relation to the broader concept of adaptation, I demonstrate how game localization incorporates creative human intervention into the technological nature of the game media. In the context of further developments of TS in Japan I argue that game localization, which has deep roots in Japan, can be a fruitful research domain that both facilitates insight into related Japanese practices and feeds into further developments of the discipline in Japan.

Game localization

While software localization is well established in the industry and is recognized in TS to the extent of being incorporated into translator training at universities (Folaron 2006), the same is not true for game localization. Although this practice has been in existence in the industry for a few decades, game localization has gathered momentum in TS only relatively recently (O'Hagan 2007). In his revised edition of *Introducing Translation Studies*, Munday (2008: 190) refers to "video game translation" as "a blend of audiovisual translation and software localization," highlighting it as an example of the knock-on effect of technology on translation. While somewhat simplified, this description nevertheless indicates how this new practice as a "blend" does not neatly fit within a single existing category of translation.

Since the concept of localization is already tightly bound to software, for the purposes of this chapter I adopt the most common term *game localization* (rather than *game translation*) to refer to the whole specialized process of making games available in markets other than their home market. Use of this term stresses the fact that video games are essentially a piece of software (Frasca 2001: 4). Under Frasca's definition, video games are treated as "any forms of . . . entertainment software, either textual or image-based, using any electronic platform." While a detailed explanation of the evolution of software localization is beyond the scope of this chapter, the term serves to highlight the changes in the nature of language transfer as a result of the source text shifting to digital form. As Frasca's definition indicates and as has been discussed in earlier studies of game localization (e.g. O'Hagan and Mangiron 2004; Mangiron and O'Hagan 2006), the understanding of games as entertainment is also significant, as it links to the skopos of this practice. In particular, entertainment based on a substantial user interaction with the game system is also a key concept in understanding the medium of video games. The fact that game localization prioritizes the product's entertainment value affects the micro- and macro-strategies used in translation and localization. Here I use the term *translation* in its narrow sense of converting verbal messages in one language into another, while *localization* refers to the broader process of "taking a product and making it linguistically and culturally appropriate to the target locale (country/region and language)" (Localization Industry Standards Association 1998: 3) by combining translation and software engineering.

In response to the demands of globalization and the rising cost of software and hardware development, the game industry relies on global sales of games. Even though Japan has a relatively large domestic market, which means it is not always necessary for developers to go global (Edge Staff 2008), this global aspect highlights the inherent significance of game localization. Often simply described as "the process of translating the game into other languages" (Chandler 2005: 12), game localization involves a specialized set of technical processes and procedures that overlap with the software localization process applied to business software (see Esselink 2000) and yet entail a number of distinct differences.

For example, in terms of the language directionality involved in game localization, Japan's central position in the game industry has made Japanese a main source language alongside English. This contrasts with other types of utility software localization, which take place almost exclusively from English, reflecting the dominant status of the US business software industry. Japanese exports of game software (Japanese games localized into target languages) continue to far outstrip imports of foreign games (games localized into Japanese). According to 2009 game trade statistics in the 2010 CESA Games White Paper (Computer Entertainment Supplier's Association 2010: 119–20), exported Japanese games accounted for 506 billion yen, as opposed to the figure for imported foreign games at 3.2 billion yen.[1] Although this is not a precise measure of how many games are actually localized to and from Japanese, one can reasonably infer that as far as game localization is concerned Japanese is predominantly a "donor" rather than "receptor" language, to use Hermans' terminology (2009: 98) regarding language directionality in translation. Importantly, however, European versions of Japanese games are often translated from their English-language versions, as is prominent in Nintendo practices, rather than directly from the Japanese original, on the assumption that the extent of transformation will be less (Uemura, pers. communication, June 11, 2010). Nevertheless, major Japanese publishers such as Square Enix are attempting to translate directly from Japanese for all locales (Mangiron 2004).

While sharing localization elements that are common with other software products, such as translation of the user interface (UI), games require the translation of many different types of in-game text, including more literary as well as functional and technical text. The cinematics that are now regularly inserted in games also require translation in a form similar to subtitling and/or revoicing.

One of the key differences found in games concerns the presence of country-specific age rating systems that can significantly affect translation and localization decisions. Germany's Unterhaltungssoftware SelbstKontrolle (USK) is the most stringent example and is a mandatory process (Chandler 2005: 32). Rating systems often reflect wider sociocultural issues, including ideological and moral stances, as well as the religious beliefs of the given country. Although compliance with rating systems is, in most cases, not mandatory, retailers will usually not stock titles that lack ratings, so they have an important impact on game localization. Ratings necessitate adjustments at the microlevel, with changes of verbal elements in translation as well as macrolevel changes in broader nonverbal elements (Kohler 2005; Yahiro 2005). Yahiro's comparative study (2005: 10–36) highlighted how early Nintendo role-playing games (RPGs) intended for a relatively young age group in Japan had to undergo various changes in order to be sold in the US market. These changes concerned references to alcohol and religion, sexual expressions, and discriminating remarks against minority groups. Interestingly, these changes were imposed in line with the internal guidelines of Nintendo of America, a separate company set up to oversee Nintendo's business in North America (NA). In the early days before independent national ratings boards were established in each territory,[2] game companies such as Nintendo and Sega set up their own voluntary regulations, modifying their games to make them acceptable for the intended age group in the target market. This was also to avoid "moral panic" reactions from the general public, whose sentiment at the time was often negative, treating games as violent antisocial products (see Kent 2001: 461–80).

Aside from requirements arising from ratings, one further factor that distinguishes game localization from the localization of more utility-oriented software is that the product's fundamental properties—such as game character design, story, and game mechanics—might also be subject to change to suit the tastes of a particular target territory.[3] Game localization also needs to meet the complex demands arising from being part of popular global culture, with universally recognized common characteristics expected of all games, as well as territory-specific preferences[4] in playing style, game genres, game platforms, and so on. In this way game localization entails a complex negotiation and transformation process on both technical and cultural levels in addition to consideration of linguistic issues, with the ultimate goal being to meet market demands and entertain the end user.

A new localization strategy afforded by technology

Games have undergone considerable technological transformations since the release of the early consoles in the mid-1980s. In addition to impressive graphics, today's game consoles allow online as well as offline play and also serve as a home entertainment hub with additional capabilities of storing music, pictures, and so on. In this way the distinction between game consoles and computers is constantly being blurred.

The development of games as software is particularly significant. Here the target text (TT) or locale can be considered as one manifestation of the source code that is the backbone of the product constituting the source text (ST). Unlike the translation of a text in print, localized games in their transformation yet retain some physical tie to the ST in the form of the source code. This relates to what Manovich (2001: 36) calls the "variability" of software, whereby software is "not something fixed once and for all, but something that can exist in different, potentially infinite versions." Because of this characteristic,[5] we can argue for treating localized games as variations of an ST. At the same time, despite the continuum at a technological level between the ST and TT, each locale can take on a quite different "look and feel" from the original ST, with the TT expected to be more comparable to locally produced counterparts (Localization Industry Standards Association 2003: 11). This dimension in turn affords a broader scope for localization strategies.

In the 1990s advances in game technology leading to the overall enhancement of game console capacities through the use of CD-ROM, for example, allowed cinematic sequences to be inserted in games more readily. Today they are a typical feature of games (Kohler 2005: 5), to the extent that games themselves are becoming like interactive movies. These cinematic elements perform various functions such as introducing game characters, setting the scene and providing a back-story, as well as showcasing the latest technologies (Egenfeldt-Nielsen et al. 2008: 176–7). The use of movies in games has in turn forged a closer link between game localization and audiovisual translation (AVT), although AVT techniques such as subtitling and revoicing are often used differently in game localization (Mangiron and O'Hagan 2006).

Perhaps one of the most significant relatively recent advances in game technologies in the context of localization is the incorporation of human voiced dialog. This has literally lent voice to animated game characters—by voice actors for the original and by revoicing for localized games. One of the early cases of using human voiced dialog was the PlayStation2 RPG title *Final Fantasy X* (Square Enix, first released in 2001), which had 90 percent of its dialog voiced by a team of 100 voice actors (Kohler 2005: 122). In comparison with the previously mechanical and less believable computer-generated speech sounds, human voices have made the narrative come alive, increasing the realism of games. Voiced dialog may be applied to highlight the personal traits of different game characters through a deliberate use of regional accents both in the original and localized games, often conveying humor (Andersson 2009; Mangiron and O'Hagan 2006).

Such an application of technologies can in turn create a challenge for the localizer. Although revoicing is expensive, it is often fully exploited, especially with the localization of major titles destined for commercially significant territories, which are served by the most expensive "full localization." According to Chandler (2005: 15), full localization entails translating the "text, voiceover, manual, and packaging," whereas partial localization does not involve revoicing of the voiceover files. This reflects the high cost involved in revoicing, especially for a game with a large number of characters. Among many examples of innovative use of voicing the dialog in a localized version is the best-selling Japanese RPG *Dragon Quest VIII* (Square Enix, 2004), where the dialog that appears only in written form in the original is voiced in a localized version. The game's creator, Yūji Horii, explains how voiced dialog was thought to better serve players of the localized version, whereas in the home version the written form was adequate for conveying the intended emotion (quoted in Onyett 2005: n.p.).

In this way new technical capabilities have opened up fresh possibilities, adding a new dimension to existing translation strategies such as compensation, as in the case of adding regional accents where there were none in the original or adding voicing in a localized version that originally used written dialog (Mangiron and O'Hagan 2006). The "voiced dialogue" seems to offer a means for further fine-tuning of localization so as to deliver greater player immersion and an enhanced gameplay experience in some games. These solutions are, to some extent, addressing comments often heard from end players to the effect that localized games are "lacklustre" or "an afterthought" compared with the original (Chandler 2005: 4). The reasons behind such comments are likely to derive both from clear-cut problems such as poorly translated and localized games with blatant linguistic mistakes and from less obvious aspects such as some loss of realism, with localization possibly perceived as a negative filter. For some hard-core gamers, the typical loss in localized versions is often associated with censorship applied to games, in turn driving them to undo such manipulations through subversive actions known as translation hacking (Muñoz Sánchez 2009: 178).

Because today's video games are multimedia and multifaceted, the process of localization is highly complex. While new technical capabilities have opened up new ways to enhance the look and feel of localized games, they have also created more room for errors. In cases of a "linguistic plot stopper," the actual gameplay itself is hindered by a translation error where the player of the localized version is prevented from "finishing a mission or even the entire game" (Dietz 2006: 125). Dietz cites the example of an adventure game requiring players to pronounce the correct magic sentence, which was not possible in the German locale because of the different word order used in the German translation.

Unique Japanese rerelease model with a new voice

Building further on the technical affordance of incorporating human voiced dialog in games, I refer below to an example to demonstrate how certain unique Japanese contexts and new technical capacity have manifested themselves in a novel practice of game localization. The case in point is a particular rerelease model that I call the "reverse localization model"[6] (O'Hagan 2009). This is used most systematically by one of the major Japanese game developers/publishers, Square Enix, alongside some more ad hoc examples by other Japanese publishers such as Nintendo, Konami, and Capcom.[7] Considered as a global corporation able to negotiate the global media culture, Square Enix has a track record of delivering internationally successful games (Consalvo 2006). Consalvo (2006: 120) regards its products as "evidence of a hybrid culture" where different cultures are successfully mixed through the firm's overseas subsidiaries, without succumbing to "a totalizing system." She continues:

> Distinctions still remain between the games that Square Enix produces for the Japanese market, and those that successfully sell abroad. Those products destined for global consumption are carefully localized to ensure that their international flavor is not *too* foreign for non-Japanese tastes. (Consalvo 2006: 120)

This section focuses on one localization approach by Square Enix that serves to highlight how a leading Japanese game company has been exploiting technological affordance in localizing its products. For some of its major titles, such as the *Final Fantasy* (FF) and *Kingdom Hearts* series, Square Enix periodically releases so-called "International" or, in the case of the latter series, "Final Mix" editions that are usually exclusive to the Japanese market. These editions are derived from an earlier NA version of the original Japanese game, but they are specifically prepared to reintroduce them into the Japanese market. Discussion of this reverse localization model is limited here to the FF series, as *Kingdom Hearts* adds an extra layer of complexity linked to Disney movies, as detailed in Mandiberg (2009),[8] whereas the FF series is of purely Japanese origin.

The NA market is typically considered the most significant export territory for Japanese games, with statistics for 2009 (Computer Entertainment Supplier's Association 2010: 119) showing that this territory accounts for over 50 percent of Japanese game software exports, with the USA and Canada respectively constituting 46.4 percent and 5.1 percent of total export sales. Therefore the NA market is usually prioritized in terms of the game release schedule and resource allocation for full (as opposed to partial) localization. As mentioned earlier, full localization entails revoicing all Japanese dialog into English, as well as usually providing English subtitles for those who wish to listen to the original Japanese sound track. In effect, the FF International Editions port the NA version back into Japanese but leave the voiced dialog in English, supplementing it with newly created Japanese subtitles. Due to liberties taken in the NA version when translating the original Japanese dialog into English, subtitles need to be provided anew, rather than reusing the original Japanese script. Since these editions are usually released only for the Japanese market, the game's UI is in Japanese. The idea is that Japanese players are able to access in their own language the feel for playing the NA version, which tends to incorporate extensive adaptation not only in the translated text at the microlevel but also at the macrolevel, involving other fixes and extras, sometimes with altered or new gameplay features.[9]

This model therefore creates an unusual reverse localization, whereby the original basic game features are retained but all the voices are dubbed in English with Japanese subtitles. Here the language of the "voice" plays a pivotal role. This model is not only theoretically interesting, but apparently also commercially viable. As mentioned earlier, Japan has a large domestic consumer base for video games, including hard-core fans who are prepared to invest in virtually the same game they have already purchased and played. The comprehensive strategy guide for *Final Fantasy X-2 International + Last Mission* (Square Enix, 2004), which is the International edition of *Final Fantasy X-2* (Square Enix, 2003), suggests that the rationale behind releasing these Japanese-only editions is to let Japanese players discover what changes were made in the NA version and enjoy the foreign "feel" added to the game as a result of the revoiced English dialog.

These examples further highlight the malleable nature of software, which can undergo a metamorphosis in different locales. The International and Final Mix editions directly exploit deviations made in the major locale and leverage the changes so as to generate a separate product for reintroduction to the originating market (Japan). This approach is guided by the goal of entertainment value to the end user, thus achieving the translation skopos. The English revoicing plays a particularly important role in these rerelease versions of Square Enix games. Other key Japanese game companies, such as Nintendo, occasionally use a similar model, as in the case of どうぶつの森e (Nintendo, 2003), maximizing these malleable characteristics of the medium in their localization practices.

In this way, localization presents a new dimension that, in the tradition of Descriptive Translation Studies, calls for more in-depth study to gather further evidence so as to allow hypotheses about translation norms. This whole area of game localization study is only now emerging, while localization itself has remained under-theorized in TS despite its prevalence as an industry practice and as a focused area in translator training. Below I draw on the concept of transcreation in an attempt to frame according to a translation perspective the little-known approaches and transformations that take place during game localization.

Transcreating games: Transcreation's past, present, and future manifestations

These rerelease editions illustrate how game localization is broadening translation practices and therefore affecting norms. From a purist's point of view, the reverse localization model described above might seem merely a business model resulting from the pursuit of commercial goals and thus adding nothing to the conceptualization of translation. Yet this practice illustrates how technological changes are affecting the nature of source texts and also expectations about target texts in the global digital media landscape. The ultimate goal of game localization—that is, to create a product that entertains the end player—seems to justify taking a broad range of liberties during the localization process so as to adjust the game to target-user parameters. Some of the localization approaches seem highly creative, sometimes in an effort to enhance the user experience and at other times necessitated by various constraints inherent in the process, such as space limitations (Mangiron and O'Hagan 2006). At the same time, game localization can be characterized by a more literal (e.g. UI elements, certain proper names) and prescriptive approach (e.g. in the imposed use of platform-specific terminology as well as operation-related constraints[10]).

While game localization thus calls for both literal and creative strategies, it is the latter that highlight new dimensions of game localization and distinguish it from software localization for utility applications. Using the concept of "transcreation," Mangiron and O'Hagan (2006: 13) have identified translatorial creativity as one defining characteristic of game localization, where even "functionality must be achieved with a high degree of creativity and originality." Building on this prior work, this section further discusses the concept of transcreation in the specific context of Japanese game localization.

Viewing translation strategies as a cline between "more derivative" and "more primary," Munday (2009: 8) points to the increasing interest within TS in the crossover between translation and creative writing. The latter includes concepts such as translocation and adaptation, as the goal is equivalent impact on the target audience (as in the case of translating classic Greek drama for a contemporary audience in a new culture) rather than equivalent renditions. Also drawing on the concept of transcreation in reference to the Brazilian poet and theorist Haroldo de Campos, Munday frames the functional and creative orientation of translation strategies as follows: "The anthropophagic, transcreative use of the original in order to 'nourish' new work in the target language breaks the notion of faithfulness to the original text as a necessary criterion for translation." Transcreation and the metaphor of anthropophagy are mainly attributed to Haroldo de Campos, whose ideas were first made accessible to the English-speaking world by Vieira (1999). More recently Nóbrega and Milton (2009) have discussed the immense influence on literary translation of the Campos brothers, Haroldo and Augusto, within the framework of translators as agents of change. In the context of postcolonial theory the cannibalism metaphor is used both as "a violation of European codes and an act of homage" (Bassnett and Trivedi 1999: 4–5) whereby the translator devours the ST to break away from it and produce the TT as a fresh creation, not a copy.

Originally conceived in the context of the translation of poetry, which is feasible only "under the sign of invention" (de Campos 1969, qtd in Cintão 2009: 827), the cannibalist metaphor of transcreation can also be applied to the localization of modern digital entertainment such as video games. The treatment of translation as a "two-way transcultural enterprise" that asserts "the autonomy of the translator/recreator while problematizing the question of authorship in translation" (Vieira 1999: 106) seems to help explain the creative process involved in game localization. Localization is facilitated by the variability of software, which allows a rebirth of the original with a new "look and feel" by combining the technical operations of software engineering and the act of creative human intervention. This concept embraces the often radical transformation of the ST into the TT on the user-layer while retaining the core source code on the technical layer shared between the ST and TT.

In game localization, the transcreative approach is enhanced when the human translation process is combined with the defining characteristics of software products, which continue to reinvent themselves through fixes, patches, and so on, incorporating additional features or removing unpopular features. In the case of rerelease editions, a transcreated locale (rather than the original) becomes the new ST, in a manner ostensibly similar to relay translation, yet with a deliberate goal of supplying inspiration for another locale. In this series of operations, game localization takes a broad adaptive approach according to the user preferences of the given target market. This in turn offers further insight into the techno-orientalism mentioned earlier, where technology and culture come together in creating East-West and West-East cultural hybridization, as illustrated by the reverse localization model from Japanese into an NA locale then back into Japanese.

In the domain of localization, the term *adaptation* is widely used (e.g. Esselink 2000) as a relatively neutral description, whereas in TS in general this term tends to inspire negative connotations that imply a lesser form of translation, as highlighted in AVT forms such as subtitling (Díaz Cintas and Remael 2007: 9). The free strategies of adaptive methods have, however, been regarded more positively in some Asian countries, including Japan. For example, Chan (2009: 392–3) traces the Japanese tradition of adaptation as applied to translating Chinese fiction from the later years of the seventeenth century into the nineteenth century, when it began to also include source texts from the Western repertoire. Chan argues that adaptation is not a superseded and antiquated practice in Japan. The Japanese term *hon'an* for adaptation "connotes transmutation" and includes the "rewriting of source texts—even the extensive manipulation," as opposed to *hon'yaku* (translation), which chiefly pointed to "correspondence" similar to the literal translation applied mainly to scientific and medical texts (Chan 2009: 393). Chan (2009: 397), further asserts that under an intertextual framework the division between author and translator is erased, giving the translator diverse roles as a text-handler with "free rein to modify and adjust, play with and manipulate, as well as tease out the meanings." "Locales," which are regional variations of the original video game as a result of a broad range of operations applied by the game localizer, can be best explained under the broad framework of adaptation, specifically linked to transcreation.

In addition to the view that adaptation has been rather widely and successfully implemented in some Asian translation traditions, Chan signals in the broader translation community a change toward advocating this hitherto somewhat maligned concept:

> The current privileging of concepts like *appropriation*, *transposition*, *transmutation*, and *transcreation* means that a subtle shift has occurred, as a result of which adaptation can be rethought and re-evaluated. Together with this some older views about adaptation should be debunked. (Chan 2009: 397)

Such trends toward "privileging" concepts related to a broad sense of adaptation are particularly prominent in the field of advertising. For example, Bernal Merino (2006: 32–3) notes how the concept of transcreation has come to be used by "a new wave of companies seeking to distance themselves from traditional translation firms." In turn, Ortiz-Sotomayor (2007: n.p.) remarks how the advertising industry is latching on to the concepts of transcreation and adaptation to stress the particularly creative dimensions involved in translation for advertising—although in the translation industry in general it is understood that "a good translator also transcreates, localizes and adapts" (here the meaning of "localization" differs from the one used in this chapter in reference to the process of converting products presented on an electronic platform to meet user parameters in the target market).

Along with the revived concept of transcreation and the general adaptive approach used in certain industry sectors (e.g. advertising industries), game localization provides further evidence of a new translation practice headed in the same direction. As a highly technologized medium, video games widen the scope of such transcreative operations into a broad range of micro- and macro-operations, as already regularly embarked on by leading Japanese game companies, with many more ad hoc instances than just the Square Enix example discussed here.

A future direction in Japan for further maturing of Translation Studies

TS has today grown to establish a solid basis for explaining a diverse range of translation phenomena. As the discipline matures, however, some scholars have begun to question its Western-centric focus and to call for a broadening of the discipline (e.g. Tymoczko 2007), leading in effect to "decentering Translation Studies" (Wakabayashi and Kothari 2009). "Translating Others" (Hermans 2006) has now become one of the key concerns in TS, bringing to light translation practices and phenomena that were previously little known and therefore not accounted for in mainstream translation theory. With this new focus on translation beyond the confines of Europe, TS is well positioned to continue to grow as an academic discipline in Japan, building on foundations that have been in preparation for some time (Mizuno 2007: 1–2).[11]

This chapter has focused on the emerging research domain of game localization to argue that it could provide a future direction for TS in Japan and usefully contribute Japanese perspectives to further internationalization and expansion of the discipline. Exploring how a leading Japanese game company with a wealth of experience in delivering digital entertainment to the world stage has been developing an innovative translation and localization approach, provides insights into rapidly developing new translation practices and therefore contributes to building new norms. In particular, such new practices are driven by the nature of video games, which combine culture and technology to exemplify new technological artefacts that have significant implications for translation. This chapter has highlighted the view that when the ST consists of software, a TT is merely a manifestation of many different variations of the ST while retaining a physical link via core source code to the base form. In turn, the framework of transcreation, which itself has been reincarnated in contemporary contexts, seems to provide a good fit for explaining the rather broad and liberal approaches taken in game localization, albeit in limited examples covered in this chapter. Nevertheless, the powerful metaphor of cannibalism, where the translator ingests the ST as nourishment in order to give birth to a TT as a new creation, highlights the translator's deep engagement in the process of recreating the source. In this scenario, the translator's presence as an active agent is promoted rather than suppressed. This illustrates how new technological environments could further harness human creativity, thus exemplifying "localization as humanization," rather than "dehumanization" as observed in certain other approaches applied in software localization (Pym 2004: 184). A journey with game localization could potentially open up a new vista for TS in Japan and elsewhere.

Notes

1   CESA (2010: 120) regards the data on the import figure for foreign games as indicative only, due to the discarding of some data as a result of some incomplete survey responses. This suggests that the indicated figure is lower than the actual amount. To fill in the gap, it is useful to note that earlier data by the Japanese Ministry of Economy, Trade and Industry (METI) in 2006 suggested that the game export market was over 80 times the size of the market for imports of foreign games in Japan (O'Hagan 2006: 242).

2   The official game rating system in the United States was established in 1994 as the Entertainment Software Rating Board (ESRB). It replaced the internal guidelines laid out by Nintendo of America (Kent 2001: 479–80), which was well known for sanitizing games. Its Japanese counterpart, the Computer Entertainment Rating Organization (CERO), was not established until 2002.

3   Although the industry is well known for soliciting user feedback during the development of games, such as beta testing by gamers, it might be naive to believe that game companies are always driven by and in full understanding of customer preferences. For example, game scholars such as Dovey and Kennedy (2006: 60–2) highlight "the extraordinarily self-contained and self-replicating nature" of game production, which suggests that customer preferences are more based on the game companies' perceptions of these preferences.

4   According to the 2010 CESA Games White Paper (Computer Entertainment Supplier's Association 2010: 126, 147), the three most popular game genres in

Japan were Role playing games, Action, and Adventure in that order, whereas the US counterparts were Sports, Action, and Family. While console games are more popular in Japan and the United States, PC games are more common in Europe (Kerr 2006).

5   Mandiberg (2009) also develops a detailed argument on translation versus localization in reference to Manovich's characterization of new media as variability.

6   For prior studies of this reverse localization model in reference to "International" or "Final Mix" editions of Japanese games, see Mandiberg (2009) and O'Hagan (2005, 2009).

7   What I call "reverse localization model" is sometimes referred to as "recursive import" in commercial contexts. For a list of examples, see http://tvtropes.org/pmwiki/pmwiki.php/Main/RecursiveImport, accessed August 30, 2011.

8   Mandiberg's 2009 study of *Kingdom Hearts: Final Mix* (Square Enix, first released in 2002) suggests an added issue with this particular game since it is a cocreation by Disney and Square Enix, so it had explicit links to English-language sources in Disney movies from the outset. This makes the reverse localization model especially problematic, although it is "more interesting as international equates to 'mixture'" (n.p.), true to the name of the edition. Nevertheless, it is beyond the scope of the present chapter to comment in any detail on Final Mix editions associated with this particular series.

9   http://finalfantasy.wikia.com/wiki/International, accessed August 30, 2011.

10 In the game industry, simultaneous shipment (sim-ship) has become the norm, especially among US and UK publishers, so as to allow localized games to be released at the same time as the original game. Sim-ship creates significant constraints for localizers and translators, as translation starts even before the game is finalized. This often leads to a lack of the contextual information that is usually available for other types of translation.

11 One of the key recent initiatives to get TS off the ground in Japan was its official inclusion in the former Japan Association of Interpretation Studies (JAIS), renamed as the Japan Association of Interpretation and Translation Studies (JAITS) in 2008.

References

Andersson, T. 2009. "Game Localisation and the Game—How Localising Accents and Dialects Affects the Game Experience." Unpublished BA thesis: Dublin City University.

Aoyama, Y. and H. Izushi. 2003. "Hardware Gimmick or Cultural Innovation? Technological, Cultural, and Social Foundations of the Japanese Video Game Industry." *Research Policy* 32: 423–44.

Baker, M. and G. Saldanha. 2009. "Introduction to the Second Edition." In *Routledge Encyclopedia of Translation Studies*, edited by M. Baker and G. Saldanha, 2nd rev. edn. London: Routledge, pp. xx–xxii.

Bassnett. S. and H. Trivedi. 1999. "Introduction: Of Colonies, Cannibals and Vernaculars." In *Post-Colonial Translation*, edited by S. Bassnett and H. Trivedi. London: Routledge, pp. 1–18.

Bernal Merino, M. 2006. "On the Translation of Video Games." In *The Journal of Specialised Translation* (*JOSTRAN*) 6: 22–36. www.jostrans.org/issue06/art_bernal. pdf, accessed August 20, 2010.

Chan, T. L. 2009. "At the Borders of Translation: Traditional and Modern(ist) Adaptations, East and West." *Meta* 54(3): 387–400.

Chandler, H. 2005. *The Game Localization Handbook*. Massachusetts: Charles River Media.

Cintão, H. P. 2009. "Translating 'Under the Sign of Invention': Gilberto Gil's Song Lyric Translation." *Meta* 54(4): 813–932.

Computer Entertainment Supplier's Association (CESA). 2010. *2010 CESA Games White Paper*. Tokyo: CESA.

Consalvo, M. 2006. "Console Video Games and Global Corporations: Creating a Hybrid Culture." *New Media & Society* 8(1): 117–37.

—. 2011. "MOOs to MMOs: The Internet and Virtual Worlds." In *The Handbook of Internet Studies*, edited by M. Consalvo and E. Charles. Malden, MA: Wiley-Blackwell, pp. 326–47.

Díaz Cintas, J. and A. Remael. 2007. *Audiovisual Translation: Subtitling*. Manchester: St. Jerome Publishing.

Dietz, F. 2006. "Issues in Localizing Computer Games." In *Perspectives in Localization*, edited by K. Dunne. Amsterdam and Philadelphia: John Benjamins, pp. 121–34.

Dovey, J. and H. W. Kennedy. 2006. *Game Cultures: Computer Games as New Media*. Berkshire: Open University Press.

Edge Staff. 2008. "GC Asia: Understanding Asia." In *Edge Online*. www.next-gen.biz/ news/gc-asia-understanding-asia, accessed February 20, 2011.

Egenfeldt-Nielsen, S. E., J. E. Smith, and S. P. Tosca. 2008. *Understanding Video Games*. New York and London: Routledge.

Esselink, B. 2000. *A Practical Guide to Localization*. Amsterdam and Philadelphia: John Benjamins.

Folaron, D. 2006. "A Discipline Coming of Age in the Digital Age." In *Perspectives in Localization*, edited by K. Dunne. Amsterdam and Philadelphia: John Benjamins, pp. 195–222.

Frasca, G. 2001. "Rethinking Agency and Immersion: Video Games as a Means of Consciousness-raising." Essay presented at SIGGRAPH 2001. http://siggraph.org/ artdesign/gallery/S01/essays.html, accessed July 28, 2010.

Hermans, T. (ed.) 2006. *Translating Others*. Manchester: St. Jerome Publishing.

—. 2009. "Translation, Ethics, Politics." In *The Routledge Companion to Translation Studies*, rev. edn, edited by J. Munday. London: Routledge, pp. 93–105.

Kent, S. L. 2001. *The Ultimate History of Video Games*. New York: Three River Press.

Kerr, A. 2006. *The Business and Culture of Digital Games: Gamework/Gameplay*. London and Thousand Oaks: Sage Publications.

Kohler, C. 2005. *Power Up: How Japanese Video Games Gave the World an Extra Life*. Indiana: BradyGames.

Localization Industry Standards Association (LISA). 2003. LISA The Localization Industry Primer. 2nd edition. http://www.ict.griffith.edu.au/~davidt/cit3611/ LISAprimer.pdf, accessed February 18, 2011.

Mandiberg, S. 2009. "Translation (Is) Not Localization: Language in Gaming." UC Irvine: Digital Arts and Culture 2009. www.escholarship.org/uc/item/6jp2f8kwm, accessed September 28, 2010.

Mangiron, C. 2004. "Bringing Fantasy to Reality: Localizing Final Fantasy." *Globalization Insider LISA Newsletter* 13(1.3).

Mangiron, C. and M. O'Hagan. 2006. "Game Localization: Unleashing Imagination with 'Restricted' Translation." In *The Journal of Specialised Translation* (*JOSTRANS*) 6: 10–21. www.jostrans.org/issue06/art_ohagan.pdf, accessed August 15, 2010.

Manovich, L. 2001. *The Language of New Media*. Cambridge, MA: MIT Press.

Mizuno, A. 2007. *Hon'yaku e no shōtai* (Invitation to Translation Studies in Japan) 1: 1–2.

Munday, J. 2008. *Introducing Translation Studies: Theories and Applications*, 2nd edn. London and New York: Routledge.

—. 2009. "Issues in Translation Studies." In *The Routledge Companion to Translation Studies*, rev. edn, edited by J. Munday. London: Routledge, pp. 1–19.

Muñoz Sánchez, P. 2009. "Video Game Localisation for Fans by Fans: The Case of Romhacking." In *The Journal of Internationalisation and Localisation* 1: 168–85.

Nóbrega, T. M. and J. Milton. 2009. "The Role of Haroldo and Augusto de Campos in Bringing Translation to the Fore of Literary Activity in Brazil." In *Agents of Translation*, edited by J. Milton and P. Bandia. Amsterdam and Philadelphia: John Benjamins, pp. 257–78.

O'Hagan, M. 2005. "Multidimensional Translation: A Game Plan for Audiovisual Translation in the Age of GILT." In Proceedings of *EU High Level Scientific Conferences: Multidimensional Translation* (*MuTra*) *2005*. www.euroconferences.info/ proceedings/2005_Proceedings/2005_O'Hagan_Minako.pdf, accessed June 20, 2011.

—. 2006. "Manga, Anime and Video Games: Globalizing Japanese Cultural Production." *Perspectives* 14(4): 242–7.

—. 2007. "Video Games as a New Domain for Translation Research: From Translating Text to Translating Experience." *Tradumàtica 05 Localització de videojocs*. www.fti. uab.es/tradumatica/revista/, accessed August 7, 2010.

—. 2009. "Putting Pleasure First: Localizing Japanese Video Games." *TTR—Traduction, Terminologie, Rédaction: études sur le texte et ses transformations* (La Traduction au Japon/Translation in Japan) 22(1): 147–166.

O'Hagan, M. and C. Mangiron. 2004. "Game Localization: When 'Arigato' Gets Lost in Translation." In *Proceedings of New Zealand Game Developers Conference Fuse 2004*. Dunedin: University of Otago, pp. 57–62.

Onyett, C. 2005. "E3 2005: Interview with Yuji Horii: We Talk Dragon Quest VIII." http://ie.ps2.ign.com/articles/617/617479p1.html, accessed August 8, 2010.

Ortiz-Sotomayor, J. M. 2007. "Multiple Dimensions of International Advertising: An Analysis of the Praxis in Global Marketing Industry from a Translation Studies Perspective." In *Proceedings of the EU High-Level Scientific Conference Series MuTra 2007: LSP Translation Scenarios*. Vienna: University of Vienna.

Pym, A. 2004. *The Moving Text: Localization, Translation, and Distribution*. Amsterdam and Philadelphia: John Benjamins.

Square Enix. 2004. *Final Fantasy X-2 International + Last Mission Ultimania*. Tokyo, Square Enix.

Taylor, T. L. 2011. "Internet and Games." In *The Handbook of Internet Studies*, edited by M. Consalvo and E. Charles. Malden, MA: Wiley-Blackwell, pp. 369–84.

Tymoczko, M. 2007. *Enlarging Translation, Empowering Translators*. Manchester: St. Jerome Publishing.

Vieira, E. 1999. "Liberating Calibans: Readings of Antropofagia and Haroldo de Campos' Poetics of Transcreation." In *Post-Colonial Translation*, edited by S. Bassnett and H. Trivedi. London: Routledge, pp. 95–113.

Wakabayashi, J. and R. Kothari (eds). 2009. *Decentering Translation Studies: India and Beyond*. Amsterdam and Philadelphia: John Benjamins.

Yahiro, S. 2005. *Terebi gēmu kaisetsu joron: Assemblage* [Towards a theory of video games: assemblage]. Tokyo: Gendai Shoten.

11

Community Interpreting in Japan: Present State and Challenges

Makiko Mizuno

Introduction

The concept of community interpreting was virtually unknown in Japan until around the beginning of the 1990s. Throughout modern history, Japan had always been a country sending immigrants rather than receiving them. However, the bubble economy (an economic boom that occurred between the latter half of the 1980s and the early 1990s) attracted a large number of immigrant workers from all over the world, particularly from other parts of Asia and from South America. Since then the number of such newcomers has continued to increase. Registered foreigners in Japan hit a record high of about 2.21 million in 2008, or 1.74 percent of the total population (Immigration Bureau of Japan). The number has been declining since 2009 because of the economic recession and the effects of the great East Japan earthquake which occurred in 2011, but it is still perceived as high by the Japanese population.

Until the time of the bubble economy, most foreign nationals in Japan were Koreans who had been living there for a long time and who often spoke Japanese as their first language. Currently, however, the majority of foreign nationals are newcomers, and many are not able to communicate fully in Japanese, which makes their presence more conspicuous.

Non-Japanese-speaking foreign nationals face institutional, cultural and, most importantly, linguistic barriers in their daily lives. This has led to greatly increased demand for community interpreting in various settings such as schools, government offices, hospitals, and courtrooms. This paper surveys the current state of community interpreting in Japan, both in practice and in terms of research on this important topic.

The position of community interpreting in Japan

Scope of the term "community interpreting"

Legal interpreting has been known to the Japanese public since the latter half of the 1980s because of the increasing number of foreigners involved in crimes in Japan (Ministry of Justice), but it was not until around 2005 that linguistic support in areas such as healthcare and education came to be called *komyunitī tsūyaku* (community interpreting). This relatively new term in Japan borrows the English word "community." Some people define it narrowly, excluding the legal area. This is partly because the system of legal interpreting in criminal proceedings is controlled by the national government, which clearly differentiates it from other areas of community interpreting. In 2003 the Japan Association for Interpreting and Translation Studies (JAITS), the largest academic association for interpreting studies in Japan, launched a community interpreting Special Interest Group, and this group's research includes legal interpreting.[1] The author takes the position that legal interpreting is a part of community interpreting, because non-Japanese nationals who need interpreting in criminal proceedings are mostly from the local community and legal interpreting also includes civil cases and legal consultations in which local foreign residents are involved.

Lack of public measures

In many countries, especially long-established immigrant-receiving nations, community interpreting has been handled within the framework of social welfare as a part of immigration policy. A public agency such as an immigration bureau deals with a range of services for immigrants, including interpretation and translation services. In Japan, however, community-based interpreting has been treated as part of international friendship activities, and it has been the norm for many local jurisdictions to register volunteer interpreters or "goodwill interpreters" who perform various types of jobs, including healthcare interpreting, and sometimes even legal interpreting. The reason for this attitude is historical. Foreigners, especially those who do not speak Japanese, have long been regarded as temporary visitors who are not expected to become permanent residents. The Japanese government is not yet prepared to cope with long-term residency and immigration, so language services for non-Japanese speakers have been made available only on an ad hoc basis.

Another important factor that hampers development of comprehensive and systematic approaches to community interpreting and translation in Japan is bureaucratic sectionalism. Legal interpreting is under the jurisdiction of the Ministry of Justice; healthcare interpreting is under the Ministry of Health, Labour, and Welfare; and school interpreting is under the Ministry of Education, Culture, Sports, Science, and Technology. There is no single government organization that handles all matters relating to immigrants in Japan.

Community interpreting and conference interpreting

In Japan "interpreting" usually refers to conference interpreting, which includes many kinds of interpreting settings such as diplomatic negotiations, conferences, lectures, business negotiations, television broadcasts, and even interpreting in sport or entertainment. Conference interpreting is a firmly established profession with high social status and pay, and although Japan has no system for certifying conference interpreters, the market mechanism helps ensure high-quality interpreting. By contrast, there is no market mechanism for community interpreting because the difference between professionals and volunteers is not clear, which leads to low pay.

Another difference between community and conference interpreting is the language combination. In community interpreting, the languages in most demand include Chinese, Korean, Portuguese, Spanish, and Tagalog. The number of fluent speakers of these languages who are also fluent in Japanese is very limited compared with the number of fluent speakers of both English and Japanese, which is the most sought-after language combination for conference interpreting. Shortages in human resources make it difficult to control the quality of community interpreting.

Community interpreting and sign language interpreting

In many countries, sign language interpreting is an integral part of community interpreting. In Japan, however, sign language interpreting is regarded as a matter of social welfare under the jurisdiction of the Ministry of Health, Labour, and Welfare, whereas foreign language interpreting in the community is handled by organizations such as international friendship associations in each district or various nonprofit organizations. Bureaucratic sectionalism also plays a role. Sign language interpreting and spoken language interpreting have therefore been treated as separate areas, and there has been no attempt to integrate them.

Although there is no governmental move to establish a certification system for spoken language interpreting, the Ministry of Health and Welfare (as it was known until 2001) has had a certification system for sign language interpreting since 1989, and many local governments have their own system for certifying sign language interpreters. Only certified interpreters are sent to legal or healthcare venues, thereby ensuring a high quality of sign language interpreting. Interpreters certified at the national level are regarded as more qualified than those certified by local governments.

The National Center of Sign Language Education conducts annual training programs for nationally certified and locally certified sign language interpreters. There are separate educational boards for the two groups and the contents of the programs are decided separately, but the training sessions are held on the same dates.

In terms of research, however, spoken language interpreting is more advanced, because studies of conference interpreting have a relatively long history in Japan and have significantly influenced studies of community-based, spoken language interpreting. The first publication to deal with sign language interpreting in the framework of legal interpreting was a book by Matsumoto and colleagues (1992). Lately, as community interpreting has attracted increasing attention, there have been moves among sign language interpreters and researchers to learn about theories of community-based interpreting, because they have realized that the circumstances surrounding sign language interpreting are very similar to those surrounding community interpreting, especially in terms of interpreter ethics and roles. In recent years, there have been increasing opportunities to exchange ideas and opinions between the two fields.

Main areas and characteristics of community interpreting

Like other countries, Japan needs community interpreting in three main areas: the legal system, healthcare, and local government. This last area covers diverse matters related to everyday life, including help at municipal offices, support in public school education, and interpreting for consultations on such matters as housing, tax, labor problems, and domestic violence. In comparison with conference interpreting, the characteristics of community interpreting are as follows (Mizuno 2008: 12–16):

1. The non-Japanese-speaking clients are local residents, whereas the clients for conference or business interpreters are people in Japan temporarily for a certain purpose.
2. There is a power differential between the two parties, mainly in terms of knowledge and information and sometimes authority. Service providers such as medical doctors, schoolteachers, and government officials usually have more knowledge and information than the non-Japanese-speaking clients, and in police interrogations the investigators symbolize the state's authority. By contrast, conference interpreters work between parties who are equal, at least in principle.
3. A great variety of languages are used in community interpreting, as noted earlier. Moreover, community interpreters have to deal with people from a wide range of backgrounds and with very diverse speech styles and registers. There are also regional differences, such as a high demand for Portuguese in Shizuoka, Aichi, and Gunma prefectures or for Chinese in the Tokyo metropolis and Osaka Prefecture. By contrast, the speech styles and registers that conference interpreters handle are, in most cases, those of the well-educated, and they are rather uniform.
4. Cultural differences are more significant in community interpreting settings. The matters at hand are closely related to the personal lives of immigrants and often deeply rooted in their culture, so problems tend to occur because of misunderstandings stemming from cultural differences. Conference interpreters seldom face such problems.
5. Community interpreting and translating are closely related to the protection of basic human rights. The notion of language rights is well known in the West, where it has been developed since the days of the civil rights movements as one of the rights of minorities. It was not until recently, however, that community interpreting came to be regarded in Japan as a way of guaranteeing the rights of non-Japanese-speaking residents to access public services. The right to a fair trial, safe healthcare, and school education can be protected only with the aid of interpreters. By contrast, conference interpreting is generally unrelated to the issue of human rights.

Legal interpreting

Legal interpreting is one of the two most important areas of community interpreting (the other being healthcare interpreting), because people's lives are potentially at stake. In Japan it is the only area of community interpreting that has a nationally established system. Legal interpreting began to draw attention at the end of the 1980s with the rapid increase in the number of foreigners involved in criminal cases in Japan. After peaking in 2003, the number started to decline gradually, mainly because tougher regulations led to a decrease in illegal stayers. In 2010, 3,321 out of the 71,061 defendants who were tried at district and summary courts (the lowest court in the Japanese hierarchy) nationwide needed a legal interpreter (General Secretariat, Supreme Court of Japan 2012). The most needed language was Chinese (31.1%), followed by Filipino (11.8%), Korean (11.3%), Portuguese (10.2%), and Spanish (7.3%) (General Secretariat, Supreme Court of Japan 2012).

Assignment and training of interpreters

As of April 2011, a total of 4,052 interpreters of 61 languages were on the lists of courts nationwide (General Secretariat, Supreme Court of Japan 2012). Two kinds of training opportunities are provided by each of Japan's eight high courts. The Court Interpreting Seminar is for novice interpreters of lesser-used languages, and it teaches basic knowledge and skills through mock sessions. The Court Interpreting Follow-up Seminar is for interpreters with a certain level of experience who can cope with simple court cases. They learn more advanced knowledge and skills in order to be able to interpret in complicated and difficult cases. These seminars are held only once a year, and they cover only a limited number of languages, so interpreters of many languages never have the opportunity for training. The General Secretariat of the Supreme Court of Japan has issued self-study handbooks for court interpreters in 21 languages—only a small proportion of the languages for which interpreting services are required.

The police headquarters in each prefecture has a special center to deal with interpreting. When English or Chinese is needed for interviews or interrogations, in-house interpreters who are full-time employees of the police headquarters are usually used, but for other languages or when there is no in-house interpreter available, private citizens registered as interpreters are used. Some prosecutor's offices have their own list of interpreters, but others use the interpreters registered at the police headquarters in their jurisdiction. Training programs for interpreters are offered in some jurisdictions, but not in others.

When a suspect is arrested, he or she is entitled to consult an on-duty lawyer free of charge. If the suspect is not able to speak Japanese, the local bar association procures an interpreter. Prefectural bar associations have their own system of registering interpreters, and some hold training sessions in collaboration with local interpreters. In October 2006, a new system was launched for providing suspects with a public defender before indictment. Under this system, the Japan Legal Support Center[2] is in charge of securing and dispatching interpreters.

In 2009 the Legal Research Foundation of the Japan Federation of Bar Associations launched a research group to study quality control of court interpreting, and as part of its activities, this group organized a training program as a pilot project focusing on the lay judge system (see below). This two-day program for interpreters, consisting of a mock trial and a training seminar, was held five times in 2009 and 2010. Its emphasis was not only on teaching about court proceedings and legal terms, but also analyzing linguistic and communicational matters in court settings.

Introduction of the lay judge system

In May 2009, Japan introduced a lay judge system as an important element of its judicial reform. Under this system six randomly selected citizens from the list of eligible voters serve as lay judges and, together with three professional judges, decide whether the defendant is guilty. In the case of a guilty verdict, they also determine the sentence. The crimes dealt with in lay judge trials are felonies that can involve the death penalty or indefinite imprisonment (e.g. murder, robbery resulting in death or injury, arson, or smuggling stimulant drugs for profit).

The introduction of the lay judge system has transformed the entire landscape of criminal trials in Japan and presented many new challenges for court interpreting. The most noticeable change occurred in language use. The specialized terms and expressions used in trials have been simplified to make court proceedings easier for ordinary people without legal training to understand. This has reduced the burden on court interpreters in terms of understanding difficult legal discourse.

Compared with conventional trials, where the emphasis is on documentary evidence,[3] under the new system testimonies are regarded as more important. Under the principle of direct trial, what is presented orally in court is the only evidence on which the judgment may be based, which means that what is said and how it is said is of great importance. Moreover, compared with professional judges, who are expected to be able to see the facts objectively, lay judges can be more emotional and can have a tendency to focus more on the defendant's character, mentality, and feelings (Hotta 2009: 120–3). Thus the mode of expression in court has a greater influence on lay judges' decision making, so it is particularly important for interpreters to render the nuances and registers of testimonies accurately. For these reasons, the demand for properly trained interpreters with high interpreting skills is much greater in lay judge trials than in conventional trials.

The first lay judge trial for a non-Japanese-speaking defendant was conducted in Saitama Prefecture in September 2009, and by the end of 2010, there were 141 interpreter-mediated lay judge trials nationwide (General Secretariat, Supreme Court of Japan). Many problems related to court interpreting have surfaced, including interpreting errors and communication breakdown.

Quality control

In the past two decades, the system of appointing legal interpreters has improved significantly in each judicial branch in Japan. In most cases non-Japanese-speaking suspects' right to an interpreter of their native language is now guaranteed, although there have been a few cases of relay interpreting when a very minor language was involved. In terms of quality control, however, there has not been much progress. Accuracy is the most crucial element in legal interpreting, but there have been several cases in which inaccurate interpreting became grounds for an appeal.

A recent court case known as the Bernice Case, which was the first English interpreter-mediated lay judge trial, presented serious problems related to the court interpreting. This was a stimulant drug smuggling case in which the defendant appealed to a high court on the grounds that the quality of interpreting in the lower court was very poor and that her right to a fair trial had therefore not been guaranteed. To determine the quality of the lower court interpreting, the defending lawyer commissioned four linguists, including the author, to submit their expert opinions to the higher court. It was discovered that more than 60 percent of the defendant's relatively long utterances were interpreted with some errors, such as omissions or inaccurate renditions. Nevertheless, the appeal was rejected. In his reason for the judgment, the judge stated that it is impossible to interpret everything with 100 percent accuracy, so the interpreting in the first trial had been acceptable. Not acknowledging the poor quality of court interpreting seems to be the general stance of the judiciary at present.

As in the Bernice Case, there are still many poor-quality interpreters working in Japanese courts, mainly because Japan has no certification system for court interpreters. Almost anyone can register at a court or police station. Although it is relatively easy to check the interpreter's past career and experience or educational background, there is no mechanism for screening language ability and interpreting skills, especially for lesser-used languages. This lack of certification mechanisms is regarded by many researchers in this field as the biggest problem in the Japanese system of legal interpreting (Mizuno 2008: 71).

Healthcare interpreting

Healthcare interpreting is another important area of community interpreting, but it was not until much later than legal interpreting that it began to attract attention in Japan.

Past developments and present status

Since around 2000 there have been sporadic movements toward providing better language services in healthcare settings. For example, Multilanguage Information Center Kanagawa has been training healthcare interpreters of many languages in cooperation with the Kanagawa prefectural government. Other organizations, such as the Medical Interpreters Association in Hyogo Prefecture and the Medical Interpreter Network Tokai in Aichi Prefecture, have their own programs for training healthcare interpreters, holding regular study sessions on various topics. Generally speaking, these programs have four main pillars—medical knowledge and terminology, interpreting skills, cross-cultural issues, and interpreter ethics.

In 2005, Suita city in Osaka Prefecture launched a system to certify community interpreters in cooperation with an extragovernmental organization, Suita Inter-people Friendship Association (SIFA). SIFA has been conducting programs for training and testing interpreters, mainly focusing on healthcare interpreting. Those who pass the test receive certification from the city government and are sent to interpret at hospitals that have ties with SIFA. This was the first time in Japan that a local government had established a system to certify community interpreters. Lately, an increasing number of prefectures and municipalities have been making efforts to establish a local system to register, train, and dispatch interpreters to medical settings.

Some Japanese hospitals and clinics promote a system of healthcare interpreting, stationing interpreters on a regular basis or requesting their services as necessary. At the university level, a noteworthy initiative is Aichi Prefectural University's launching of a program to teach local residents Spanish and Portuguese and train them as medical communication supporters. Besides regular seminars, the university has held symposiums to educate people about this issue. Such trends have boosted public awareness of communication problems in healthcare settings and enhanced awareness among healthcare providers about the quality of interpreting.

The professionalization of healthcare interpreters has come to be recognized as an important issue. There have been several conferences and symposiums to discuss such issues, sponsored by many of the above-mentioned organizations. Against this background, the Japan Association of Medical Interpreters (JAMI), a nationwide organization, was launched in 2009 to carry out activities aimed at establishing proper compensation for and status of healthcare interpreters. JAMI drafted a code of ethics for healthcare interpreters in 2011.

Challenges

Although there has been great progress in healthcare interpreting in Japan, difficulties remain in terms of quality control. There are serious shortages of interpreters who can provide quality services, because there is no certification system and most interpreters work on a volunteer basis or are paid just enough to cover their travel expenses. The system relies on the goodwill of these interpreters. Yet without financial security, people with talent and skills might not continue as healthcare interpreters.

To solve these problems, healthcare interpreting needs to be officially regarded as a public service and public funds need to be allocated for this purpose. This is the biggest challenge for healthcare interpreting in Japan right now. Establishing a system of interpreter training that incorporates language training, especially for the most needed languages, is also necessary to solve the problem of quality control.

A system to protect interpreters is also needed. Few hospitals and clinics have measures (e.g. influenza vaccinations) to prevent interpreters from contracting diseases. Moreover, in healthcare settings interpreters are apt to have traumatic experiences and develop mental problems as a result, so they should be provided with easy access to counseling.

Recent trend

A noteworthy trend in recent years is the Japanese government's promotion of medical tourism.[4] This is aimed at wealthy people abroad who want to have sophisticated medical examinations or treatment in Japan. Interpreting costs should be included in the packages provided by travel agencies or covered by overseas travel insurance. This would guarantee appropriate fees for interpreters, who would be required to have a high level of interpreting skills, and it would also enhance their motivation. It might, however, have an adverse effect on healthcare interpreting in the community in that good interpreters will move to medical tourism, exacerbating the shortage of quality interpreters in the community. Avoiding a bipolarization of quality in healthcare interpreting will be a major challenge if this new trend takes off.

Areas related to local government

Education

According to a report compiled by the Ministry of Education, Culture, Sports, Science, and Technology, the number of foreign children who need communication support in public schools stood at 28,511 in 2010. Of these, 9,477 spoke Portuguese, 6,154 Chinese, and 4,350 Filipino, with these three languages accounting for more than 70 percent of the children in need of support. Some studies have revealed that many non-Japanese children needing communication support drop out of school or do not attend school at all. In Japan, the requirement for compulsory education does not apply to non-Japanese children. Low motivation for study due to the language barrier is among the main reasons for their not attending school (Kojima et al. 2004: 161).

Against this background, many local governments, especially in regions that have concentrations of foreign nationals, have made efforts to establish a system to support non-Japanese children. For language support, they regularly send bilingual educational supporters to local schools. These supporters do not have clear status as interpreters. In many cases, they play multiple roles, such as teaching Japanese to the children, assisting teachers in class, counseling children in trouble, translating letters from the school to parents, and interpreting during home visits by teachers or at parent–teacher association meetings. Thus interpreting is only one part of their work. Like healthcare interpreters, these supporters are a kind of paid volunteer, and their financial reward is very small. In some cases, they are paid by the day, and in other cases by the month.

Typically, educational supporters are local Japanese who are bilingual or students from abroad studying at Japanese universities. In 2009 the Shiga prefectural government decided to employ non-Japanese who had lost their jobs in the recent economic recession as educational supporters in local schools, and it is expected that other local governments will take similar measures to help foreign residents.

Other areas

Other local government-related areas of community interpreting are highly diversified, and systems vary from place to place. In most cases, interpreters are called "language volunteers" and do not receive compensation for their work. Child-rearing, domestic violence, and matters related to social welfare (e.g. livelihood support) are the main areas of consultation in which interpreting services are needed. There are also many inquiries and consultations about the pension system or health insurance for which interpreters with knowledge of public systems are required.

An increasing number of local international centers have recently introduced telephone interpreting services. When they receive an inquiry from a non-Japanese-speaking person, they use a special telephone system (Triophone) to connect this person with the staff of the local government office and an interpreter.

Returnees from China

One unique aspect of Japanese community interpreting is that only returnees from China[5] are entitled to the official support system,[6] of which interpreting services are a part. Nevertheless, even the system for returnees from China is far from satisfactory, because there is a shortage of quality interpreters and interpreting services are not intended to cover all their needs (Iida 2010).

Development of research on community interpreting

Until the 1980s there were practically no publications in Japan on interpreting. In the 1980s the contributors in this field of study were conference interpreters, who mainly focused on issues related to conference interpreting and its historical, societal, or cultural background. Elsewhere (Mizuno 2007) I have described in detail the development of studies on community interpreting in Japan, noting that research on legal interpreting started first, followed by research on interpreting in healthcare and other areas.

Research on legal interpreting

Research on legal interpreting began in the late 1980s at the initiative of practicing lawyers and legal scholars, who focused their studies mainly on foreign laborers' human rights (Tezuka 1989). Their work led to broad recognition that foreigners in Japan face problems of noncommunication or miscommunication, which implies a violation of their right to a fair trial. Some researchers (Ebashi 1990, Okabe 1991) focused on the systems of other countries, especially the United States, where legislation for court interpreting was advanced. The Osaka Bar Association (1991) compared Japanese laws and regulations on legal interpreting with international laws on this topic.

Practicing interpreters later collaborated with lawyers in the study of legal interpreting, which led to a greater focus on interpreting itself. Mizuno (1995, 1996), Tsuda (1997), and Watanabe and Nagao (1998) are representative of such studies. Many of the interpreters who participated in such collaboration were members of the Japan Judicial Interpreters Association (JJIA), which was established in 1993 and dissolved in 2007.[7] Based in the Kansai region, JJIA aimed to share information and give members opportunities to learn interpreting skills and legal terminology, as well as about ethics and court proceedings. Members often conducted mock trials using scenarios that had been prepared by lawyers, and they exchanged opinions and ideas on issues that surfaced during these mock trials. This kind of collaboration helped interpreters understand the legal system and terminology and helped lawyers recognize the difficulties that interpreters face. The book *Shihō tsūyaku* (Legal interpreting) (Watanabe et al. 2004) was published as a result of such collaborative work. It illustrates many stages of criminal procedures and describes various situations in which interpreters might face difficulties.

Beginning in 2000, the Ministry of Justice dispatched researchers, mainly from academia, to countries in which legal interpreting systems were considered to be well developed.[8] They gathered information about the laws governing legal interpretation, how legal interpreters are certified and assigned, and so on. The data were then compiled into a report on each country by each research group, and these reports were submitted to the Ministry. This led to significant publication of studies on overseas legal interpreting, including Mizuno (2004), Tsuda (2007), and Nishimatsu (2007).

Researchers' attention has recently shifted toward linguistic approaches in legal interpreting. With the introduction of the lay judge system, the question of how discourse in court influences verdicts by lay judges has become a concern for both linguists and lawyers, so the pragmatics of court discourse and interpretation has attracted the attention of researchers. Studies have addressed the equivalence between an original speech and its interpretation (Mizuno 2006), the choice of lexis based on corpus linguistics (Nakamura and Mizuno 2009), and interpreter footing (participation status) based on discourse analysis (Yoshida 2008).

Since 2007 the author and other researchers interested in linguistic analysis of court interpreting have been conducting research based on interpreter-mediated mock trials,[9] and since 2009 this project has been awarded a Grant-in-Aid for Scientific Research by the Japan Society for the Promotion of Science. The project team has analyzed data from mock trials in order to identify the impact of interpretation on the impressions and decision making of lay judges[10] (Nakamura et al. 2008; Nakamura and Mizuno 2010; Watanabe et al. 2010). These studies were strongly influenced by existing studies such as Berk-Seligson (1990) and Hale (2004). The data from the mock trials were also used in a study of court interpreters' stress and fatigue (Mizuno and Nakamura 2010), which supported the results of earlier studies such as Moser-Mercer et al. (1998).

Research on healthcare interpreting

Japanese research on healthcare interpreting began to appear after 2000. Systems in other countries such as the United States, Australia, Canada, and European Union nations were surveyed in Ishizaki, Nishino, and Borgman (2004); Multilanguage Information Center Kanagawa (2006); and other works. Some studies dealt with related themes such as healthcare interpreter education (Hori 2006). A noteworthy statistical study on support systems for foreigners in medical settings was conducted by KDDI Research Institute, Inc. in 2005. This study is unusual in that it addresses the use of machine translation systems in medical treatment settings.

Japanese academic associations have also begun to focus on issues of healthcare interpreting. In 2004 Biwako Forum for International Medical Services, which focuses on cross-border medical activities, made healthcare interpreting one of its main pillars, and studies on issues such as the roles of healthcare interpreters and the mental health of interpreters have been introduced in their biannual meetings. The JAITS[11] and the Japan Association for Public Service Interpreting and Translation, which are academic associations that focus on interpreting and translation, both recognize healthcare interpreting as an important area of study.

The roles of healthcare interpreters often become a focus of research, such as in Nadamitsu (2008). Existing studies (e.g. Angelelli 2004 and Hale 2007) serve as useful references for Japanese researchers. Ideas about life and death, treatment, hygiene, and dietary habits are related to culture, so how to bridge the cultural gap is an important issue that is closely related to interpreters' roles (Itō et al. 2004). Interpreter ethics have also often become a topic of study. For example, Mizuno (2005) compares ethical principles among different areas of community interpreting, including healthcare interpreting.

Research on interpreting in other areas

From around 1990, many local governments began to conduct surveys to identify the linguistic needs of foreigners residing in their jurisdiction. Although the focus of these surveys was on social services, no significant research was conducted on the issue of interpretation until after 2000.

With growing concern about education for children who do not speak Japanese, the issue of linguistic supporters is now attracting attention. Kojima and colleagues (2004) is a collaborative study by the local government, private organizations, and academics that surveyed the status of education for non-Japanese children, focusing on Kani city in Gifu Prefecture as a pilot area. Miyajima and Ōta (2005) examine the problem of foreign children not attending school and the challenges for a multicultural society. Iida (2010) focuses on interpreters in the context of public support for returnees from China and analyzes problems relating to interpreting services.

Present problems and future prospects

Quality control

As mentioned above, Japan has no system for certifying interpreters. Even for legal interpreting, which is regulated by the nation, there is no system for certification or for adequate training. In this situation, it is difficult to control the quality of interpreting.

Nor are there fixed guidelines about how to use interpreters. For example, in lay judge trials, which sometimes last over 6 hours, some courts use two interpreters but others use only one interpreter throughout, without considering potential fatigue. In medical settings, when interpreting is expected to be very difficult (e.g. when a patient is seriously ill or difficult medical matters are to be discussed) two or more interpreters might be needed. The most efficient ways to use interpreters (including their number) need to be considered so as to ensure high-quality interpreting. Current and future research is expected to provide relevant information.

Compensation

In most cases, community interpreting is practiced on a volunteer basis, and interpreters' financial rewards are very small. For example, healthcare interpreters are paid only about 3,000–5,000 yen (approximately 37–63 USD as of May 2012) per visit, which sometimes lasts more than 3 hours.

The highest-paying interpreter job is court interpreting. Court interpreters are paid by the hour. However, since the normal duration of a session is about one hour, except in the case of lay judge trials, the remuneration is not overly generous. By contrast, conference interpreters are paid a half-day fee even if the actual interpreting work undertaken only lasts an hour.

Community interpreters are required to have a high level of interpreting skills, because accuracy is of utmost importance when dealing with situations in which people's lives are potentially at stake. Proper compensation is the key to securing quality human resources. More financial support from the public sector is urgently needed.

Professionalization of interpreters

As already noted, Japan has no official system to certify interpreters. Conference interpreting, however, is a high-paying job, and if the market mechanism works, those who perform poorly will be excluded from the market. In terms of social status and reward, conference interpreters are treated as professionals, so they have a strong motivation for improving their skills. Community interpreters working on a volunteer basis cannot be expected to have such strong motivation.

With the rapid internationalization of Japanese society, there will always be foreign people living in local communities, and it is impractical to continue relying on the goodwill and volunteer spirit of individuals for communication with these groups. Fortunately, there is increasing awareness that community interpreters should be professionals, thanks to the awareness-raising activities of many organizations. User education will be the next step to make this awareness more concrete among those who actually use interpreters.

Conclusion

Community interpreting in Japan has made great strides in the past three decades, but many issues remain. With rapid internationalization, Japan can neither avoid nor postpone establishing a system that meets international standards for interpreting.

In recent years, community interpreting has attracted considerable attention from Japanese researchers, and the volume of related publications has increased dramatically. The number of Japanese participants in international conferences that focus on community interpreting, such as the Critical Link,[12] has gradually increased, as has the number of opportunities to share information on the Japanese situation.

Most early studies on community interpreting in Japan were either case studies based only on personal experience or an introduction of non-Japanese systems. In recent years, however, there has been a shift to more scientific data-driven studies. It is expected that findings from these studies will contribute significantly to improving the status of community interpreting in Japan in the coming years.

Notes

1   The author is the founder of this special interest group. Its rationale is that the clients in legal interpreting (including in civil cases, such as divorce cases or industrial accident cases) are local residents, so it is clearly a part of community interpreting.

2   This Center was established in 2006 as one of the three pillars of Japan's judicial reform.

3   In conventional trials, judges base their judgment mainly on the investigator's record of oral statement. Details of the contents of such documentary evidence are not directly presented in court, but judges are at liberty to examine them anywhere at any time.

4   Travel agencies and translation-service companies will participate in the tour packages, which will combine medical checkups with sightseeing trips.

5   In the chaos of Japan's defeat in World War II, many children of Japanese settlers in Manchuria were left behind in China. In 1981, an official project was launched for them to visit Japan and look for their blood relatives. Many have chosen to live in Japan, but most have communication problems because they cannot speak Japanese.

6 In order to help Chinese returnees lead a stable and independent life, the Japanese government provides them with vocational training, public housing, and welfare benefits for three years after their return, as guaranteed under the 1994 Law to Promote the Smooth Reentry of Japanese Nationals Left Behind in China and to Support Their Independence Following Reentry.

7 JJIA activities were mainly focused on raising awareness of legal interpreting as a profession. After more than a decade, the interests of its leading members shifted to more academic activities, and there was no strong motivation among them to continue the organization.

8 The United States (2000), Germany, France, and Sweden (2001), Australia (2002), the United Kingdom and Spain (2003), Taiwan, Singapore, and Hong Kong (2004) and Switzerland and the Netherlands (2005).

9 In Japan, researchers are not allowed to obtain linguistic data from real trials.

10 For example, according to Nakamura and Mizuno (2010), a comparison of mock lay judges' impressions of a defendant whose testimony was interpreted in three different ways—that is, politely, bluntly, or with many fillers and hesitation—showed that the blunt version and the version with many fillers and hesitation scored low in terms of conveying an impression of intelligence, trustworthiness, and convincingness.

11 See the archive of papers at www.soc.nii.ac.jp/jais/Kaishi_Archive/index.html.

12 Critical Link International is an international, non-profit organization committed to the advancement of the field of community interpreting in the social, legal, and health care sectors. The international Critical Link conference has been held every three years since 1995.

References

Angelelli, C. 2004. *Medical Interpreting and Cross-Cultural Communication*. Cambridge: Cambridge University Press.

Berk-Seligson, S. 1990. *Bilingual Courtroom*. Chicago: Chicago University Press.

Ebashi, T. 1990. "Saiban o ukeru kenri to tsūyakunin o tsukeru kenri" [Right to trial and right to an interpreter]. *Review of Law and Political Science* 87(4): 21–75.

General Secretariat, The Supreme Court of Japan. 2012. "Gozonji desuka hōtei tsūyaku" [Do you know about court interpreting?]. (Pamphlet)

—. www.saibanin.courts.go.jp/topics/pdf/09_12_05–10jissi_jyoukyou/h22_siryo1.pdf, accessed May 4, 2012.

Hale, S. 2004. *The Discourse of Court Interpreting*. Amsterdam: John Benjamins.

—. 2007. *Community Interpreting*. Basingstoke and New York: Palgrave Macmillan.

Hori, T. 2006. "Graduate-Level Medical Interpreting Education and Its Challenges: A Case of the Graduate School of Osaka University of Foreign Studies." *Interpretation Studies* 6: 155–74.

Hotta, S. 2009. *Saiban to kotoba no chikara* [Trials and the power of language]. Tokyo: Hituzi Shobō.

Iida, N. 2010. "The Present Condition and Problems of Community Interpreters Involved in the Support System for Returnees from China: A Study of Interpreter's Roles." *Ritsumeikan University Graduate school of Core Ethics and Frontier Science* 21: 75–88.

Immigration Bureau of Japan. www.immi-moj.go.jp/toukei/index.html, accessed August 1, 2010.

Ishizaki, M., K. Nishino, and P. Borgman. 2004. "Medical Interpreting and LEP Patients in the USA." *Interpretation Studies* 4: 121–38.

Ito, M., Y. Nakamura, and A. Kobayashi. 2004. "Zainichi gaikokujin no boshi hoken ni kansuru tsūyaku no yakuwari" [Role of interpreters in mother-child healthcare for foreigners in Japan]. *Shōni hoken kenkyū* [Journal of Child Health] 63(2): 249–55.

KDDI Research Institute, Inc. 2005. *Study on Models of Support for Medical Treatments of Foreigners in Japan through Information Technology.* KDDI Research Institute, Inc.

Kojima, Y., Y. Nakamura, and A. Yokō. 2004. *Gaikokujin no kodomo no kyōiku kankyō ni kansuru jittai chōsa* [Report on the educational environment for foreign children]. http://square.umin.ac.jp/boshiken/repo15/no8.1.pdf, accessed December 20, 2010.

Matsumoto, M., S. Ishihara, and O. Watanabe. 1992. *Chōkaku shōgaisha to keiji tetsuzuki* [The hearing-impaired and criminal procedures]. Tokyo: Gyōsei Press.

Ministry of Education, Culture, Sports, Science and Technology. www.mext.go.jp/b_menu/toukei/chousa01/nihongo/1266536.htm, accessed May 5, 2012.

Ministry of Justice. *The Criminal White Paper.* www.moj.go.jp/housouken/houso_hakusho2.html, accessed May 19, 2011.

Miyajima, T. and H. Ota. (eds). 2005. *Gaikokujin no kodomo to Nihon no kyōiku* [Foreign children and education in Japan]. Tokyo: University of Tokyo Press.

Mizuno, M. 1995. "Shihō tsūyaku shikaku nintei seido no kanōsei ni tsuite" [Possibility of introducing a certification system for legal interpreters]. *Jurist* 1078: 100–5.

—. 1996. "'New Comers' in Japan and Their Language Barriers: On the Issue of Language Problems in the Criminal Procedure." *Memoirs of Institute of Humanities, Human and Social Science, Ritsumeikan University* 64: 35–84.

—. 2004. "Future Prospects of the European Legal Interpreting System." *Interpretation Studies* 4: 139–56.

—. 2005. "Contents and Philosophy of Codes of Ethics in Conference, Community, Legal and Healthcare Interpreting." *Interpretation Studies* 5: 157–72.

—. 2006. "Possibilities and Limitations for Legally Equivalent Interpreting of Written Judgments." *Speech Communication Education* 19: 113–31.

—. 2007. "The History of Community Interpreting Studies in Japan." *Linguistica Antverpiensia, New Series* (5/2006), Hoger Institute voor Vertalers en Tolken, 69–80.

—. 2008. *Introduction to Community Interpreting.* Osaka: Osaka Kyōiku Tosho.

Mizuno, M. and S. Nakamura. 2010. "Fatigue and Stress of Court Interpreters in Lay Judge Trials." *Kinjo Gakuin Daigaku Ronshū, Studies in Social Science*, 7(1): 71–80.

Moser-Mercer, B., A. Kunzli, and M. Korac. 1998. "Prolonged Turns in Interpreting: Effects on Quality, Physiological and Psychological Stress (Pilot Study)." *Interpreting* 3(1): 47–64.

Multilanguage Information Center Kanagawa. 2006. *Best Practice of Language and Healthcare*. MIC Kanagawa.

Nadamitsu, Y. 2008. "The Status, Roles, and Motivations of Medical Interpreters." *Interpretation Studies* 8: 73–95.

Nakamura, S. and M. Mizuno. 2009. "The Linguistic Analysis for the Second Mock Trial: Issues Involving Interpreters' Choices of Lexis." *Interpreting and Translation Studies* 9: 33–54.

—. 2010. "Court Experiment: Impact of Interpreting on Impressions of Mock Lay Judges." *A Statistical Study of Language Use in Trials under the Lay Judge System*. The Institute of Statistical Mathematics Cooperative Report 237: 53–66.

Nakamura, S., M. Mizuno, T. Asano, and R. Yoshida. 2008. "Impacts of an Interpreter on a Witness Testimony—A Mock Trial and a Pilot Research." Proceedings of the 18th FIT World Congress on CD-ROM.

Nishimatsu, S. 2007. "The Court Interpreters in Japan and in the United States of America." *Interpretation Studies* 7: 189–204.

Okabe, Y. 1991. "Amerika gasshūkoku no hōtei tsūyakunin ni kansuru mondai" [Issues about court interpreters in the United States]. *Osaka University Law Review* 40: 723–76.

Osaka Bar Association. 1991. *Symposium: Foreigners and Criminal Cases*. Osaka: Osaka Bar Association.

Tezuka, K. 1989. *Gaikokujin rōdōsha* [Foreign labourers]. Tokyo: Nihon Keizai Newspaper.

Tsuda, M. 1997. "Human Rights Problems of Foreigners in Japan's Criminal Justice System." *Migration World Magazine* 25(1–2): 22–5.

—. 2007. "A Study of the Public Certification System for Interpreters and Translators in Sweden." *Interpretation Studies* 7: 167–88.

Watanabe, O. and H. Nagao. (eds). 1998. *Foreigners and Criminal Proceedings*. Tokyo: Seibundō Press.

Watanabe, O., H. Nagao, and M. Mizuno. 2004. *Shihō tsūyaku* [Legal interpreting]. Tokyo: Shōhakusha Press.

Watanabe, O., M. Mizuno, and S. Nakamura. 2010. *Jissen: Shihō tsūyaku* [Practices of legal interpreting]. Tokyo: Gendaijinbun-sha.

Yoshida, R. 2008. "Court Interpreters' Footing: Discourse Analysis on the Mock Trial Data." *Interpretation Studies* 8: 113–31.

Index

Lightning Source UK Ltd.
Milton Keynes UK
UKOW06f0007240816

281289UK00007B/160/P

9 781472 526502